The Meaning of American Federalism

Mrs. Powel: Well Doctor what have we got a republic or a monarchy?
Dr. Franklin: A republic, if you can keep it.

September 18, 1787, diary of James McHenry

A publication of the Center for Self-Governance

THE
MEANING OF

AMERICAN FEDERALISM

*Constituting a
Self-Governing Society*

Vincent Ostrom

ICS PRESS

Institute for Contemporary Studies
San Francisco, California

This book is a publication of the Center for Self-Governance, which is dedicated to the study of self-governing institutions. The Center is affiliated with the Institute for Contemporary Studies, a nonpartisan, nonprofit public policy research organization. The analyses, conclusions, and opinions expressed in ICS Press publications are those of the authors and not necessarily those of the Institute for Contemporary Studies, or of the Institute's officers, directors, or others associated with, or funding, its work.

Inquiries, book orders, and catalog requests should be addressed to ICS Press, 720 Market Street, San Francisco, CA 94102. (415) 981-5353. Fax (415) 986-4878. For book orders and catalog requests call toll free in the contiguous United States: (800) 326-0263.

Index compiled by Judith Evans
Cover design by Ben Santora

0 9 8 7 6 5 4 3 2 1

Library of Congress   Cataloging-in-Publication Data

Ostrom, Vincent, 1919–
       The meaning of American federalism : constituting a self-
  governing society / Vincent Ostrom.
        p.   cm.
       "A publication of the International Center for Self-Governance."
       Includes bibliographical references and index.
       ISBN 1-55815-393-4
       1. Federal government—United States. 2. The Federalist.
I. Title.
JK311.O78 1991
321.02'0973—dc20   91–11825
                                                  CIP

To Elinor
in appreciation of
the intellectual adventures
we have shared

CONTENTS

III
SOME EMERGENT PATTERNS OF ORDER

IV
CONCLUSION

FOREWORD

How can a society so constitute itself that its members will be
free participants in a self-governing order and not merely
the subjects of the state?

Through an analysis of American federalism that returns to
the classic sources—*The Federalist* and the writings of Tocqueville—this book explains the conditions necessary for creating
and maintaining a self-governing society and describes how such
a system works. In a world in which government by central authority has become increasingly discredited, this issue is as important as it was 150 years ago when Tocqueville observed that
American "society governs itself for itself."

Federalism is commonly understood as a theory of government that uses power to check power amid opposite and rival interests. Authority is limited, and no single body exercises supreme
control nor has a monopoly over the use of force in society. But
the idea of federalism is rendered trivial when applied only to the
coexistence of state and national governments. Rather, federalism
offers no less than an enabling basis for the development of self-
organizing and self-governing capabilities under conditions of
equal liberty and justice.

This book also illuminates the importance of institutional
analysis in dealing with problems in the contemporary world. We
face a basic challenge in recognizing and understanding the institutional foundations on which systems of governance and social

arrangements are established in modern societies. Vincent Ostrom has previously addressed this challenge in the ICS Press studies *Rethinking Institutional Analysis and Development*, edited with David Feeny and Hartmut Picht, and *Local Government in the United States*, with Robert Bish and Elinor Ostrom, as have John Clark and Aaron Wildavsky in *The Moral Collapse of Communism*, also published by ICS Press. Faith in the reformability of human societies underlies these efforts to understand institutions and to explicate the conceptual foundations of self-governance.

For those who are seriously concerned with understanding the American system of governance and how it can be used to address problems of collective choice and action, whether in neighborhoods or in the international arena, *The Meaning of American Federalism* offers rich rewards.

Robert B. Hawkins, Jr., President
Institute for Contemporary Studies

ACKNOWLEDGMENTS

The chapters of this book represent inquiries that have proceeded at different levels of analysis over some thirty years. Chapter 6, "The Organization of Government in Metropolitan Areas: A Theoretical Inquiry," an essay written in collaboration with Charles M. Tiebout and Robert Warren, was originally published in *The American Political Science Review* 55 (December 1961): 831–42. Permission from the American Political Science Association and from Robert Warren to publish here is gratefully acknowledged. Chapter 7 was originally written with Elinor Ostrom in response to an invitation by E. S. Savas for presentation at a colloquium concerned with alternatives for delivering public services, sponsored by the Diebold Institute for Public Policy Studies, Inc. That paper was revised with helpful editorial suggestions by Savas and appeared as "Public Goods and Public Choices" in *Alternatives for Delivering Public Services: Toward Improved Performance*, edited by E. S. Savas and published in 1977 by Westview Press, Boulder, Colorado. Both presentation of the paper and its initial publication were made possible by a grant from the Diebold Institute for Public Policy Studies, Inc. Permission to publish here is gratefully acknowledged.

Over a period of nearly twenty years, I have had occasion to participate in several colloquia and conferences organized by Daniel Elazar and the Center for the Study of Federalism at Temple University. It was in this context that the concept of covenant was seriously explored for its religious and political significance and different conjectures about the meaning of American federalism were advanced and explored. Earlier versions of Chapters 2, 3, and 4 were published in *Publius: The Journal of Federalism.* An early version of Chapter 2 appeared as "Hobbes, Covenant and Constitution," *Publius* 10 (fall 1980): 83–100. The fall 1980 issue of *Publius* includes several contributions on the concept of covenant in a theory of federalism. An initial presentation of the issues addressed in Chapter 4 was given in "The Meaning of Federalism in *The Federalist:* A Critical Examination of the Diamond Theses," *Publius* 15 (winter 1985): 1–22. This was part of a larger symposium with contributions from Paul Peterson and Jean Yarborough. Some of the issues addressed in Chapter 3 were also presented in "An Inquiry Concerning Liberty and Equality in the American Constitutional System," *Publius* 20 (spring 1990): 33–52. Permission to publish here is gratefully acknowledged. An early version of my efforts to explore generally the meaning of American federalism appeared in "Can Federalism Make A Difference?" *Publius* 3 (fall 1973): 197–238.

My concerns about the problems of normative inquiry have also been stimulated by colleagues who participated in the research group on guidance, control, and performance evaluation in the public sector led by Professor Franz-Xavier Kaufmann, Center for Interdisciplinary Research, Bielefeld University, Federal Republic of Germany; a panel organized by Mark Sproule-Jones at the 1983 meeting of the Public Choice Society; and a conference organized by Harold Berman and John Witte, "Religious Dimensions of American Constitutionalism," at the Law School, Emory University, April 7–8, 1988. Chapter 8 benefited from the intellectual exchange occurring in a conference, "*Res Publica:* East and West," held in Dubrovnik, Yugoslavia, October 10–14, 1988. I much appreciate the intellectual stimulation from discussions with colleagues on these occasions. Somewhat related essays have been published as "A Fallibilist's Approach to Norms and Criteria of Choice" in F. X. Kaufmann, G. Majone, and V. Ostrom, eds., *Guidance, Control, and Evaluation in the Public Sector* (Berlin and New York: Walter de Gruyter, 1986); "The Meaning of Value Terms," *American Behavioral Scientist* 28 (November/December 1984): 249–62; and "Religion and the Constitution of the American Political System," *Emory Law Journal* 39 (winter 1990): 165–90.

Chapter 5 was originally prepared for presentation at a symposium on the Supreme Court's decision in *Garcia* v. *San Antonio Metropolitan Transit Authority* (1985), sponsored by the U.S. Advisory Commission on Intergovernmental Relations, and was published in *Federalism and the Constitution: A Symposium on Garcia*, M152 (Washington, D.C.: ACIR, 1987). Discussions with Robert Hawkins, Lawrence A. Hunter, Ronald Oakerson, and John Kincaid, both in planning the conference and in revising papers for publication, were most helpful.

My deepest debt is to colleagues at the Workshop in Political Theory and Policy Analysis with whom I have maintained continuing conversations about patterns of order and development in human societies. American federalism has been a recurrent point of departure for these discussions as the world has become increasingly familiar with such terms as *glasnost* and *perestroika*. Works by Antoni Kaminski, Ronald Oakerson, Dele Olowu, Elinor Ostrom, Roger Parks, Amos Sawyer, Branko Smerdel, Mark Sproule-Jones, Theo Toonen, Susan Wynne, James Wunsch, and T. S. Yang are important complements to my efforts here.

Finally, I much appreciate the concerns of Robert Hawkins and his colleagues at the Institute for Contemporary Studies for problems of self-governance, and I am grateful for their support of this publication. I especially appreciate the sympathetic reading and helpful suggestions of J. M. B. Edwards, who as copyeditor could contest my use of language on behalf of potential readers.

I

INTRODUCTION

Instead of presuming that "the state" rules or "the government" governs, can we conceptualize and think about the constitution of order in human societies that might be self-governing? That is the core issue being addressed in this volume. The possibility of societies' achieving self-governance depends upon numerous conditions and especially upon the emergence of patterns of polycentricity that might apply to the whole system of human affairs.

We cannot explore these ideas so long as our thinking about order in human societies is dominated entirely by reference to "the state" or "the government." We must open our minds to other ways of thinking about ourselves, our relationships with others, and how peoples might constitute patterns of rule-ordered relationships in their societies. *My puzzle is your challenge.* Can we deal with the facts of rule-ordered relationships and contemplate how a system of such relationships might be constituted without reference to "the state" or "the government" at the center of our thinking? Can we contemplate societies where people are capable in some meaningful sense of governing their own affairs? If we are willing to consider that possibility, we may open ourselves to new frontiers of inquiry and new potentials for development. Such a possibility is of Copernican proportions for the constitution of order in different societies and of major significance for the contemporary world.

All possibilities are subject to limits. We cannot have the best of all possible worlds; but our degree of choice always turns upon the availability of alternatives. Can we help clarify what these might be?

ONE

The Meaning of American Federalism

O ne of the important puzzles about the governance of human societies turns upon the relationship of federalism to the widely held aspirations of people in various parts of the world for something called "democracy." The term democracy implies that people govern. "The government," however, is plainly not the people. People vote and elect representatives who participate in the government. Voting is a very slender thread, hardly strong enough to let us presume that people, by electing representatives, govern. The ordinary use of language strongly implies that the government governs. How do we resolve this dilemma?

I doubt that there is any single resolution. If people rely only upon the pronouncements of those who aspire to leadership, democracy will be universally proclaimed—a form of demagoguery, not democracy. To honor democracy by words alone creates false illusions. If democracy has an essential place in the unfolding of human civilization, the part that people play in the governance of societies must turn upon much more than voting in elections.

In my own efforts to come to terms with what it means to be a citizen in a democratic society, I have come to regard the concept of federalism as of basic importance. My concern is with general features of a system of governance that would be appropriate to circumstances where people govern rather than presuming that governments govern. When the problem is posed this way, conceptualization and definition become difficult.

LANGUAGE AND MEANING IN POLITICAL DISCOURSE

The term "federalism" has generally been associated with the development of the American system of government. Federalism was the key design concept used in the formulation of the U.S. Constitution of 1789. The explanation of the draft of that constitution offered by Alexander Hamilton, John Jay, and James Madison was entitled *The Federalist*. While federalism was its key design concept, the U.S. Constitution established reference to only one of the constituent elements—a limited national government—in a more general system of governance.

The critical conceptual difficulty in constituting a federal system of governance was directly addressed in essays 15 and 16 of *The Federalist*, but serious ambiguities in language still remain. Hamilton argued that an essential attribute of a government is its capacity to enforce law. A confederation, as traditionally conceived, could not meet this defining criterion for a government. The Articles of Confederation had established an organization of states, not a government. The Congress of the United States under the Articles of Confederation could not enforce its own resolutions. Hamilton argued that the concept of a confederation had to be reformulated. In his view, individuals are the basic constitutive element in each unit of government. Each unit of government must be able to articulate the aspirations of people, respond to the demands of individuals, and enforce its resolutions with regard to individuals, not to collectivities as such. Each unit would be autonomous in itself and have both executive and judicial authorities to enforce its resolutions as laws. Hamilton's reformulation of the concept of confederation is, in my view, an essential attribute of what has come to be known as a federal system of government.

Serious ambiguities continue to exist because both Hamilton and Madison were not careful to distinguish between "federal" and "confederation" in their discourses. What was proposed by the Philadelphia Convention of 1787 was variously referred to as a confederation, a federal government, the Union, and the general government. This conceptual confusion persists today among scholars and among those who have special responsibility for construing the meaning of the U.S. Constitution.

The first general application of the concept of federalism to a system of autonomous units of governments occurred in the formulation of the U.S. Constitution. The primary referent, then, was the authority of a limited national government in its relationship to state governments. The basic conception is reflected in the name: the United States of America. One of the attributes used as a standard definition of federalism is a system of government where authority is exercised concurrently by a national government and state or provincial governments. With such a definition, the focus is upon a two-tiered structure of government. Thus William Riker, in his *Federalism*, explicitly states this definition as follows:

A constitution is federal if (1) two levels of government rule the same land and people, (2) each level has at least one area in which it is autonomous, and (3) there is some guarantee (even though merely a statement in a constitution) of the autonomy of each government in its own sphere. [1964, 11]

All federal systems have reference to multiple units of government, each of which has an autonomous existence. A two-tier arrangement might thus qualify as a federal system. It is entirely possible, however, for a state to draw upon the concept of a federal system in constituting its own internal system of governance as did the California constitutional convention in 1879. There are those who refer to federated cities (Zimmerman 1972). General laws pertaining to the incorporation of municipalities, where decisions to incorporate are made by local citizens with the authority to formulate and modify the corporate charters, have all the attributes that I would associate with a federal system of governance.

I see no reason why national governments should represent the ultimate achievement among human beings in fashioning systems of governance. Efforts to deal with standard forms of international organizations are subject to the basic flaw that Hamilton identified with confederation. The United Nations is an *organization* of *nation-states*, not a government. Hamilton would have considered it absurd to refer to such an organization as a "government." Yet the efforts of the nations of Western Europe to fashion a European Community are taking on some of these attributes. Since these attributes relate to the standing of individuals and other units of government, we might begin to think of a federal system of governance being fashioned in the European Community. To treat Western Europe as though it were constituted only by reference to nation-states is to misunderstand what is occurring there. Europeans cannot shape the future of their societies only by reference to nation-states as such. How these arrangements are worked out is a matter of profound constitutional significance for the future of Europe with considerable bearing upon what is meant by a federal system.

The crucial issue is that the concept of federalism enables people to break out of the conceptual trap inherent in a theory of sovereignty that presumes there must exist some single center of supreme authority that rules over society. If the nations of Europe exist as single centers of supreme authority, then there can be no European Community. Conversely, if the European Community were organized by reference to a single center of supreme authority, there could be neither national nor local autonomy. So long as such a concept of sovereignty is presumed necessary to a system of government, I cannot imagine how it is possible for democracies to exist in domains that reach out to continental proportions.

Relying upon mere words in a constitution, as Riker suggests, is a very weak way to characterize a democratic or federal system of governance. The name Union of Soviet Socialist Republics would seem to imply a federal system of democratic government. The term "soviet" refers to councils. But anyone who is aware of the key concepts that Lenin drew upon to design the Soviet experiment would know that he placed critical emphasis upon strict secrecy and strict discipline subject to the central leadership of the

Communist party. Lenin presumed that the whole country could be run like the German postal system. Despite the use of such words as "union," "soviet," and "republic," the Soviet Union was none of these (Kaminski 1992). It was an autocracy run by the Communist party leadership. It is possible that the Gorbachev reforms may achieve constitutional alterations consistent with a federal system of democratic government. But that would be a system of government much different from the one conceptualized by Lenin and ruled over by Stalin.

Systems of governance have reference to many attributes. Attributes applicable to the coexistence of entities identified as a national "government" and state or provincial governments again bring us back to the puzzle of whether it is governments that govern or whether the existence of democracies implies that people govern in some meaningful sense. This puzzle leads us to a radically different concept embedded in the term "federalism."

In several of his works on federalism, Daniel Elazar points to the derivation of the word federalism from the Latin term *foedus*, which means covenant (See, for example, Elazar and Kincaid 1980). *Foedus* has much the same meaning as the Hebrew term *b'rit*, which is fundamental to biblical traditions pertaining to covenantal relationships with God and with those who choose to govern their relationships with one another by covenant. "Federal theology" in the sixteenth and seventeenth centuries was a covenantal theology developed by some Protestants to conceive a system of church governance that drew upon Old Testament concepts of covenants and New Testament accounts of early Christian congregations; it was sharply opposed to the doctrine of apostolic succession relied upon by the Roman Catholic church in the constitution of its system of governance. The Puritans of New England were congregationalists who adhered to federal theology, and in the Mayflower Compact the first Puritans made the commitment to covenant with one another in constituting civil bodies politic. This commitment can be viewed as a basic precommitment to a federal system of governance. It adds an important dimension to federalism as pertaining to multiple units of government.

The commitment of American Puritans to a covenantal approach has an interesting parallel to a seemingly strange use of language in Switzerland. German-speaking Swiss still refer to confederation as *Eidgenossenschaft*. *Genossenschaft* means association or comradeship. *Eid* refers to oath. An *Eidgenossenschaft* is an association bound together in a special commitment expressed by reciprocal oaths. A Swiss citizen is referred to as an *Eidgenosse*, that is, a covenanter—a comrade bound by oath. The source of authority resides, then, in a covenant that each is bound to uphold in governing relationships with another. Authority grounded in comradeship—collegiality—has quite different connotations from authority viewed as *Herrschaft*—lordship—the standard German term translated as "authority." It implies domination. Swiss and Dutch confederations existed before the Pilgrims' journey to New England, and the Pilgrim Church still stands in Leiden, giving testimony to the existence of a self-governing congregation nearly four centuries ago.

Once we begin to understand that the way people think and relate to one another is a most fundamental feature in the governance of human affairs, we can appreciate that "governments" can exercise only a limited role in the governance of a society. Concepts of covenants, constitutions, and multiple units of government all fit together in relation to a "federal" system of government. The focus cannot be upon governments alone but needs to include how people think and relate to one another and how the whole complex system of relationships gets put together. We can then begin to understand how a concept like democracy might be a meaningful one, one that might make us think of people really governing. In short, descriptions of what "governments" do no longer suffice if we are to understand systems of governance in democratic societies.

The term "federalism" has quite different connotations to those who associate the French Revolution with their aspirations for democracy. During the period of the Convention, which was dominated by Robespierre and the Jacobin clubs, some of their opponents called for provincial autonomy in a federal system of government. During the Terror, federalists were thought of as betraying the revolution and thus as committing treason against the French Republic. From this perspective, federalism has come to be associated in some French traditions of thought with conservative provincialism opposed to revolutionary progress. The American Revolution and the French Revolution gave expression to quite different ways of conceptualizing systems of governance.

In my efforts to understand how a democratic system of governance works, I have found it necessary to reexamine much of the conventional wisdom in contemporary political science. To this end, I have pursued lines of inquiry into basic issues in political philosophy, political economy, history, epistemology, philosophical anthropology, analytical jurisprudence, sociology, and cognitive psychology. Public administration has usually been at the core of my concern because the operational context of any system of government turns upon what gets done. To administer implies to bring into use or operation—to transform concepts and ideas into states of affairs. What gets done turns upon how institutions as systems of rule-ordered relationships work. How institutions affect the structure of incentives for people to act is one of the key considerations in the study of any system of governance. The constitutional level of analysis assumes a special significance in democratic societies because it is in the context of constitutional choice that the terms and conditions of government get specified as systems of rules that apply to those who exercise rulership prerogatives.

If constitutions are to be effective—to be more than words on paper—it is necessary to understand how to design systems of governance for democratic societies in contrast to autocracies. This question, in turn, drives one back to explore basic ideas about how people think and relate to one another. It is an essential feature of a democratic society that people, as they live their lives and shape their aspirations, should think of and experience themselves in certain ways.

TOCQUEVILLE'S ANALYSIS OF THE AMERICAN EXPERIMENT

I consider Tocqueville's *Democracy in America* to be the single most important study of a democratic society. In his analysis, he considers three types of factors to be important in understanding how a society functions. The first factor he identifies as "the peculiar and accidental situation in which Providence" places people (Tocqueville [1835] 1945, 1: 288). I construe this category to refer to the environmental and material conditions that are available to people in fashioning their lives. The second factor is "the laws," which I construe broadly to refer to institutions—the working rules of going concerns (Commons [1924] 1968). The third factor is the "manners and customs of the people." In discussing this factor, Tocqueville refers to *the habits of the heart* (his emphasis) and to "the mass of those ideas which shape their character of mind" ([1835] 1945, 1: 299). I therefore construe manners and customs to include habits of thought—cognition. We might think of people as having characteristic habits of the heart and mind that get linked in shaping human activities.

In assessing the relative importance of these factors in his concluding assessment of the "causes which tend to maintain democracy in America," Tocqueville gives first priority to the habits of the hearts and minds of Americans. Relating to one another by convenantal methods might then be construed to be the most important factor in conceptualizing a federal system of governance. The laws, or institutions, are identified as the second of the most important factors contributing to the maintenance of democracy in America. Among these factors Tocqueville gives priority to three:

> The first is that federal form of government which the Americans have adopted, and which enables the Union to combine powers of a great republic with the security of a small one.
>
> The second consists of those township institutions which limit the despotism of the majority and at the same time impart to the people a taste for freedom and the art of being free.
>
> The third is to be found in the constitution of the judicial power. I have shown how the courts of justice serve to repress the excesses of democracy, and how they check and direct the impulses of the majority without stopping its activity. [Ibid., 299]

Human societies and their systems of governance, drawing upon Tocqueville, can be thought of as complex configurations of relationships, including the natural endowments reflected in the "peculiar and accidental situation" in which people find themselves, the institutions that structure patterns of relationships among people, and the habits of the heart and mind that shape the ways people think and feel about themselves and about their relationships with others. It is in such a context that the meaning of federalism needs to be examined if we are to understand the relationship of federalism to democracy.

The impulse to unravel such strands of inquiry is usually provoked by puzzles that lead one deeply into a subject. The work of Alexis de Tocqueville, more than anyone else's, has continued to provoke my inquiries. In *Democracy in America* ([1835] 1945, 1: 89) he observes that "the appearance of disorder which prevails on the surface leads one to imagine that society is in a state of anarchy; nor does one perceive one's mistake until one has gone deeper into the subject." These words have provided me with a basic rule of thumb: Be skeptical of surface appearances—and be prepared to go deeper into the subject. Assertions about "chaos" usually imply that some deeper pattern of order prevails, different from that anticipated by an observer (Huckfeldt 1990).

The paragraph with which Tocqueville concludes his first chapter on the geography of North America has provoked me to conjecture that the theory of American federalism was of Copernican proportions in the development of political theory.

> In that land the great experiment of the attempt to construct society upon a new basis was to be made by civilized man; and it was there, for the first time, that theories hitherto unknown, or deemed impracticable, were to exhibit a spectacle for which the world had not been prepared by the history of the past. [(1835) 1945, 1: 25]

Such an observation implies that the essays by Alexander Hamilton, John Jay, and James Madison published as *The Federalist* were more than propaganda published in the course of a political campaign and deserve to be treated as a serious contribution to political theory. The assertion in Harold Lasswell's and Abraham Kaplan's *Power and Society* that Tocqueville comes "dangerously close" to "brute empiricism" (1950, x) suggests to me that they did not understand the magnitude of the revolution in political theory that had taken place. In *The Political Theory of a Compound Republic* (1987), I have attempted to expound the theory used by Hamilton and Madison in their effort to explain the U.S. Constitution. It is somewhat surprising to find how few major works in modern political theory give serious attention to the work of Hamilton, Madison, or Tocqueville.

In opening his discussion of the administration of government in New England, Tocqueville offers a comment that is a challenge to any serious student of political theory, political economy, or public administration.

> Nothing is more striking to a European traveler in the United States than the absence of what we term the government, or the administration. Written laws exist in America, and one sees the daily execution of them; but although everything moves regularly, the mover can nowhere be discovered. The hand that directs the social machinery is invisible. [(1835) 1945, 1: 70]

Since Adam Smith, economists have viewed competitive markets as achieving an ordering of relationships as if an invisible hand were at work. Most contemporary scholars assume that "the government" exercises a highly visible hand in the administration of society. Tocqueville recognized that the highly centralized system of French administration exercised a clearly visible hand in maintaining tutelage over French society. Instead of an overarching system of bureaucratic administration, the American system of overlapping jurisdictions and fragmentation of authority comes much closer to meeting the criteria Max Weber identified with democratic administration (Rheinstein 1954, 330–34). In *The Intellectual Crisis in American Public Administration* (1989), I have argued that an institutionally rich federal system of government yields a different system of public administration, functioning more as an open, competitive public economy, from what one would expect under a bureaucratic system of administration.

In the concluding paragraph of a chapter called "The Principles of Sovereignty of the People," Tocqueville also observes that "in some countries a power exists which, though it is in a degree foreign to the social body, directs it and forces it to pursue a certain track. In others the ruling force is divided, being partly within and partly without the ranks of the people" ([1835] 1945, 1: 57). I construe these references to imply that the first type of country is an autocracy, where a state rules over society, and that the second type includes representative institutions, as with a king-in-parliament. Tocqueville, however, goes on to observe: "But nothing of the kind is to be seen in the United States; there society governs itself for itself" (ibid., 57).

If a "state" is conceived as a monopoly of authority relationships and the coercive use of force in a society, then a society governed by a great multitude of governments, many of which have their own police, cannot be conceptualized as a state. I prefer to think of such an arrangement as a "system of governance" or simply as a "political system," recognizing that the feature of being a monopoly need not apply to all systems of governance. Madison, in essay 39 of *The Federalist*, makes an important allusion when he refers to "that honorable determination which animates every votary of freedom, to rest all our political experiments on the capacity of mankind for self-government" (Hamilton, Jay, and Madison [1788] n.d., 243). If a federal system of government entails a great multitude of governments, each organized on principles of self-government, we might view such an arrangement as constituting a self-governing society where "society governs itself for itself."

SOME CONTEMPORARY REFLECTIONS

In *The Political Theory of a Compound Republic* (1987, 25), I have suggested that federalism can be characterized as *constitutional choice reiterated* to apply to many different units of government

where each is bound by enforceable rules of constitutional law."
This is consistent with a view of American federalism as the constitution of order for a self-governing society. Alternatively and
equivalently, such a society might be conceived as a constitutional
political economy for a self-governing society.

The term "constitutional political economy" comes from
the work of James M. Buchanan, the economist who was
awarded the Nobel Prize in economics for his work at the constitutional level of analysis. Most of this work has addressed itself to government as a single entity (see, for example, Buchanan
1975). Here I am concerned with federalism as a system of governance composed of many units of government. This approach
opens new horizons of inquiry because important processes
occur at both the intraorganizational and the interorganizational levels of analysis.

Economists recognize the importance of the interorganizational level with reference to markets. But surprisingly few economists have focused upon the interorganizational level with
reference to public economies as distinguished from market economies. Highly federalized systems of government permit the
emergence of quasi-market conditions in public economies, and
these conditions have important implications for the public quality of life. Invisible-hand effects can be expected to occur in public
economies concerned with the production and use of public
goods and services as well as in market economies concerned with
the production and distribution of private ones.

Further, a system of government organized on principles of
separation of powers with checks and balances implies a sharing of
power among independent decision structures. Using power to
check power amid opposite and rival interests (to combine phrases
from Montesquieu and Madison) implies that such a system of
government will have equilibrating tendencies. When veto conditions are met, power is shared within constraints that more closely
approximate agreement and consensus than majority rule. In such
circumstances law acquires a publicness of meaning that comes to
apply alike to those formulating law, those using law, those enforcing law, and those judging the application of law.

In a society that works under such contingencies, it is more appropriate to presume that policies *emerge* from the interaction of multiple centers of authority than to presume that they are *made* by some single center of ultimate authority. Words on paper enacted by legislatures need not meet constitutional and jurisprudential standards of valid legislation. In a democratic society, legislative enactments are deserving of critical scrutiny and are appropriately challenged in alternative decision structures. Valid policies emerge from diverse processes of due deliberation. Collective actions, as distinguished from collective decisions, depend upon what people do in responding to the opportunities and exigencies of life. If there is a shared community of understanding and a reasonable level of consensus about how to address common problems, people will exercise a significant influence in monitoring, facilitating, and constraining one another's behavior rather than presuming that it is only governments that govern.

Government in a democratic society, then, is not simply a matter of command and control but of providing multiple structures that have reference to diverse methods of problem solving. Together, these methods enable people to process conflict in peaceful and constructive ways and to search out more effective ways of achieving resolutions. People have diverse interests but they work out effective complementarities of interest to achieve interdependent communities of interest. Processes of contention and adjustment occur as though an invisible hand were at work, rather than a visible hand exercising command and control over a society (Lindblom 1965).

I view American federalism as a system of government in which a serious effort has been made to come to terms with the possibility that people might, in some significant sense, "govern" and to avoid presuming that "the government" governs. The American federal system obviously has reference to multitudes of governments—a national government, fifty state governments, at least 80,000 units of local government, and great numbers of corporations, cooperatives, unions, clubs, families and kinships, and other forms of voluntary associations governed in accordance with their own charters, bylaws, and mutual understandings. "Governments" govern in a limited sense. But in this configuration of relationships, people have a decisive place in governing affairs. People coordinate complex patterns of interaction with one another while taking account of diverse communities of relationships. So people too govern. The constitution of order in a self-governing society turns upon how those configurations of relationships get put together.

This collection of essays reflects my efforts to come to terms with the meaning of American federalism with reference to its implications for the constitution of order in democratic societies. I believe that 1989 was a decisive juncture in the unfolding of human civilization. If what emerges serves to advance human civilization, it will be because people come to appreciate the creative potential of self-organizing and self-governing arrangements. Something like federal systems of governance—we should not presume that American federalism is the only way—will be of decisive significance. There is something to be learned from what Tocqueville referred to as "the great experiment . . . to construct society upon a new basis."

Viewed from other places in the contemporary world, American government is apt to be seen as American national government or even as "presidential government." These are serious errors. There may be expedient reasons why African heads of state chose to rely upon a metaphor of presidential government. In the Soviet Union, autocratic rule—dictatorship—is now called "presidential rule." If Africans were to concern themselves more with covenanting with one another to form civil bodies politic, they would appreciate that African peoples draw upon diverse ways of conceptualizing patterns of order in their societies. There is as much to be learned from stateless societies as from those that emerged as "kingdoms" and "empires" before the intrusion of European empires. Modern democratic societies cannot be imposed from the top. They emerge as people learn to cope with the problems of collective organization associated with their shared interdependencies.

Some of the same problems exist among the nations extending from the Baltic to the Mediterranean in what is variously referred to as Middle or Eastern Europe. Relying upon national governments to govern is only one element that needs to be addressed. The constitutional foundation for people's assuming responsibility for governing their own affairs in the context of both markets and public economies requires diverse types of institutional arrangements. Further, the place of diverse ethnolinguistic communities in Eastern Europe and the relationship of their nation-states to one another depend upon multinational structures of relationships having the characteristics of federative arrangements. American federalism may be instructive about some of these possibilities.

Americans themselves may also have a great deal to learn from reconsidering the relationship of federalism to something called "democracy." An affliction, which might be called "political modernism," has plagued much of the world since the late nineteenth century. Both Bentham and Marx presumed to know the natural laws of human societies. Both Walter Bagehot and Woodrow Wilson presumed that they could see social "reality" without drawing upon ideas or conjectures to inform their observations. The idea that commonwealths or human societies are fashioned by human beings who draw upon concepts and aspirations to create their social reality was neglected. It was as though knowing nothing were a virtue, ensuring an open-mindedness in the study of human affairs. Induction was presumed to be the basis for the discovery of behavioral regularities. Social theory might then be developed by aggregating inductive generalizations in a behavioral science of society. The challenge of the scientific enterprise was presumed to lie in the future. What lay in the past was mythology, misunderstanding, and error.

Too many American scholars have turned their backs on the roots of their own civilization without understanding how to appreciate the way that other civilizations are constituted or the place of ideas in the continuing emergence of Western civilization. Reading Tocqueville for them is like reading a political travelogue. I make these comments because they are autobiographical observations about the perspectives I earlier held in my life as a scholar, before I came to appreciate the role of ideas and language in human cultural evolution and in all forms of artisanship reflected in human actions. It was in that interval that my relearning began with an appreciation that we as individuals always function in a cultural milieu constituted by semiautonomous cognitive systems that come to us from the past and give us capabilities for facing the future. We may contribute new ideas in the emergence of new knowledge, technologies, and patterns of social organization, but whether we do so will depend upon communication with and acceptance by others of ideas that are ways of realizing our mutual aspirations.

Habits of thought may be transformed over time. What people see as the challenge of a new era may lead them to take much for granted and neglect the essential requisites for life in human communities. It is possible for civilizations to advance *and* to decline.

THE SCOPE OF THIS INQUIRY

The following essays, written over a period of thirty years, represent my effort to rethink and extend the frontiers of my conjectures about the place of federalism in the constitution of American democracy. Chapter 6, "The Organization of Government in Metropolitan Areas," which was written with Charles Tiebout and Robert Warren, is the earliest; "*Res Publica*" (Chapter 8) and "The Covenantal Basis of American Federalism" (Chapter 3) are more recent. They fall into different sections in this presentation but complement one another.

Part II is concerned with the meaning of American federalism and some of the implications that follow from its conceptual attributes. Here, I am concerned with concepts and the computational logics that are associated with concepts. I proceed on an assumption that human thought has its representational characteristics, associated with conceptualizations, as well as its computational characteristics, associated with logical reasoning. Thus, we think by reference to conceptual-computational logics.

The conceptual-computational logic of Hobbes's theory of sovereignty is quite different from that appropriate to the organization of a democratic society of continental proportions. What we today call federalism is a fundamental part of the computational logic appropriate to a compound republic as conceptualized by Montesquieu and reformulated by Hamilton and Madison. These issues are addressed in Chapter 2.

There are, however, deeper roots at the foundation of both Hobbes's theory of sovereignty and the theory of American federalism. These roots have borne fruit in the way Americans express their commitments to one another and their aspirations for the future. Concepts from the very depths of the Jewish and Christian religious traditions are drawn upon—concepts implying a computational logic that can be used both as a method of normative inquiry and in fashioning patterns of mutual understanding among human beings. These matters are pursued in Chapter 3.

Chapter 4 is concerned with construing the meaning of "federalism" in *The Federalist*. The issue was earlier engaged by Martin Diamond, a distinguished scholar of American constitutional history. My reading of *The Federalist* is quite different from Professor Diamond's, and the differences in our respective interpretations are of considerable importance for an understanding of federalism and democratic theory.

Chapter 5 is a critique of the way that Justice Harry A. Blackmun has construed the meaning of federal form with reference to American federalism. Federal form, in his interpretation, implies the eclipse of federalism and the nationalization of the American system of government. This essay presents my critique of contemporary developments in American society that place American democracy at risk.

Part III shifts away from conceptualizing a federal system of governance as such and turns to features that have become important in the unfolding of the American federal system of governance at work. Important conceptual problems are still involved, but the relevant concepts apply to what emerges from the patterns of interaction at an interorganizational level of analysis with reference to multiorganizational arrangements. The reference in Chapter 6 is to the organization of government in metropolitan areas, where that system of governance is viewed as a polycentric order.

I view these patterns of relationships as emergent properties of a federal system because I agree with the authors of an address to the citizens of California that federal principles can apply to a system of governance within a state as readily as they can be applied to the United States.

Chapter 7 is an essay, originally entitled "Public Goods and Public Choices," that I wrote with my wife and colleague, Elinor Ostrom. This essay is concerned more with how federal systems of governance contribute to the emergence of public economies and industry structures with different structural characteristics than with either market economies or systems of administration relying upon principles of bureaucratic organization to achieve command and control over public affairs. Chapter 7, "Public Goods and Public Choices," goes beyond Chapter 6 in more fully elaborating a theory of goods and in extending the implications of a theory of federalism arising from the organization of open and competitive public economies. Both chapters apply economic reasoning to public-sector problems in the context of what might be called political economy, narrowly construed.

Chapter 8 opens an area of inquiry concerned with the meaning of the term "republic." I cannot accept the presupposition that republican government is representative government. Elections and representation may be essential features of republican government, but the Latin term *res publica* implies something like an open public realm. I pursue the implications of such a conception so that we can see public opinion, civic knowledge, and a culture of inquiry as emergent properties arising from the constitutional features of American federalism.

In Chapter 9, "Polycentricity," I am concerned with the way that the structural characteristics of a political system, where power is used to check power amid opposite and rival interests, give expression to processes for resolving conflicts and achieving order in self-governing societies. The American federal system provides the structural conditions for processes that contribute to problem-solving capabilities. Patterns of order and rivalries go together in a dynamic system of governance. These structures and processes elucidate information, articulate alternative ways to address problems, stimulate innovation, and facilitate the emergence of arrangements to address problems in new ways by changes of policy, changes in institutional arrangements, or both. These are the dynamics of a polycentric system of order grounded in self-organizing and self-governing capabilities in contrast to a command-and-control system directed from the top.

Finally, in Chapter 10, I draw some conclusions from this inquiry and conjecture about their implications for the contemporary world. I view the several essays as an inquiry about the constitution of order in democratic societies. I do not look upon the American experiment as the only way to deal with the constitution of order in democratic societies or my own formulations as being the definitive exposition. We can learn only as we sympathetically engage one another in light of people's efforts in diverse societies to organize their own social realities while striving to improve human potentials.

The thrust of the argument in this volume pertains to the conceptions and structural characteristics of a federal system of governance as a particular regime-type that is highly pluralistic in its structure. I have not been concerned with detailed descriptions of particular structures. I assume that these are relatively well known. My concern is with how American federalism can be conceptualized as a regime that enables people to be first their own governors; to exercise substantial latitude in associating with others; to share in the exercise of legislative, executive, and judicial prerogatives; and to exercise the basic prerogatives of constitutional choice in setting, maintaining, and altering the terms and conditions of governance. Minimal emphasis is placed upon command and control. Primary attention is given to the way that the structures serve to process conflict and achieve conflict resolution. Process is the key to the way the system works. Contestation is the activating force that drives the system. The method of normative inquiry inherent in the Golden Rule is the method that makes it work successfully in achieving conflict resolution. Through it, diverse interests achieve complementarities with one another in communities of relationships marked by innovation, reciprocity, and productivity.

The regime-type characteristic of American federalism, in turn, can be contrasted with other regime-types. The questions of how those are conceptualized, structured, and work to achieve results need to be on the larger agenda of inquiry, so that people in diverse societies may learn from one another's experience. Harold Berman's *Law and Revolution* (1983), Ray Huang's *1587: A Year of No Significance* (1981), Antoni Kaminski's *Institutional Order of Communist Regimes* (1992), Richard Pipes's *Russia under the Old Regime* (1974), Alexis de Tocqueville's *Democracy in America* ([1835] 1945) and *The Old Regime and the French Revolution* ([1856] 1955), and Amos Sawyer's *Emergence of Autocracy in Liberia* (1992) provide us with important points of departure.

II

Conceptualizing the Meaning of American Federalism

If, as Tocqueville did in *Democracy in America*, we view the United States of America as a great experiment to construct society upon a new basis, we are required to consider the theory that informed the experiment.

Every experiment, in contrast to blind trial and error, is based upon certain conceptions that get expressed in the design of that experiment. If we are to understand the meaning of American federalism, it is important to view those conceptions or ideas in light of people's approach to designing institutions of government. Chapter 2 contrasts the conceptions and computations inherent in a theory of sovereignty with the conceptual-computational logic inherent in American federalism. Chapter 3 explores the basic metaphysical (religious) and epistemological presuppositions that provide the foundation for the American theory of federalism. Chapter 4 examines the meaning of federalism as addressed by arguments advanced by Alexander Hamilton and James Madison in *The Federalist*. At issue are the contrasting interpretations of Martin Diamond and myself in reading *The Federalist*. Critical readers need to check both interpretations against their own reading of the relevant texts. Chapter 5 is a critical assessment of what can be expected to occur as a general theory of limited constitutions in a federal system of government is abandoned for a presupposition that the American national government is competent to decide on all matters of government in American society.

TWO

HOBBES'S *LEVIATHAN* AND THE LOGIC OF AMERICAN FEDERALISM

Those of us who are concerned with the study of federal systems of governance confront some fundamental methodological problems in deciding how to proceed with our inquiries. By fundamental methodological problems, I mean the basic conceptions and computations that are used to frame our inquiries. We are required to confront this issue as we raise questions about the nature of political and social phenomena. If human beings, at least in part, create their own social realities, we need to clarify whether there are alternative ways to create such realities.

To the degree to which choice is possible and alternative possibilities are available, we might anticipate that different conceptions may be used to design, create, and maintain different social realities. This principle applies to all forms of artisanship. Different conceptualizations can be used by architects, for example, to design and construct various types of buildings. Different types of architecture depend upon both different conceptualizations and different computational logics for putting together different types of structures. Knowledgeable architects presumably use a language that enables them to communicate in a coherent way about the conceptual-computational logics that are an essential part of a theory of architecture.

In exploring the question of whether the conceptual-computational logic associated with federal systems of government differs from that associated with unitary systems of government, we need to take a step backward to view our problem in the context of the constitutional era of the seventeenth and eighteenth centuries. Thomas Hobbes, in *De Cive* ([1642] 1949) and *Leviathan* ([1651] 1960), addressed the constitutional level of analysis during the era of Cromwell's effort to constitute a commonwealth as an alternative to the English monarchy. The central thrust of Hobbes's analysis is that a unity of power is the only way to create a stable commonwealth. John Locke challenged Hobbes with reference to a separation of powers, and the Baron de Montesquieu proposed confederation as the basis for a viable republican system of governance. Alexander Hamilton and James Madison addressed themselves to the failure of confederation and to the conditions for a viable federal system of governance.

The analyses offered by Walter Bagehot in *The English Constitution* ([1865–1867] 1964) and by Woodrow Wilson in *Congressional Government* ([1885] 1956) and his essay "The Study of Administration" (1887) have dominated political analysis in the twentieth century. Bagehot's theses about parliamentary government and Wilson's thesis about bureaucratic administration as the principle of good administration that applies to all governments alike have left us with an intellectual heritage where a combination of parliamentary government and bureaucratic administration are presumed to be the appropriate form for any modern system of democratic government. In that formulation no justification exists for a federal system of governance.

It is only as we step back to the seventeenth and eighteenth centuries that we can recapture the structure of the contending arguments and account for differences in the computational logics that are inherent in unitary and federal systems of governance. The computational logic associated with a unitary system of government is best represented in the theory of sovereignty formulated in Hobbes's *Leviathan*. The computational logic appropriate to republican or democratic institutions in a federal system of governance is best represented by the efforts of Montesquieu, Hamilton, Madison, and Tocqueville. The latter provided us with the computational logic of American federalism.

HOBBES'S *LEVIATHAN*

Hobbes's *Leviathan* represents a remarkable achievement in laying out a computational logic that applies to the constitution of a system of governance in human societies. I refer to the structural characteristics of this system of government as "Leviathan"— Hobbes's mortal god. There are at least six sets of computations in Hobbes's analysis: (1) the initial statement of his methodological presuppositions, (2) his exposition of the computations that are characteristic of human choice, (3) his analysis of man in a "state of nature," (4) his formulation of the articles of peace that lay the foundations for human community, (5) his theory of sovereignty (that is, his Leviathan), and (6) his specification of a sovereign's accountability to God and the natural punishments that follow from errors of judgment.

Hobbes presumes that commonwealths are human artifacts— human creations to serve human purposes. As nature is God's creation, commonwealths or, more broadly, patterns of order in human societies are human creations. These artifacts are a distinct class in the world of artifacts because human beings both make up the matter (constituent elements) of commonwealths and serve as the designers or "artificers" of commonwealths. Human societies are artifacts that contain their own artisans (Greene 1978). Human nature, then, is deserving of special attention for the sake of understanding both human beings as the basic constituent elements of commonwealths (societies) and the artisanship required to create commonwealths.

Hobbes's methodological plea to his readers is to use their own resources as human beings to derive an understanding both of human nature and of the science that is applicable to the creation of commonwealths. He presumes that a common biological heritage is the source of a basic "similitude" of thoughts and passions that characterizes all mankind. What is variable among human beings is largely derived from the accumulated learning that accrues as a cultural heritage overlaying the common biological heritage. It is possible, then, for anyone to use his or her resources as a human being to come to an appreciative understanding of the rudimentary foundations of human nature and of how others think and feel. This requires a studied effort to cross the thresholds of languages and cultures. As a result, the task facing the student of commonwealths is "harder than to learn any language or science," but Hobbes's effort to cover this ground will presumably reduce "the pains left to another" (Hobbes [1651] 1960, 6). The ultimate key to political understanding lies in the resources that each of us can mobilize as individual human beings to understand other human beings and in estimating the consequences that follow as human beings choose to act in hypothetical situations. This use of our resources is what I understand "methodological individualism" to mean—to use individuals as the basic unit of analysis in the social sciences.

In part 1, "Of Man," Hobbes seeks to clarify the basic attributes of human nature. Hobbes turns first to cognitive processes that are characteristic of both man and beast. Perceptions of the external world are acquired through the senses and are transformed into images by the central nervous system. An association of images enables creatures, which learn, to develop foresight presuming something like cause-and-effect relationships. Reflecting upon images to engender new associated relationships is the source, then, of the imagination with which human beings are so richly endowed. The imagination is the source of new ideas, potential advances in knowledge, and innovations.

The distinctive characteristic of human beings is speech (language) "consisting of names or appellations, and their connexions; whereby men register their thoughts; recall them when they are past; and also declare them to one another for mutual utility and conversation" (Hobbes [1651] 1960, 18). It is this factor that is decisive in the constitution of human societies, "without which, there had been among men neither commonwealth, nor society nor contract, nor peace, no more than amongst lions, bears, and wolves" (ibid.).

It is language, then, that enables human beings to use symbols to represent events and relationships. Events and relationships are symbolized by the assignment of names. Human beings transform trains of thoughts (associations of images) into trains of words that can be used in a computational logic to develop science as a "knowledge of consequences" (ibid., 29), derived from the dependence of symbols and their connections to one another in ways that reflect named events and relationships. Reason derives from language (names and connections worked out in a computational logic). Children do not learn to reason, Hobbes argues, "till they have attained the use of speech" (ibid.).

All voluntary action is thus based in thought amplified through human capabilities to reason and thus to estimate the consequences associated with alternative forms of action. The other form of computation made in taking voluntary action has reference to internal indicators that reflect human feelings, sentiments, or passions. These can be characterized as appetites and aversions. These internal indicators are an initial ground for distinguishing good (for which one has appetites) and evil (for which one has aversions). Deliberation, then, involves two sets of computations: first, the calculations associated with consequences of alternatives and, second, the weighing of alternatives in relation to preferences (appetites and aversions or benefits and costs). Choice thus involves conjectures, deliberation, and selection.

The two sets of computations are interactive. Human beings can learn of consequences that flow from acting upon a passion: "Passions unguided are for the most part mere madness" (ibid., 48). They can also acquire appetites or aversions derived from experience. Human beings, then, acquire a cumulative skill in obtaining "those things which a man from time to time desireth" (ibid., 39). This Hobbes calls felicity, and I construe to be equivalent to "the pursuit of happiness." It is a cumulative condition that accrues with maturation.

His summation of the "general inclination of all mankind" is that each individual has "a perpetual and restless desire for power after power, that ceaseth only in death" (ibid., 64). The "power" of a man is defined as "his present means to obtain some future good" (ibid., 56). I construe his postulate to mean that human beings continually strive to use present means to achieve some future apparent good that unfolds in a succession, one activity after another, that ceases only in death. There is a continual striving for something better, whether as manifest in the saint who seeks to bring him- or herself closer to God or in the despot who aspires to gain dominance over others. All human beings have a capacity to think for themselves, and their choices will reflect their own computation of the alternatives they consider to be available. People are never perfectly obedient automata; they always strive to better themselves. This is the source of all political contingencies.

Hobbes's analysis of man in a state of nature I construe to be a mental experiment to establish a zero base for political analysis. His state of nature is devoid of any political conditions or constraints. There is no law, no authority, no "mine" or "thine," none of the arts grounded in words, and everyone is free to take what one can get and defend what one has got (ibid., 83). Each individual is essentially equal to each other individual and is motivated to seek his or her own good. Conditions of scarcity are presumed to prevail. In such circumstances Hobbes infers that conflict will occur and that conflict, in the absence of any political constraint, will escalate to a point where people end up fighting with one another—a state of war of each against every other individual.

The computational conclusion of this thought-experiment is counterintentional. Each individual sought his or her own good but realized misery instead. The argument can be viewed as offering a proof of the insufficiency of the pursuit of unconstrained self-interest in the constitution of human societies. An unconstrained pursuit of self-interest will yield to human propensities to fight rather than to pursue peaceful and mutually productive relationships.

Hobbes's analysis of man in a state of nature, other than as a hypothetical thought-experiment, is seriously flawed because it neglects the distinctly human capability for speech and the opportunity that speech would afford human beings to address themselves to the puzzle that those who sought their own good realized misery instead. Given human capabilities for communication through speech, we might expect them to communicate with each other and derive ways to avoid fighting and develop more constructive ways of relating to one another. This is what Hobbes does in the next step in his analysis—to establish the conditions for peace as an alternative to war.

In chapters 14 and 15 of *Leviathan,* Hobbes specifies some nineteen rules that he refers to as "natural laws" (or "dictates of reason") for establishing the conditions for peace as an alternative to war. These "articles of peace"—all based upon presumptions of equality in interpersonal relationships—are summarized as I have come to understand them in Table 1. The basic computational logic in each of these rules, Hobbes tells the reader, can be understood by reference to a single rule: *"Do not that to another, which thou wouldst not have done to thyself"* (ibid., 103, his emphasis). The Golden Rule, for Hobbes, provides a method of normative inquiry that is characterized by a fundamental symmetry in computing the basic structure of order in human societies: I act in relation to others as I would have others act in relation to me. The rule may be generalized if I put myself in the place of others and others in my place so that our respective "passions" and "self-love" add nothing to the weight. Then we can understand the grounds for establishing peaceful communities of relationships among individuals who consider themselves to be free and equal (see Chapter 3 for further elaboration).

The articles of peace, however, are insufficient for the organization of human societies. They are but rules—words—and rules are not self-formulating, self-maintaining, or self-enforcing. They persuade in the sense of obliging one's conscience, but they do not necessarily compel or control one's actions. In human actions, temptations arise and reign. Unless rules can be enforced they cannot be made binding in human relationships even when they appeal to one's reason and one's conscience. Without enforceable rules, some will be tempted to act at variance with the rules; and men who act in accordance with their conscience may then become the "prey" to others (ibid.). Hobbes's theory of sovereignty, then, is addressed to the problem of how to make rules binding in human relationships. The basic symmetry in the rules that are constitutive of Hobbes's state of peace yields to basic asymmetries in rule-ruler-ruled relationships.

TABLE 1	Hobbes's Articles of Peace
Article 1:	That one seek peace and follow it, but be prepared to defend oneself.
Article 2:	That one be willing, in the quest for peace, when others are willing, to lay down one's right to all things and be content with so much liberty against others as one would allow others against oneself.
Article 3:	That individuals perform their covenants made.
Article 4:	That one act in relation to others so they will have no cause for regret.
Article 5:	That everyone strive to accommodate oneself to the rest.
Article 6:	That upon caution of future time, a person ought to pardon the offenses past of them that, repenting, desire it.
Article 7:	That in retribution of evil for evil, persons look not at the greatness of the evil past but at the greatness of the good to follow.
Article 8:	That no one by deed, word, countenance, or gesture declare hatred or contempt of others.
Article 9:	That everyone acknowledge another as one's equal by nature.
Article 10:	That at the entrance into the conditions of peace, no one reserve to oneself any right which one is not content should be reserved to every one of the rest.
Article 11:	That if one be trusted to judge between one person and another, one deal equally between them.

continued on next page

TABLE 1 *continued*

Article 12:	That such things as cannot be divided, be enjoyed in common, if it can be, and if the quantity of the thing permit, without stint, otherwise proportional to the number of them that have right.
Article 13:	That such things as cannot be divided or enjoyed in common require that the entire right to the whole thing, or else, making the use alternative, be determined by lot.
Article 14:	That distribution by lot be determined by an agreement among the competitors or by first seizure.
Article 15:	That all who mediate peace be allowed safe conduct.
Article 16:	That they that are at controversy submit their right to the judgment of an arbitrator.
Article 17:	That no one is a fit arbitrator of one's own cause in relation to the interest of another.
Article 18:	That no one in any cause ought to be received for arbitrator to whom greater profit or honor or pleasure apparently arises out of the victory of one party rather than another.
Article 19:	That in controversies of fact those who judge should give no more credit to one witness than to another but should call additional witnesses until the question is decided by the weight of evidence.

Summary Rule: *Do not that to another, which thou wouldst not have done to thyself.*

SOURCE: Hobbes, *Leviathan,* chs. 14, 15.

Hobbes's resolution of this problem is based upon a presupposition that a unity of power is necessary to the unity of law and that the unity of power and of law are necessary to the peace and concord of commonwealths. He expresses his presumption in this way: "For it is the *unity* of the representer [ruler], not the unity of the represented [ruled], that maketh the person [that is, commonwealth as a personated aggregate of individuals] *one*" (ibid., 107). The unity of the commonwealth depends upon a unity of power. This is the basic presupposition that applies to unitary systems of governance.

Hobbes's theory of sovereignty is an articulation of the basic computations that follow from the unity of power. A unity of power entails a monopoly over the powers of governance, including the powers of the sword, that are necessary to the maintenance and enforcement of rules of law and the defense of a commonwealth. Such a conception necessarily implies that rulers are the source of law; as such they are above the laws that they promulgate; and rulers cannot themselves be held accountable to a rule of law by other human beings in a commonwealth. From this formulation it follows that the prerogatives of rulers are unlimited, inalienable, absolute, and indivisible. These are the basic attributes of sovereignty that apply to the internal structure of a commonwealth; and these apply in any organization of authority relationships that has the necessity of being a monopoly. Whenever we define a state as a monopoly of the legitimate exercise of force in a society, Hobbes's attributes of sovereign authority necessarily apply as a manifestation of monopoly. Unity of power implies a monopoly of authority relationships in a society.

Rule-ruler-ruled relationships create the most profound tensions in human societies. The power of the sword (of instruments of coercion, in other words), is necessary to derive the advantages of rule-ordered relationships: "And covenants, without the sword, are but words, and of no strength to secure a man at all" (ibid., 109). Instruments of evil, symbolized by the sword, are necessary to derive the common good of peaceful relationships. Human societies, as a consequence, can be viewed as Faustian bargains: people must learn how to live with the use of instruments of evil to do good. It is easy for those with the best of intentions to become the source of the greatest evils. This tension is always present in all societies and can never be ignored.

Rule-ruler-ruled relationships must also involve fundamental inequalities in human societies. Those who enforce rules must necessarily exercise an authority that is unequal in relation to those who are the objects of enforcement efforts. The only question is the degree to which constraints can be interposed upon those inequalities. I presume that the rule-ruler-ruled relationship is the most fundamental source of inequalities in human societies. I, thus, expect all human societies to manifest fundamental inequalities inherent in rule-ordered relationships. Complete equality among human beings in human societies is an impossibility.

How does Hobbes attempt to reconcile the basic symmetry inherent in the conditions of peace with the radical asymmetry between rulers and subjects? This issue is addressed in chapter 31, "Of the Kingdom of God by Nature," in *Leviathan*. There he identifies his laws of nature as being God's law (ibid., 235) in the sense that they are "immutable and eternal" (ibid., 104). He leaves no room for doubt by referring to those laws of nature (God's law) as being presented in chapters 14 and 15 of his treatise (ibid., 235). How, then, do human beings avoid the circumstance of offending against the laws of God by too much civil obedience or of transgressing the laws of the commonwealth through fear of offending God (ibid., 232)? Hobbes's resolution is to specify that the radical asymmetry inherent in his theory of sovereignty is subordinate to the fundamental symmetries of his laws of nature, which he views as the laws of God in the sense that they are immutable and eternal. The logical sufficiency of his political theory turns, then, upon the accountability of those who exercise sovereign prerogatives to God. They are binding upon the sovereign as the sovereign is accountable to God rather than to other human beings.

In the absence of a sovereign's accountability to God (that is, to be bound by the rules of peace), the natural punishments will then prevail:

> There is no action of man in this life that is not the beginning of so long a chain of consequences as no human providence is high enough to give a man a prospect to the end. And in this

chain there are linked together both pleasing and unpleasing
events, in such manner as he that will do anything for his plea-
sure must engage himself to suffer all the pains annexed to it;
and these pains are the natural punishments of those actions
which are the beginning of more harm than good. And hereby
it comes to pass that intemperance is naturally punished with
diseases, rashness with mischances, injustice with the violence
of enemies, pride with ruin, cowardice with oppression, negligent government of princes with rebellion, and rebellion with
slaughter. For seeing punishments are consequent to the breach
of laws, natural punishments must be naturally consequent to
the breach of the laws of nature, and therefore follow them as
their natural, not arbitrary, effects. [Ibid., 240–41]

The association of the negligent government of princes with
rebellion and rebellion with slaughter occurs because successful
rebels find it necessary to use the sword as their instrument of
governance; rebels create their own autocracy to exercise the prerogatives of rulership. Rulers change, but the patterns of rulership
remain the same.

Law viewed as the command of a sovereign is a precarious way
to constitute patterns of order in human societies. There are no
effective ways to challenge the arbitrary exercise of public authority by a sovereign and no effective ways to deliberate about the
constitution and reconstitution of systems of governance in
human societies. These are the counterintuitive implications of
presuming that there must be some single ultimate center of authority in the governance of each society: the more authority is
unified, the more irresponsible it becomes.

In presenting his theory of sovereignty, Hobbes characterizes
his formulation as "the only way" (ibid., 112) to constitute a com-
manding power sufficient to maintain order and security in a
commonwealth. There can, then, only be unitary states. He recognizes that the forms of government may vary among monarch-
ies, aristocracies, and democracies. But, in the case of a
democracy, it too would be a unitary state where only one assembly of all citizens would exercise the prerogatives of government.
Citizens in this case would be both rulers and subjects, but the

unity of power would be preserved by having but one assembly where binding decisions could be made by a plurality of votes. A majority, in such circumstances, would be the smallest plurality to yield an exclusive decision. It is in the working out of the relationship of democracy to constitutional rule and to federalism that Montesquieu and the American authors of *The Federalist* provide us with an alternative to Hobbes's theory of sovereignty.

DEMOCRACY, CONSTITUTIONAL RULE, AND FEDERALISM

Hobbes's characterization of democracies as rule by assemblies of all citizens who will come together neglects a crucial consideration: in order to have *rule by assemblies*, it is logically necessary to have a shared community of understanding and agreement about the *rules of assembly* and what it means to govern by assembly. There are sets of calculations of what it means to govern by assembly that must be taken into account in the organization of an assembly and in the conduct of its proceedings. In establishing the terms and conditions of governance in an assembly, these require stipulation in much the same way that the articles of peace might be specified as the basis for organizing relationships among individuals. We might then distinguish between rules that apply to the terms and conditions of assembly and rules enacted by an assembly to apply to the ordinary exigencies of life. The former would be constitutional in character and, if enforceable with regard to the exercise of governmental prerogatives, might be regarded as constitutional law. The latter might be characterized as ordinary law, or laws that apply to citizens as subjects of law.

Government by assembly, then, necessarily depends upon generally accepted rules of assembly. Hobbes presumes that it is the unity of the representer, not the unity of the represented, that makes the commonwealth one. His view is open to serious objection. In the case of rule by a democratic assembly, the representer (the assembly) and the represented (the citizens) are the same people. A democracy cannot be achieved until there is sufficient unity of the representer and/or represented to specify the terms and conditions of government applicable to a democratic assembly. We thus confront the possibility that a democratic people might draw upon the articles of peace, covenant with one another, and constitute a system of governance in which each official could be held accountable to others for the exercise of a limited public trust.

Within a formulation that might apply to a simple, direct democracy, important issues arise both in relation to the proceedings of an assembly and to the assignment of authority to those who act on behalf of an assembly. Matters pertaining to eligibility for membership, setting the time and place of meetings, a quorum, voting rules, orders of proceedings, and so on, all establish the terms and conditions of assembly. The assignment of specialized authority to direct the proceedings of an assembly, to exercise interim authority, to act on behalf of an assembly in the discharge of executive prerogatives, to represent an assembly in external affairs, and to provide for the common defense all involve agency relationships for which a democratic constitution would require that such authority in each case be limited and accountable to an assembly as a public trust. The prerogatives of an assembly are limited by rules; and the prerogatives of those who act on behalf of an assembly are subject to limits placed upon agency relationships. Limits can be maintained only so long as democracies rely upon multiple agency relationships. To rely upon a single individual to act as the sole agent on behalf of a democracy is to run great risk that the sole agent will become the effective sovereign—the master who rules over society.

There is a puzzle that arises in direct, simple democracies that long led to the conclusion that a democracy is necessarily confined to a very limited domain. First, the territorial domain is limited by the distance citizens can travel to participate in an assembly. Second, all democratic assemblies are subject to strong oligarchical tendencies. The first condition requires no explanation.

The oligarchical tendencies inherent in all deliberative assemblies, explained by Madison in essays 55 and 58 of *The Federalist*, arise from a biological constraint that applies to all human beings: no one can listen to and understand more than one speaker at a time. This means that orderly proceedings in any deliberate assembly beyond a very limited size depend upon the exercise of leadership prerogatives to set the agenda, recognize speakers, and order the proceedings. As assemblies increase in size, the prerogatives of the leadership become increasingly dominant and the voice of the ordinary member becomes more and more attenuated. There comes a point, probably confined to a very few hundred participants, where coherent debate is difficult; and the prerogatives of the leadership predominate. This problem can be alleviated somewhat by moving to representative institutions, but problems of size still pose difficulties. This problem is resolved in the British House of Commons, for example, by confining debate largely to those who exercise leadership positions among the two major parties. The back benches form the cheering sections, and deliberation becomes a form of public theater. The rules allocating debate to each member for a fixed number of minutes in the U.S. House of Representatives means that debate there is of limited coherence. The U.S. Senate, as the smaller body, conducts the more coherent debate. These oligarchical tendencies inherent in deliberative assemblies are counterintentional, operating without regard to the intentions and character of the participants, and also counterintuitive for those who believe that elections and decisions by majority vote are sufficient to sustain a democracy.

Simple, direct democracies, then, were always exposed to institutional failures arising from the usurpation of authority by those who exercised leadership prerogatives and agency relationships. If the people acquiesce in the usurpation of authority by a dominant leader, Hobbes argues in *De Cive*, the death of democracy occurs ([1642] 1949, 97). A democracy survives only so long as the rule of assembly is maintained with effective limits upon those who exercise leadership prerogatives and serve as agents of the assembly.

Limits upon size also carry a correlative vulnerability to aggression by powerful neighbors. Montesquieu recognized this basic relationship when he observed: "If a republic be small, it is destroyed by foreign force; if it be large, it is ruined by internal imperfection" ([1748] 1966, 181). If both small and large republics are destined to failure, the viability of democratic republics is severely limited.

Montesquieu suggested that confederation would be a way of resolving this problem. Small republics might join together in a confederation until they had aggregated sufficient strength to defend themselves against foreign aggression. By keeping small republics within a confederate republic, the virtues of small republics could be maintained. If corruption arose in some part of a confederate republic, remedies could be sought through alternative instrumentalities of government. Montesquieu, thus, viewed confederation as a way of "withstanding an external force" and of preventing "all manner of inconveniences" that arise from "internal corruption" (ibid., 182).

The American effort to draw upon Montesquieu's conception of a confederate republic to organize the United States of America under the Articles of Confederation was, however, accompanied by serious institutional failure. This problem was diagnosed by Alexander Hamilton, and an alternative conceptualization was advanced that I shall distinguish by referring to it as a federal republic.

Hamilton argues, consistent with Hobbes, that government implies a capacity to make rules binding as enforceable laws. A confederate assembly, which depends upon member republics to enforce law, is not a government in the proper signification of that word. Its resolutions are not binding as rules of law but constitute mere recommendations to member republics. If a confederate republic as a "government" mobilizes sanctions to enforce its resolutions in relation to a member republic, it can do so only by an exercise of sanctions against a collectivity. Reliance upon collective sanctions implies that sanctions are being exercised against innocent bystanders as well as those who are culpable of wrongdoing. Reliance upon sanctions against collectivities is thus contrary to the requirements of justice. Justice can be done only if the prerogatives of government are exercised with reference to individuals. Thus a federal system of government requires that each unit of government be constituted with reference to the persons of individuals. A government of governments is, for Hamilton, an absurdity that is contrary to the essential requirements of government: it cannot enforce its resolutions as binding rules. Hamilton's analysis is of far-reaching importance. His formulation of the principle that individuals are the basic units in the constitution of order in human societies deserves to be treated as one of the most fundamental theorems in a political science.

In light of this formulation, the task that the Philadelphia Convention of 1787 faced was to constitute a *limited* national government that extended its jurisdiction to all individuals in its domain in the context of a more general federal system of government. A limited national government exercises governmental prerogatives that are confined to its domain, concurrently with limited state governments that exercise independent powers of government within their domains. The states, in turn, might exercise a limited prerogative with reference to local units of government that in turn exercise limited, independent governmental prerogatives with reference to local affairs. Both Montesquieu's confederate republics and Hamilton's federal republics were efforts to constitute *compound republics*, not simple, unitary republics. The compound nature of federal republics requires what Hamilton refers to as a *general theory* of *limited constitutions:* limits to the prerogatives of each unit of government are to be maintained by reference to a general system of constitutional law. The computations that apply to the constitution of a federal republic require reference to quite a different formulation from the one Hobbes specifies in his theory of sovereignty. The strong emphasis upon subordination is indicated by his formulation that each sovereign has the exclusive, unlimited, inalienable, and indivisible powers of rulership, "and everyone besides, his SUBJECT" (Hobbes [1651] 1960, 112, Hobbes's emphasis). By contrast, Montesquieu articulates the basic structure of a republic that is capable of maintaining liberty by using *power to check power* (Montesquieu [1748] 1966, 200). Madison articulates the same principle by saying that the constitution of a popular system of government depends upon using a principle of *"opposite and rival interests"* that extends through "the whole system of human affairs," including "the supreme powers of the State" (Hamilton, Jay, and Madison, [1788] n.d., 337–38, my emphasis).

The basic computations that apply to a general theory of limited constitutions in organizing federal republics can be conceptualized

in the following way. Each unit of government is subject to the terms
and conditions as specified in a constitution that serves as a legal
charter specifying the way that authority is distributed and shared in
that unit. Specifying the terms and conditions of the constitution is
subject to distinguishable processes of constitutional decision making; those who exercise governmental powers cannot on their own
authority establish or alter the terms and conditions of a constitution. The mark of a democracy turns critically upon the capacity of
the people through processes of constitutional decision making to
control the basic distribution and sharing of powers to govern by
provisions of constitutional law. If power is to be *distributed* and
shared on the basis of *opposite and rival interests,* then all persons can
have access to some powers of government and no one need be in a
position to exercise unlimited powers. Conditions of asymmetry
must be met so that law can be effectively enforced; but the inequalities can be limited so that everyone has a voice in the processes of
government, and no one exercises an unlimited authority.

Citizens in a federal republic have as recognizable roles in the
exercise of rulership as they would within the assembly of simple,
direct democracies. These roles are specified through rules assigning the authority of citizens to participate in establishing limits
upon the authority of government, in specifying the means by
which citizens participate, directly or indirectly, in the processes of
government, and in other processes of constitutional choice. The
basic architecture of a limited constitution, then, has reference to
the authority of individuals and limits upon the authority of government; it distributes the powers of government among diverse
decision structures, assigning both powers and limits to the exercise of those powers, and specifies the conditions for the direct or
indirect participation of people in the powers exercised by the different structures of governance. I shall refer briefly to each of these
sets of calculations.

Constitutional provisions that are traditionally referred to as
"bills of rights" typically specify limits upon governmental authority and assign authority, as inalienable rights, to individuals as
persons or citizens. The rights in question include freedom of
communication, protection of property, the enforcement of con-

tracts, rights of association including religious association outside the confines of governmental control, and rights to due process of law. It should be strongly emphasized that these are not private rights but public rights exercisable by individuals in the context of interpersonal relationships. Freedom of speech and press have their significance in maintaining an *open public realm* for discourse among people in a democratic society about public affairs, a realm not subject to control by governmental authorities. Such freedoms are essential to an independent exercise of the public prerogatives of citizenship and are not confined to purely private relationships and matters of individual conscience. A right to due process of law also implies that citizens have the authority to command the services of officials—judges—to enforce demands that other officials, including judges, discharge their prerogatives in proper, nonarbitrary ways. A right to due process of law also implies lawful limits upon the exercise of governmental prerogatives by officials. A right to trial by jury, in turn, implies that the judicial process must include provision for juries, and thus for the direct participation of citizens in the judicial process. The enforceability of contracts implies that individuals can enter into arrangements for specifying rules that are binding and enforceable in their mutual relationships. As a result, individuals can establish terms and conditions of association that are binding upon one another in governing their mutual affairs under mutually agreeable arrangements that allow for substantial spontaneity. Because contractual arrangements are a binding source of law, it follows that statutory enactments of legislatures are not the sole source of law. Constitutional guarantees of the right to bear arms clearly imply that no monopoly over instruments of coercion can exist in such a society.

I construe constitutional guarantees applied to the authority of persons and citizens as inalienable rights which recognize that individuals are first their own governors in a democratic society. If individual citizens can be presumed to exercise the basic authority specifying the terms and conditions of government and to know what it means to govern, they can exercise the basic responsibility for governing their own affairs while taking account of the interest of others. Either persons or citizens can be relied upon to govern their own affairs and to constitute most social and economic relationships by voluntary association. In democratic societies, people acting individually and voluntarily with others govern their own affairs without being subject to the ever-present tutelage of government. Thus, it is not governments that assume the primary responsibility for governing in democratic societies. Governments only exercise a complement of authority that is necessary for taking collective decisions pertaining to collective goods, including the good of common systems of law, enjoyed in common by communities of individuals.

The architecture of constitutional arrangements in the American federal republic also has reference to a separable assignment of authority among distinct decision structures in each unit of government. Distinguishing legislative, executive, and judicial instrumentalities of government clearly implies the existence of a division of labor and a separation of powers in the exercise of authority in any society where those distinctions occur. Such structures also imply multiple agency relationships. Constitutions assign authority to multiple agents functioning in legislative, executive, and judicial instrumentalities of governance. The merit of such arrangements was specified by Locke and recognized in his *Second Treatise of Government* ([1690] 1947).

The critical constitutional issue turns upon the way that such structures are linked to one another. Where limits occur, one would anticipate that those limits imply checks; and where a reciprocal set of limits exists it would be proper to conceptualize a separation of powers as being accompanied by "checks and balances." If there are limits to the exercise of legislative authority, if executive officials are confined to act in accordance with rules of law in the exercise of executive prerogatives, and if judges can exercise independence in adjudicating disputes pertaining to the application of law, then something like a system of checks and balances exists. Power is then used to check power through opposite and rival interests; and we can suppose that such a society is constitutive of public deliberation about the affairs of diverse communities of interest in accordance with established rules facilitating a due process of law. Rules of law, then, serve as a metric for ordering relationships in such societies.

The third set of provisions usually entailed in the architecture of a democratic constitution provides for ties that link the exercise of authority by citizens to the exercise of authority in governmental decision structures. These provisions specify how citizens participate, directly or indirectly, in the structures and processes of the diverse decision structures of government. Provisions for jury trials imply that citizens participate directly in judicial decision making. The same principle applies to the exercise of the investigatory and monitoring authority of grand juries. Elections become ways in which citizens either participate indirectly in the exercise of governmental authority by selecting those who do exercise governmental prerogatives or directly through various forms of initiative and referendum.

These participatory ties anchor the exercise of governmental authority to the same community of people who exercise the prerogatives of individuals to act with spontaneity and freedom in the organization of society at large. The structural characteristics of custom and law are meshed one with the other by (1) the way that the constitutional prerogatives of individuals have an autonomous standing apart from the prerogatives of government, and (2) the way that individuals participate, directly or indirectly, in processes that pertain to the formal decision structure of government. The participatory links are means by which distributed authority is shared in the governance of society. Individuals govern their own affairs, participating in the voluntary governance of relationships with one another in the society at large and in the more formalized institutions of government. In these circumstances custom, convention, and law become consonant with one another under conditions that make it possible to think of societies as being self-governing. Members of the society rule through a variety of different instrumentalities of government rather than simply being "subjects" where "the" state "rules over" society. Principles of self-governance prevail in place of Hobbes's principles of sovereignty, and these principles of self-governance require both that power be used to check power and that power be shared in accordance with rules of law.

Where principles of constitutional choice can be reiterated to specify appropriate charters for all the different units of government in a federal system, we can appreciate the merit of Montesquieu's suggestion that a confederate republic might avoid the exigencies of failure that were associated with both small and large republics. The reformulation advanced in fashioning a constitution for a federal American republic in 1787 was of fundamental importance in establishing the viability of Montesquieu's conception. The computational logic that applies to the design of a federal republic is radically at variance with the computational logic of Hobbes's theory of sovereignty. Yet the computational logic that applies to human nature, the hypothetical contingencies of "man in a state of nature," and the postulated conditions that are constitutive of human communities can serve as the theoretical foundations for compound systems of democratic republics as well as for Hobbes's Leviathan. There is an alternative way to structure the necessary asymmetries inherent in the rule-ruler-ruled relationships: individuals as citizens can share in the prerogatives of rulership, while both citizens and officials are subject to the rule of law.

SOME CONCLUSIONS

Hobbes presumed that "it is the unity of the representer, not the unity of the represented" that gives unity to a commonwealth. Such a distinction cannot apply to a democratic commonwealth if people are to exercise the constitutional prerogatives of setting the terms and conditions of government. People need to learn and acquire experience about what it means to govern. The use of power to check power amid opposite and rival interests can at best set in motion processes that are preliminary to decisions and to actions. People can also make mistakes and are required to bear the natural consequences of their actions. There is no human providence that can ensure against mistakes. Democracies become tractable when people can learn from one another's experience, and learn to diagnose problems of institutional weakness and institutional failure. Since human societies abound with structures of relationships that are counterintentional and counterintuitive, critical thinking that goes far beyond the limits of common sense is required.

This, then, is why structural arrangements cannot suffice. They must be accompanied by habits of the heart and mind that encourage the use of a problem-solving mode in addressing all puzzles, difficulties, and conflicts that may arise.

Under less propitious conditions a political architecture based upon the use of power to check power can sharpen conflict and yield stalemate. In the extreme case, conflict can tear a society asunder as contending factions war interminably upon one another to gain dominance over the instruments of coercion and to exercise control over others. Bonds of community, mutual trust, and reciprocity cease to exist. One's neighbors become one's enemies.

If American federalism is to be viewed as a great experiment in the constitution of order in human society, its claim to distinctiveness is in providing an alternative to a theory of sovereignty. The constitution of a democracy depends upon multitudinous communities that function as self-governing collectivities and have recourse to overlapping and concurrent instrumentalities of government. But such arrangements are only workable in a society where people achieve a level of learning, experience, and skill that can best be characterized as a problem-solving culture. In such circumstances, people learn to address one another as colleagues capable of inquiring about puzzles, difficulties, and conflicts under the assumption that communication and enlightenment can enable human beings to avoid the perversities whereby some oppress and exploit others.

With due caution and mutual respect for one another, human beings might achieve some modest success in bearing the burdens of a Faustian bargain in which the quest for a better life comes with the authority of the sword—the power to do evil. The use of power to check power amid opposite and rival interests can induce caution and a sense of the importance of a due process of inquiry among fallible creatures who are nurtured by fruit from the tree of knowledge. But these same creatures can draw upon their own resources as human beings to understand others and help shape the conditions for mutually productive and respectful patterns of relationships with one another. Proof of such possibilities is to be found whenever people work together to solve common problems and bring common endeavors to fruition.

In our anxiety to be "modern," we are apt to neglect the wisdom that has been accumulated through the ages and made available to us as a cultural heritage. It is the achievements of the past that afford us with the capabilities for today and the prospects of tomorrow. The method of the Golden Rule means that we each can draw upon our resources as human beings to understand others, to learn from others, and find ways to live with others. But these potentials will always exist wherever individuals who think for themselves also confront the temptation to pursue their own advantage to the detriment of others. Such are the dilemmas of life in human societies, and each of us must come to terms with these dilemmas if we are to become self-governing.

THREE

THE COVENANTAL BASIS OF AMERICAN
FEDERALISM: RELIGIOUS ROOTS

I accept the basic premise that Hobbes makes when he presumes that to acquire knowledge of the political realm and how it works, any political analyst must draw upon his or her own resources as a human being. A key, then, to understanding the conception and design of American federalism as a system of governance is to understand how people think of and experience themselves as human beings, the world in which they live, and how they relate to one another.

The modern scholar in the closing decade of the twentieth century finds it difficult to bridge nearly four hundred years and imagine how people thought of and experienced themselves in the seventeenth or eighteenth century. My concern is only with concepts of fundamental importance to comprehending the meaning of American federalism. These concepts have their roots deep in the traditions of Judaism and Christianity and are profoundly important for their religious significance, but are not confined to the dogma of any particular religious orthodoxy.

In exploring these concepts it is important to appreciate what Tocqueville referred to as an affinity between religion and public opinion. The key concept here is that of a covenantal relationship between God and those who have chosen to govern themselves in accordance with God's law. The American Declaration of Independence draws upon the basic Judaic and Christian presupposition that all men are created equal in grounding its conception of a society consistent with Judaic and Christian teachings. When the Golden Rule is conceived as a method of normative inquiry, it opens the way to a community of understanding, to the development of just laws, and to drawing upon the resources of others to enhance our own understanding of ourselves and the world in which we live. It is these elements as they are bound together in covenantal relationships that give meaning to American federalism as a public philosophy—a metaphysics for citizenship in self-governing societies.

AN AFFINITY BETWEEN RELIGION AND PUBLIC OPINION

When Tocqueville referred to religion as "the first of their political institutions" even though it took "no direct part in the government of society" ([1835] 1945, 1: 305), he did so in the context of an earlier observation:

> By the side of every religion is to be found a public opinion which is connected with it by affinity. If the human mind is left to follow its own bent, it will regulate the temporal and spiritual institution of a society in a uniform manner and man will endeavour, if I may so speak, to harmonize earth with heaven. [Ibid., 300]

Tocqueville's metaphor suggests that problems of political organization reflect the most fundamental tensions in human societies. Efforts to resolve these tensions require human beings to press their inquiries back to the most fundamental presuppositions: the metaphysical foundations upon which reason is itself grounded. Public opinion thus seeks an affinity with religion. Those who repudiate religion find themselves in a paradoxical situation. They take the perspective of omniscient observers, presume themselves to be God, and proclaim their faith as a true religion.

For Marx, religion was the opiate of the people. Yet he formulates what he considers to be the inextricable laws of history, laws that became a new religion with its own orthodoxies and heresies. Anyone who takes the perspective of an omniscient observer runs the risk of playing God without appreciating that eating fruit from the tree of knowledge can yield the mortal sin of presuming to *be* God.

The challenge of harmonizing the temporal and spiritual can be expressed as Thomas Hobbes has done in *Leviathan:*

> Curiosity, or love of the knowledge of causes, draws a man from the consideration of the effect, to seek the cause; and again the cause of that cause; till of necessity he must come to this thought at last, that there is some cause, whereof there is no former cause, but is eternal; which it is that men call God. [(1651) 1960, 68]

Modern science is based upon a powerful presupposition that there is a universe—a single coherent ground for order. Human beings, given their existence as mortal creatures, cannot know the source of creation. They can, however, presuppose the existence of a transcendent order from which all other orders derive their existence. The foundation for reasoned inquiry must necessarily rest upon presuppositions that cannot themselves be proven. They can at best withstand critical scrutiny. The presupposition of a single coherent ground for order in the universe still stands. It is possible, as both Aquinas and Maimonides taught, for human beings to strive for an understanding of universals applicable to nature as God's creation and, as a result, to achieve some rudimentary appreciation of how human beings might best relate themselves to one another and to God (that which is eternal). This is why public opinion, properly grounded, has an affinity to religion and why religion, properly understood as something other than the dogma of particular sects, is fundamental to the constitution of order in human society—to the way people think and act in relation to one another.

To assert that the voice of the people is the voice of God is absurd. To assert that democracy is majority rule is equally absurd. It is also absurd, then, to consider public opinion to be simply an expression of preferences by some sample of a population. What passes for thinking—reasoned conjectures—is deserving of critical scrutiny; and critical scrutiny requires attention to the basic presuppositions that are used to ground thought, because all action is grounded in thought.

THE KEY IDEA

In his chapter "Origins of the Anglo-Americans," Tocqueville suggested that "the reader of this book [*Democracy in America*] will find in the present chapter the germ of all that is to follow and the key to almost the whole work" ([1835] 1945, 1: 28). He turned to New England to explore the idea that lay at the foundation of the "novel spectacle" (ibid., 31) that emerged from those early colonies. He pointed in particular to the Pilgrims, who were adherents of an English religious sect that has come to be known as the Puritans. The body of doctrine to which this sect adhered was "not only a religious doctrine, but corresponded in many points with the most absolute democratic and republican theories" (ibid., 32). They took their inspiration from the Old Testament and conceived of themselves as following in the traditions of Abraham, Jacob, and Moses. They ventured into the wilderness committed to adhere to God's law as conceptualized in the Judaic tradition.

The Pilgrims who landed at Plymouth constituted themselves as a society based upon an enactment that we have subsequently identified as the Mayflower Compact. This compact was undertaken with the following commitment by those who signed it:

> In the name of God, amen. *We*, whose names are underwritten, the loyal subjects of our dread Sovereign Lord King James, by the Grace of God, of Great Britain, France, and Ireland, King, Defender of the Faith, &c Having undertaken for the Glory of

God, and Advancement of the Christian Faith and the honour of our King and Country, a voyage to plant the first colony in the northern parts of Virginia; *Do by these Presents, covenant and combine ourselves together into a civil Body Politick, for our better Ordering and Preservations and Furtherance of the ends aforesaid: and by Virtue thereof do enact, constitute, and frame, such just and equal Laws, Ordinances, Acts, Constitutions, and Officers, from time to time as shall be most meet and convenient to the general Good of the Colony; unto which we promise all due Submission and Obedience.* [Lutz 1988, 26, my emphasis]

This, then, is the key idea—the germ of all that is to follow. The constitution of order in American society is grounded in the concept of covenanting with one another in the presence of God to constitute a civil body politic, *and* in a commitment to one another to act in accordance with such a concept in confronting future exigencies. The idea of covenant, derived from biblical traditions, is connected to the idea of constituting civil bodies politic. Finally, the measure of covenanting and combining "ourselves together" was to be seen in enactments taking the form of just and equal laws expressed in acts, ordinances, and constitutions.

As we saw in Chapter 1, the term *b'rit* in Hebrew and the term *foedus* in Latin both refer to the concept of covenant (Elazar and Kincaid 1980). The terms federal, federation, and confederation all drawn upon the Latin root *foedus.* The core concept in American federalism is to rely upon processes of covenanting and combining ourselves together to form self-governing communities of relationships. These relationships began in the townships of New England and were extended to colonial charters, state constitutions, the Articles of Confederation, the Constitution of the United States, and many of the emergent patterns of order that make up contemporary American society.

Donald Lutz, in *The Origins of American Constitutionalism* (1988), indicates how the concept of covenant was used to create both civil bodies politic and religious congregations. Royal letters patent required a pledge of loyalty to the Crown but left the organization of local government to the settlers provided that local law conformed to the law of England. Whenever new settlements were undertaken, the concept of covenanting and combining ourselves into civil bodies politic and religious congregations prevailed. Congregationalists are the modern descendants of Puritans. Lutz characterizes the Pilgrim Code of Law of 1636 as "the first modern constitution"; in creating it, "a free, self-governing people used a deliberative process based upon their consent to create a government" (ibid., 32). Harold Berman points to much earlier antecedents among the free cities of Europe (1983, 392–403).

The first efforts to fashion concurrent overlapping civil bodies politic were undertaken in the Fundamental Order of Connecticut in 1639, when a common government (Connecticut) was created for a region that included the towns of Hartford, Windsor, and Wethersfield "while retaining intact each town government." The Connecticut Charter of 1662 grew out of these arrangements, essentially ratifying "the federated governments developed by the colonists" (ibid.). The problem of confederation was avoided because Connecticut, as a royal chartered colony, derived a source of its authority from the British sovereign. Lutz concludes that "the federal system of 1787 was not newly devised." Rather, it emerged from some 167 years of experience in fashioning civil bodies politic by covenanting and combining together to form local units of government and colonial charters. With this cultural heritage, people were able to undertake the American Revolution, the formulation of state constitutions, the organization of Continental Congresses, the Articles of Confederation, and the Constitution of the United States. People looked to one another in constituting associations that exercised the prerogatives of government.

PRESUPPOSITIONS

The American Revolution, as proclaimed in the Declaration of Independence, represented the culmination of a struggle over republican principles of self-government and monarchical principles of imperial authority in light of a failure to modify the constitution of order in the British Empire to accommodate

American interests. Justification for this action was stated in relation to basic presuppositions about the constitution of order in human societies that were expressed in the following way:

> We hold these truths to be self-evident, [—] that all men are created equal, [—] that they are endowed by their Creator with certain unalienable Rights, [—] that among these are Life, Liberty, and the pursuit of Happiness.—That to secure these rights, Governments are instituted among Men, deriving their just powers from the consent of the governed.—That whenever any Form of Government becomes destructive of these ends, it is the Right of the People to alter or to abolish it, and to institute new Government, laying its foundations on such principles and organizing its powers in such form, as to them shall seem most likely to effect their Safety and Happiness.

The presupposition that all men are created equal is grounded in the biblical tradition that human beings stand in a position of fundamental equality before their Creator. Furthermore, this tradition teaches that all human beings derive from a common parentage. There is thus reason to believe that there is a basic "similitude" of thoughts and passions that characterizes all mankind.

On the basis of direct personal observation the assertion that all men are created equal might be repudiated as false. All human beings can be described as having variable characteristics that achieve uniqueness in each individual instance. Yet the presumption of equality grounded in the biblical tradition is of profound significance in the emergence of Western civilization. The development of social conventions that make a virtue of both justice and liberty derives from two elements: the concept of equality in relation to some transcendent order; and the possibility of achieving harmony in human affairs by choosing to order relationships in accordance with universal rules that are conceived as God's law. Individual differences exist but do not disprove the presupposition that all men are created equal, which can also serve as a valid basis for the better ordering of relationships through just and equal laws. To regard one another as free and equal in some fundamental sense may be a better way of constituting human societies than to presume that everyone is unfree and unequal.

Other decisions may turn upon other grounds. In employing a particular professional adviser, we need not assume that all lawyers are equally competent and skilled in all practices of the legal profession. We need to make distinctions that are appropriate to different levels of analysis and choice. The genetic lottery of human reproduction may be such that human beings can prudently regard one another as having equal standing in constituting long-term patterns of order even though those individuals will differ in their endowments, skills, and aspirations. Political orders are designed to last for generations, not to serve the discrete interests of specifically named individuals.

We thus face problems of recognizing that different levels of choice exist in human societies and that the modes of analysis appropriate to each level may vary. Choices at a constitutional level are quite different from choices at an operational level. To take account of how to achieve justice and liberty in a society is quite different from a choice between apples and oranges.

A choice of rules needs to be arrayed as a type of analytical problem that differs from the choice of goods and services. Diverse levels of analysis need to be brought together in assessing the performance of differently structured institutional arrangements. The question in such an analysis, then, is not a choice between apples and oranges but the comparative effect of institutional arrangements upon the supply of and demand for consumable goods and services like apples and oranges.

It is in the realm of language, culture, and what is acquired by learning that we find the source of the most significant differences that exist among human beings. It is therefore possible for some societies to place an emphasis upon inequalities as the basis for ordering relationships in human communities and human societies more generally. In some African societies, for example, each individual is presumed to be uniquely related to some founding ancestor, and one's station in life is profoundly influenced by this presumed relationship (Sawyer 1992). Chinese society also emphasizes the unique structure of relationships that each individual occupies in any given structure of social proprieties (Yang 1987). Furthermore, the burden of showing deference falls upon the person occupying the inferior position. A display of a proper order of deference wins a reciprocal expression of respect from one's superiors. A failure to display a proper order of deference is accompanied by a loss of respect from others and is itself an offense potentially subject to punishment sufficient to induce submission. Western democratic traditions have deep roots in Judaic presumptions that human beings are equal in their standing before God and that this relationship is of special significance to those who choose to maintain a covenantal relationship with God and with one another.

Human beings, accordingly, are presumed to be endowed by their Creator with Life, Liberty (the capacity to think for oneself and act in light of one's own thoughts and feelings), and a right to the pursuit of Happiness (the eternal striving for a better life that takes account of the good of others). These conditions can be appropriately realized only when human beings share a common understanding about rule-ordered relationships; and so it is that "Governments are instituted among Men." This order is a proper covenantal relationship only so long as it is consistent with a transcendent order that is the source of creation, and so long as the prerogatives of governance are justly exercised with the consent of the governed.

Basic asymmetries in the rule-ruler-ruled relationships create opportunities for rulers to act arbitrarily. The exercise of arbitrary authority comes at the cost of those aspirations and values that human beings associate with justice, liberty, and the pursuit of happiness. They may even come at the sacrifice of life itself. It is in these circumstances that the people are entitled to alter or abolish an arbitrary form of government and to institute "new Government, laying its foundations on such principles and organizing its powers in such form, as to them shall seem most likely to effect their Safety and Happiness."

These presuppositions provide the context for thinking about a proper covenantal order, that is, one in which a covenanting people chooses to act in a way that is consistent with a transcendent order, "which it is that men call God," and with their idea of one another as a people who are faithful to their covenant with God and respectful of God's creation. In other words, God's law is presumed to be both a way of thinking and a way of relating to one another.

GOD'S LAW AS A METHOD OF NORMATIVE INQUIRY

The presupposition of equality among human beings in the presence of their Creator and the presupposition of an eternal transcendent order that is the source of creation pose a twofold problem for creating civil bodies politic. One aspect of the problem is how to find rules that apply justly among equals. The other aspect is to conceptualize how just rules can serve as universal ordering principles even though human beings confront a great diversity of conditions in which they live their lives. We must come to terms, then, with a method for making normative distinctions that can apply among a community of equals and do so in a way that is consistent with fundamental ordering principles but applicable to diverse circumstances.

Law is grounded in norms, standards, or criteria of choice that distinguish between what is forbidden as against what is permitted and what is required. Law in self-governing societies is not simply a matter of command and obedience. Rather, standards are set and used by people in ordering their relationships with one another. Since this use of standards is itself a matter of choice, the rule-ruler-ruled relationship also implies that such standards need to be enforced. Temptations always exist for some to prey upon and exploit others if rules of law are not enforced. The proper application of standards by both users and enforcers of law requires impartial standards of judgment to maintain the publicness of law and the integrity of life in a society of equals. The problem, then, is how to make interpersonal comparisons to achieve knowable standards, norms, or criteria of choice for distinguishing what is forbidden from what is permitted or required.

Gratian, the Italian monk who codified canon law in the twelfth century, identified such a method when he indicated, as Brian Tierney observes, that "a principal foundation of law [is] the timeless principle that we should do unto others as we would have them do unto us" (1982, 13). This is one version of the so-called Golden Rule that is at the core of religious teachings in the Judeo-Christian tradition. Hillel, the great liberal interpreter of the Torah, suggested that this basic rule is the fundamental core when he asserted: "'What is unpleasant to thyself, that do not to thy neighbor' is the whole Law, all else is but its exposition." A few years later, Jesus of Nazareth was teaching, "Therefore all things whatsoever ye would that men should do to you, do ye even so to them: for this is the law and the prophets" (Matt. 7:12).

The Golden Rule, as a basic moral precept, is surprisingly devoid of moral content. Instead of a rule, it can better be conceived as a method of normative inquiry that enables human beings to come to a commonly shared understanding about the meaning of value terms used as norms or criteria of choice. Viewed in this way, the Golden Rule can be seen as the foundation of major intellectual efforts to develop theories of both sovereignty and constitutional rule.

Hobbes's basic methodology rests explicitly upon using the Golden Rule as a method of normative inquiry. His efforts to formulate the conditions of peace as "natural laws" turn upon norms or criteria of choice for individuals to use in relating to one another. After having expounded his "natural laws" (see the articles of peace in Table 1 of this book), Hobbes tells the reader that grasping the logical sequence of his exposition is not essential to understanding the meaning of those laws and the implicit criterion of moral judgment contained in each law. Rather, "they have been contracted into one easy sum, intelligible even to the meanest capacity" (Hobbes [1651] 1960, 103). This summation is the Golden Rule, expressed by Hobbes as "*Do not that to another, which thou wouldst not have done to thyself.*" Hobbes goes on to observe that this measure showeth him [of the meanest capacity] that he has no more to do in learning the laws of nature, but, when weighing the actions of other men with his own, they seem too heavy, to put them in the other part of the balance, and his own in their place, that his own passions and self-love, may add nothing to the weight; and then there is none of these laws of nature that will not appear unto him very reasonable. [Ibid., 103]

The Golden Rule is used as a conceptual scale—a cognitive device—for making interpersonal comparisons so that human beings can arrive at a common understanding of what is meant by standards of moral judgment and criteria for directing moral action. Standard setting, standard using, judging the application of standards, and enforcing standards in societies governed by rules of law depend, if people are to be held responsible for a proper ordering of their relationships with one another, upon a public understanding of the meaning of standards. The justification of such a method, however, stands upon a somewhat more elaborate set of calculations.

The first step in understanding the foundations of order in human societies is to understand what it means to be human. Hobbes's advice is to indicate that such an understanding is to be acquired by first learning to "*read thyself*" (ibid., 6, Hobbes's emphasis) so that one might come to understand "not this or that particular man; but mankind." This task, Hobbes says, is "harder to learn than any language or science," but one that is tractable to human inquiry.

Such a task is possible because, as Hobbes asserts, there is a basic "similitude" of thoughts and passions that is characteristic of all mankind (ibid., 6). This similitude of thoughts and passions extends to underlying cognitive and emotional characteristics rather than to the objects of human thoughts and passions. Underlying the characteristics associated with particular languages and patterns of acculturation and socialization is a potential for human beings to come to an understanding of one another grounded in the basic similitude that is characteristic of all mankind.

"*Read thyself*" is the first step in coming to an introspective understanding of how others think and feel. But the method of the Golden Rule implies a second step of taking the perspective of the other. At the same time, care must be exercised to discount one's own passions and self-love so as to add no weight to the scale. The method of normative inquiry implied by the Golden Rule, is thus a combination of introspection as a means of understanding others, taking the perspective of the other as an act of the imagination, discounting partialities, and aspiring to impartiality, all this as preliminary to a joint inquiry about the appropriateness of mutually agreeable rules and criteria of choice. Human beings can use such a method to understand the meaning of value terms and devise norms that are impartial, meet standards of fairness, and are mutually agreeable. Indeed, such a level of knowledge is presumed to be necessary to establish the competence of individuals for the governance of one's own affairs. "Self-interest rightly understood," to use Tocqueville's expression, depends upon the right understanding to be derived from the use of the method of normative inquiry grounded in the Golden Rule. This is a basis for distinguishing right from wrong and rendering moral judgment.

The method of the Golden Rule taps a level of human emotional experience that David Hume and Adam Smith identify with sympathy or fellow feeling. This is the foundation for Smith's *Theory of Moral Sentiments* (1759) and also for what Hume refers to as his "theory concerning the origin of morals" (Hume [1738] 1948, 252). This, too, is the foundation for liberty as formulated by Kant. Asking anyone to take the perspective of others, to discount one's own biases and partialities, and to aspire to impartiality as a basis for examining matters of common concern implies fundamental respect for human integrity. The Golden Rule can, then, be considered as a law of laws, and the method of normative inquiry grounded in it might also be viewed as a "road to knowledge" that "leads man to civil freedom" (Tocqueville [1835] 1945, 1: 41). It is a method by which human beings, taking the perspective of others and aspiring to impartiality, might formulate general rules to which each would agree to be bound in ordering their relationships with one another. These same standards might variously be used in setting rules, acting in accordance with rules, adjudicating rules, enforcing rules, and evaluating the consequences achieved by acting with reference to rules. Rules pertain to patterns of interdependency in human relationships. The method of normative inquiry based upon the Golden Rule is an appropriate basis for making interpersonal comparisons with reference to rules that apply to interdependent situations.

The application of the method of the Golden Rule is grounded in presuppositions of equality. Each puts herself or himself into the scale and considers the interest of the other without allowing self-love to add to the weight. Achieving impartiality as a consequence of such a balancing process implies that human beings can then understand the meaning of fairness and justice. From such a method of inquiry, one can derive a principle of equal liberty: Each person should be content with so much liberty in relation to others as one would allow others in relation to oneself.

The great experiment in fashioning a self-governing society on the North American continent had its roots in other great experiments. After Moses led the children of Israel (that is, of Jacob) out of Egypt into the wilderness of Sinai, they fashioned the beginning of an effort to constitute a political order grounded upon the laws of God. The Israelites kept alive a tradition of holding those who exercised the special prerogatives of government accountable to the standards of God's law. That standard is consistent with the consent of the governed when the method of normative inquiry is used among equals to devise impartial rules that meet standards of fairness.

THE STRUGGLE TO UNDERSTAND

The method of normative inquiry inherent in the Golden Rule is also based upon a presupposition that human beings are fallible; in arriving at criteria for moral judgment and jurisprudential reasoning, they can learn from one another. That this presupposition has more general implications for the conduct of inquiry is suggested by the metaphor of Jacob wrestling with God. Jacob's struggle with God was not an effort to dominate and subdue God but an effort to understand God. It apparently was in appreciation of this quality that Jacob was named Israel: the one who struggled with God. Israelites have an appreciation for the importance of contestation in arriving at a deeper understanding about themselves and the world in which they live. An effort to appreciate God as a transcendent order requires that fallible creatures must struggle with one another and with their understanding of the nature of order in the universe. That struggle is not to dominate and subdue others but to engage in a process of inquiry in efforts to advance human knowledge and understanding.

Among contemporary scholars, Karl Popper best reflects the metaphor of Jacob wrestling with God. This is how I construe his *Conjectures and Refutations* (1968). Arthur Koestler's *Sleepwalkers* (1959) offers an account of human intellectual achievement that is consistent with this method of inquiry. It is a method that differs from the Socratic method as reflected in the Platonic dialogues. Plato presumes that it is possible to see the light of truth. The metaphor of Jacob wrestling with God presumes that there are puzzles that go beyond the limits of human understanding.

Those who conceptualized the American experiments in constitutional governance were, in a general sense, good Israelites who appreciated that both the processes of governance and the processes of scholarship are enlightened by processes of conflict and conflict resolution. Those with whom they struggled were not the enemy to be subdued but rather colleagues, with whom one must wrestle to overcome one's own misconceptions and misunderstandings and learn from what others have to say about problems shared in common.

These problems are not all national problems applicable to societies as a whole. Instead, the domain of what is problematical may implicate human communities that range in size from the family circle and the smallest of neighborhoods to global proportions. A commitment to covenanting and combining ourselves together in civil bodies politic is a method for the governance of human societies so long as human beings are willing to use the method of normative inquiry inherent in the Golden Rule, and to struggle with one another as colleagues to overcome misconceptions and misunderstandings. This is a method for fashioning communities of understanding that seek to harmonize the spiritual and the temporal while recognizing that all human beings are fallible. Public opinion has an affinity with religious teachings of the most fundamental sort rather than with the orthodoxies of particular religious sects.

CONCLUSION

American federalism as a great experiment cannot be understood without reference to the metaphysical presuppositions that shape the hearts and minds of a people with two commitments: to a method of normative inquiry inherent in the Golden Rule; and to the struggle that fallible creatures share in coming to terms with misconceptions and misunderstandings. In this way they learn from others, and advance the frontiers of inquiry to better understand the nature of problematical situations.

A faith in the existence of a single coherent ground for order in a universe—the applicability of the Golden Rule in the senses described—is the basis, then, for using power to check power and to achieve the resolution of conflicts. Conflict provides an opportunity to elucidate information, extend horizons of inquiry, and achieve a level of common understanding consistent with a universe grounded in a coherent system of order in which unity can be achieved through diversity.

People in a federal republic are as vulnerable as Hobbes's sovereign to human fallibility and to the natural punishments that follow from erroneous judgments. So long as they are willing to struggle with one another, not to gain dominance and subdue others by force, but to increase understanding of what it means to live a life of covenantal relationships, they have the basis for the design and conduct of great social experiments. Those experiments, however, will certainly fail whenever people think of themselves as omniscient observers capable of functioning as omnicompetent overseers who know what represents the greatest good for the greatest number. This, human beings cannot know in a world plagued by counterintentional and counterintuitive relationships.

FOUR

THE MEANING OF FEDERALISM
IN *THE FEDERALIST*

Whether in developing a political science concerned with explaining political phenomena or in developing a political artisanship concerned with the design and creation of political institutions, language poses a serious problem. The fundamental nature of political phenomena is one of word-ordered relationships. People constitute order with one another by reference to rules. Rules are always stated in words. Thus, the meanings ascribed to words have a fundamental importance in human organization. If there are to be different ways of ordering relationships so that people might know what to expect, there must be ways of distinguishing meanings so that those meanings can acquire public standing. Reasoned political discourse then becomes possible.

If, however, there is no agreement about the referents for terms, and the same term is used in many different ways, reasoned discourse becomes confused and clarification requires a prolonged translation process. When critical self-consciousness in the use of language with reference to political phenomena is abandoned, it is not at all clear that the integrity of different ways of ordering political relationships can be maintained. Since political phenomena

are word-ordered relationships, one might expect those relationships to erode as the meanings of words erode. "Federalism" is one
of those terms about which there is a great deal of confusion. Still
another is "sovereignty." This list could be extended to include
many other terms, such as "state," "government," "democracy,"
"republic," "bureaucracy," "law," "justice," "power," "freedom,"
"centralization," and "decentralization." Without some publicly
shared understanding of what such terms mean, it hardly makes
sense to speak of a political science or to presume that people can
govern themselves by political structures and processes of their
own creation. The pulling and hauling of historical happenstances
would, instead, prevail.

The meaning of terms takes on special significance when a
new concept is being introduced. The only major conceptual innovation that has been identified as having originated with the
Philadelphia Convention of 1787 is that of federalism. It is the
meaning to be ascribed to that term in the explanations offered in
The Federalist that is the subject of Martin Diamond's analysis of
the meaning of "federalism" in *The Federalist*.[1]

There is reason for confusion. The authors of *The Federalist*
applied the term "federal" (foedeal) to both the government
under the Articles of Confederation and to the one proposed in
the new Constitution. The terms "confederation" and "federal"
were used essentially as synonyms and for different referents. Any
difference in meaning to be ascribed to the new concept depended
upon context. This was not unusual, since those who develop a
new concept often have difficulty in reaching a settlement about
what word to use for it.[2]

The circumstances in which *The Federalist* was written exac-
erbated such problems in the use of language. Three active, professional men (Alexander Hamilton, John Jay, and James
Madison) separately wrote some seventy-six essays published seri-
ally as newspaper articles over a six-month period. Others were
written after the serial publication ended. The essays were not
carefully edited, and no opportunity existed for revision of the
manuscript as a whole after it was in complete draft. Anyone who
has engaged in the collaborative authorship of a major manuscript

will appreciate the problems involved. The contention that these authors "chose (virtually) every word with care" (Riley 1978, 73, quotation attributed to Diamond) is plausible only to the extent that well-trained lawyers normally use language with care.[3] The authors of *The Federalist* had less opportunity, because of the serial nature of the publication, to check editorial problems arising from differences in language usage. Potential editorial problems are indicated in essay 1 of *The Federalist*, when the planned format for the series was not executed. The essay was never redrafted to conform to a revised format.

The varying interpretations of the term "federalism," in a series of essays entitled *The Federalist*, are clearly critical. Such interpretations affect one's understanding of the theory used to design the American political system and of how that system could be expected to perform. Where interpretations are forced, we can expect difficulties in developing a coherent account of what was said. These difficulties may then lead analysts to attribute less-than-honorable motives or errors to the authors. Presumably, better interpretations will confront fewer difficulties of this sort.

In an effort to clarify some of these difficulties, I draw first upon an argument advanced by Martin Diamond about the meaning of "federalism" in *The Federalist*. In making his argument, Diamond relies heavily upon essays 9 and 39. To present another interpretation, I shall turn first to Hamilton's argument in essay 9. The analysis there is concerned with the way in which "a firm Union" can serve as a barrier to faction and insurrection. Fragments from essays 55 and 58 provide an explanation for the sources of institutional failure that generated factions and insurrections among ancient republics. It is necessary, then, to supplement the analysis in essay 9 with an appropriate use of those fragments. I shall then turn to the argument in essay 39, where Madison uses *the language of the opposition* to meet them on their own grounds (my emphasis). Hamilton's effort to clarify the conceptual problems associated with confederation will then be considered in the argument offered in essays 15 and 16. This clarification should help us to understand what Madison refers to in essay 51 as "a proper federal system" (Cooke 1961, 352).

Finally, I shall summarize the argument and pursue some of its implications.

DIAMOND'S ARGUMENT

In his essay "The Federalist's View of Federalism," which I use as my primary source for stating his argument, Diamond begins by identifying the contemporary view of federalism. In the typical modern definition of federalism, Diamond identifies its essential characteristic as pertaining to a division of political authority "between member states and a central government, each having the final say regarding matters belonging to its sphere" (1961, 22). Having "the final say" has reference to sovereignty construed to mean supreme authority. For Diamond, then, federalism implies a division of supreme authority between member states and a central government.

Diamond goes on to indicate that there is "a corollary to this sort of definition that has also come to be generally accepted. . . . [T]here are three kinds of government—confederal, federal, and unitary (national)—and that the United States exemplifies the middle term" (ibid., parenthesis in original). He then clarifies his use of the three terms:

> In this view, a confederacy and a nation are seen as the extremes. The defining characteristic of a confederacy is that the associated states retain all the sovereign power, with the central body entirely dependent legally upon their will; the defining characteristic of a nation is that the central body has al! the sovereign power, with the localities entirely dependent legally upon the will of the nation. In this view, then, federalism is truly the middle term for *its* defining characteristic is that it modifies and then combines the defining characteristics of the other two forms. A *federal* system combines states which *confederally* retain sovereignty within a certain sphere, with a central body that *nationally* possesses sovereignty within another sphere; the combination creates a new and

different thing to which is given the name federal. [Ibid., 22, emphasis in original]

Diamond then contends that this "tripartite distinction [of terms] was completely unknown to the men who made the Constitution" (ibid., 23, my brackets). Instead, the terms "confederation" and "federal" were used as synonyms for the same referent. "Federal" (that is, pertaining to confederation) was opposed to unitary or national in a dichotomous set. Given this use of language, Diamond argues that the authors of the Constitution "had, therefore, in strictness, to regard their Constitution as a composition of federal and national features" (ibid.). Those who have come to be identified as "Antifederalists" regarded themselves as the true federalists; and Diamond also regards them as such.

In developing his thesis that no distinction existed between the use of the terms "confederation" and "federal," Diamond argues that Alexander Hamilton's discussion of federalism in essay 9 of *The Federalist* is, "at least, incomplete, and consequently is misleading, perhaps deliberately misleading" (ibid., 24). Madison's argument in essay 39 is used to demonstrate the "composite" nature of the American constitutional formula. When Hamilton rejects confederation as being based upon an erroneous or invalid conception, Diamond contends that he is "implicitly denouncing and rejecting a decisively federal arrangement for America" (ibid., 39). Thus Diamond concludes that "the great teaching of *The Federalist* is not how to be federal in a better way, but how to be better by being less federal" (ibid., 40). In these conclusions, Diamond implicitly accepts confederation as the correct definition of federalism.

THE ARGUMENT IN ESSAY 9 OF *THE FEDERALIST*: BARRIER TO FACTION AND INSURRECTION

In essay 9 of *The Federalist*, Hamilton adds to the advantages of a union the way in which it might serve as a "barrier against domestic faction and insurrection" (Cooke 1961, 50). He refers to the instability of the "petty Republics of Greece and Italy" that resulted in a "rapid succession of revolutions" and kept those republics "in a state of perpetual vibration, between the extremes of tyranny and anarchy" (ibid.). Factions gained dominance and used their authority to exploit others. Oppression and tyranny periodically gave way to revolution and anarchy. Factions incited insurrection.

Hamilton does not develop the reasoning that would enable one to understand why the ancient republics were especially vulnerable to institutional failure. However, Madison in essays 55 and 58 of *The Federalist* provides fragments of a theory that enables one to understand some of the conditions of institutional failure among both ancient and modern republics.

A basic constraint exists in the organization of any deliberative group: only one speaker can be heard and understood at a time. When deliberation is organized in terms of one speaker at a time, the larger the deliberative assembly, the less opportunity individuals will have to express themselves in its deliberations and the greater will be the influence of the leadership over its proceedings. "[I]n all legislative assemblies, the greater the number composing them may be, the fewer will be the men who will in fact direct their proceedings" (Cooke 1961, 395). The operation of any large deliberative assembly, whether in a direct democracy or in a representative assembly, will depend upon the selection of a few to order the agenda and control proceedings. The influence of each member in a deliberative group will decline as the number of members increases. These principles lead Madison in essay 58 of *The Federalist* to conclude:

> The people can never err more than in supposing that by multiplying their representatives, beyond a certain limit, they strengthen the barrier against the government of a few. Experience will forever admonish them that on the contrary, *after securing a sufficient number for the purposes of safety, of local information, and of diffusive sympathy with the whole society,* they will counteract their own views by every addition to their representatives. The

countenance of the government may become more democratic; but the soul that animates it will be more oligarchic. The machine will be enlarged, but the fewer and often, the more secret will be the springs by which its motions are directed. [Ibid., 396, emphasis in original]

In the ancient republics, "where the whole body of the people assembled in person," Madison argues, "a single orator, or an artful statesman, was generally seen to rule with as complete a sway, as if a sceptre had been placed in his single hands" (ibid.).

This oligarchical tendency inherent in all large deliberative bodies also has, according to Madison, an adverse effect upon the quality of deliberations. Time is not available for well-reasoned deliberations. "[T]he larger the number, the greater will be the proportion of members of limited information and of weak capacities" (ibid.). Orderly proceedings give way to "the confusion and intemperance of a multitude" (ibid., 374). In these circumstances, Madison concludes, "in all very numerous assemblies, of whatever characters composed, passion never fails to wrest the sceptre from reason. Had every Athenian citizen been a Socrates; every Athenian assembly would still have been a mob" (ibid.). All large assemblies are thus characterized by strong oligarchical tendencies. These will occur without regard to the personalities or personal merits of the individuals involved. Either a large popular assembly or a large representative assembly is subject to counterintuitive tendencies that yield the rule of a few who dominate the decisions of the many. Where majority rule prevails, coalitions form in an effort to dominate decisions. Majorities prevail over minorities; some have an opportunity to exploit others. Conflict intensifies as factional leaders struggle to gain dominance of decision processes and enjoy the fruits of victory. Conflicts easily escalate to violent struggles for dominance. Unameliorated struggle among factions drives toward extremes of tyranny or anarchy.

In essay 9 of *The Federalist*, Hamilton recognizes that some of the sources of institutional failure in ancient republics had been somewhat ameliorated in modern ones by improvements in the "science of politics," which were either "not known at all, or imperfectly known to the ancients." Among these improvements, Hamilton lists "the regular distribution of power into distinct departments—the introduction of legislative balances and checks—the institution of courts composed of judges, holding their offices during good behaviour—the representation of the people in the legislature by deputies of their own election" (ibid., 51). Hamilton then ventures one more principle that tends to reduce conditions of institutional failure among "popular systems of civil government": "The ENLARGEMENT of the ORBIT within which such systems are to revolve either in respect to the dimensions of a single State, or to the *consolidation* of *several smaller States* into *one* great *confederacy*" (ibid., 52; Hamilton's emphasis is in capitals while mine is in italics). How the "ENLARGEMENT of the ORBIT" within which "popular systems of civil government" operate will ameliorate their tendencies toward institutional failure is a central issue in *The Federalist.*

In beginning that analysis in essay 9, Hamilton acknowledged that the advantage of confederation as a barrier against faction was not a new idea. Already Montesquieu had recognized that "if a republic be small, it is destroyed by foreign force; if it be large, it is ruined by internal imperfections" ([1748] 1966, 126). The ancient republics that were governed as direct democracies were especially vulnerable to the oligarchic tendencies that Madison had articulated in essays 55 and 58 of *The Federalist.* But the problem was that if a republic remained small, it was then vulnerable to external aggression.

Hamilton correctly pointed out that the small extent of the republics that Montesquieu had in mind was much smaller than several of the American states. On the basis of Montesquieu's basic formulation, Americans would be driven to taking refuge "in the arms of monarchy, or of splitting ourselves into an infinity of little, jealous, clashing, tumultuous commonwealths, the wretched nurseries of unceasing discord and the miserable objects of universal pity or contempt" (Cooke 1961, 52–53).

But Montesquieu had contended that a confederate republic enabled people to "contrive a kind of constitution that has all of the internal advantages of a republican constitution, together with the external force of a monarchical government." Hamilton quoted Montesquieu's discussion at length, including the following definition of a confederate republic:

> This form of Government is a Convention, by which several smaller *States* agree to become members of a larger *one*, which they intend to form. It is a kind of assemblage of societies, that constitute a new one, capable of increasing by means of new associations, till they arrive to such a degree of power as to be able to provide for the security of the united body. [Cooke 1961, 53–54, Hamilton's emphasis]

The implications of such possibilities for the military security of republics are obvious, if they are workable. Montesquieu had also argued that the institutional vulnerability of republics to oligarchic tendencies could be reduced by maintaining their small size within a larger confederation. If an affliction, such as the usurpation of authority by some one person or a popular uprising, should occur in one part of a confederate republic, the other parts, Montesquieu argued, could afford remedies and assure the internal stability of the confederation.

Montesquieu's analysis had been well known to Americans. The first efforts to form the United States of America had been organized in accordance with the traditionally recognized principles of confederation. Hamilton attempted to come to terms with the defining characteristics of a confederation:

> A distinction, more subtle than accurate has been raised between a *confederacy* and a *consolidation* [Hamilton's emphasis] of the States. The essential characteristic of the first is said to be, *the restriction of its authority to the members in their collective capacities* [i.e., a government of governments], without reaching to the individuals of whom they are composed. It is contended that the national council ought to have *no concern with any object of internal administration* [i.e., lack of internal administration]. An *exact equality of suffrage* between the members has also been insisted upon as a leading feature of a Confederate Government. [Ibid., 54–55, my emphasis except where noted]

Hamilton went on to assert that "these positions are in the main arbitrary; they are supported neither by principle nor precedent." While confederations had generally adhered to these principles, the existence of exceptions led him to conclude that there was "no absolute rule on the subject." Where "the principle contended for" had prevailed, it had caused "incurable disorder and imbecility in the government"—that is, institutional failure had reached critical proportions.

Diamond takes these same three characteristics, namely, (1) a government of governments, (2) lack of internal administration, and (3) equal suffrage of the members, as both his own definition of federalism and the essential defining characteristics claimed for federalism by Hamilton's opponents. Hamilton explicitly questions the wisdom of using these conditions for designing a system of government. Diamond criticizes Hamilton's response to those who wish to see these three characteristics used in the design of the Constitution. Diamond argues that Hamilton did not answer the question at all, because all he did was assert that "they are bad things for society." "In short," Diamond contends, "it is Hamilton's refutation of his opponents' view which is 'arbitrary,' having been vindicated 'neither by principle nor precedent'" (1961, 29).

We are confronted with a very basic issue in attempting to arbitrate between Hamilton's and Diamond's contentions. Diamond proceeds on the assumption that the terms "federal" and "confederation" are synonyms for the same referent, the essential defining criteria of which are: (1) a government of governments, (2) the absence of internal administration, and (3) equal suffrage of member states. Hamilton, on the contrary, assumes that a government over collectivities, that is, a government of governments, is an erroneous or invalid conception. If, in a confederation, the states retain all the sovereign power, as Diamond contends, Hamilton would think it absurd to speak of sovereigns as being governed by a nonsovereign government. The logic of sovereignty meaning supremacy presumes, instead, that sovereigns govern subjects. Hamilton is suggesting that the traditional definition of confederation will not stand critical scrutiny because it relies upon an incoherent use of language: nonsovereign governments cannot govern sovereigns. A confederate republic cannot repress dominant factions exercising tyrannical powers without violating the supreme authority of the member state. The characteristics of abstinence from internal administration and equal suffrage are not independent defining characteristics. They are simply additional attributes of the supreme authority of member states. There is an appearance of subtlety in the use of these defining characteristics, Hamilton asserts; but the concept of confederation as traditionally defined cannot stand critical scrutiny. To speak of sovereigns governing sovereigns, or equivalently of governments governing governments, is logically incoherent given the meaning traditionally assigned to the terms "sovereignty" and "government."

Hamilton then proposes, in terms closely parallel to Montesquieu's, to redefine a confederate republic as "an association of two or more States into one State." He goes on to elaborate:

> The extent, modifications and objects of the Foederal authority are mere matters of discretion. So long as the separate organisation of the members be not abolished, so long as it exists by a constitutional necessity for local purposes, though it should be in perfect subordination to the general authority of the Union, it would still be, in fact and in theory, an association of States, or a confederacy. The proposed Constitution, so far from implying an abolition of the State Governments, makes them constituent parts of the national sovereignty by allowing them a direct representation in the Senate, and leaves in their possession certain elusive and very important portions of sovereign power. This fully corresponds, in every rational import of the terms, with the idea of a Foederal Government. [Cooke 1961, 55]

Hamilton variously uses the terms "confederate republic," "confederacy," and "foederal." He is saying that the erroneous conception inherent in the traditional definitions of these terms can be corrected by referring to a confederate republic as an association of two or more states into one state that exists as a compound republic rather than a simple unitary republic.[4] These conditions can be met so long as the member republics have independent constitutional standing pertaining to their own internal affairs ("local purposes"). Sovereignty, conceptualized as the authority to make laws, is divided so that the people of the member republics are subordinate to the authority of the Union with respect to national affairs, but are independent with respect to those governmental prerogatives that apply to the jurisdiction of the separate states or republics. The states, in turn, serve as constituent parts of the national government by their representation in the Senate. Governments do not govern governments as such. Concurrent governments reach to the persons of individuals, including citizens and officials claiming to exercise governmental prerogatives under constitutional authority. These, I assume, are the true defining characteristics of what Madison refers to as a "proper federal system" in essay 51 of *The Federalist.*

A critical issue in these discussions is what is meant by the term "sovereignty." Is it based upon a conception that in all human societies there must exist a single source of supreme authority that is the ultimate source of law, above the law, and cannot be held accountable by a society's members? Tocqueville, on the contrary, asserts in *Democracy in America* that "sovereignty may be defined to be the right of making law" ([1835] 1945, 1: 123). Hamilton asserts in essay 15 of *The Federalist* that "government implies the power of making laws." Madison, in essay 53, distinguishes a constitution from a law: a constitution is "established by the people and *unalterable* by the government, and a law [is] established by the government and alterable by the government" (Cooke 1961, 360).

If we draw upon these distinctions, constitutions might be viewed as *fundamental laws* establishing the terms and conditions of government, and the enactments of governments as *ordinary laws.* Supreme authority is exercised by the people as they set the terms and conditions of fundamental law by covenanting and combining themselves together into civil bodies politic. It is not governments that are supreme; what is supreme is the constitutional authority of people to establish and alter the terms and conditions of government. Authority to make law is then subject to a potential division of labor so long as sovereignty is defined as the authority of making law. But this definition is no longer consistent with the presumption that supreme authority resides with "the government." This is why Hamilton considered as an absurdity the idea of governments exercising supreme authority being governed by a nonsovereign government.

By contrast, Diamond summarizes the modern definition of federalism as "the 'division of political power,' [that is,] a division of supremacy (sovereignty, as used to be said) between member states and a central government, each having a final say regarding matters belonging to its own sphere" (1961, 37).

We are in the presence of a tyranny of words. People address one another but use words that put them at cross-purposes. The supremacy of law exists where people possess and exercise constitutional prerogatives to formulate the fundamental law setting the terms and conditions of government. This is not the same as presuming that supreme authority can be divided between state governments and a national government. Governments as such are not supreme. They are subject to fundamental law as formulated in constitutions and alterable by the people engaged in processes of constitutional choice.

In asserting that "the extent, modifications, and objects of Foederal authority are mere matters of discretion," I assume that Hamilton was overstating his case. He certainly would not have considered matters of national defense and foreign affairs as purely matters of discretion. Thus we have no reason for believing that Hamilton has the final say in conceptualizing federalism, even though we might accept his argument that Montesquieu's conception is unsatisfactory, and that the generally accepted criteria used both by Hamilton's opponents and, in more recent times, by Diamond and his colleagues are "more subtle than accurate" (Cooke 1961, 54). Those defining characteristics cannot be accurate if, as Hamilton contends, they are logically incoherent and based upon an erroneous conception. On the other hand, Montesquieu's notion that it is possible to have more than one government operate concurrently, so that a democratic society organized on republican principles might have reference to both smaller and larger units of government, is worthy of further development. This notion provides the key for avoiding the sources of institutional failure that afflicted ancient republics.

Hamilton's reference to the new principle of "ENLARGE-MENT of the ORBIT" within which popular systems of civil government might better operate is to the principle of federalism (Cooke 1961, 51–52). He expresses this principle in essay 9 of *The Federalist* as involving "the consolidation of several smaller States into one great confederacy" (ibid., 52). It does make sense to speak of governments of limited jurisdiction where principles of constitutional law can be used to establish limits upon those who exercise governmental authority, whether state or federal. Allusions to an extended republic presuppose a compound republic: an association of republics within a republic where all are bound by rules of constitutional law. A federal republic includes multiple overlapping units of government that act with reference to individuals rather than governments as such.

In this view, Madison's concluding paragraph in essay 10 of *The Federalist* takes on special meaning:

> In the extent and proper structure of the Union, therefore, we behold a Republican remedy for the diseases most incident to Republican Government. And according to the degree of pleasure and pride, we feel in being Republicans, ought to be our zeal in cherishing the spirit, and supporting the character of Federalists. [Ibid., 65]

The passage is to be read with special emphasis upon "the extent *and proper structure* of the Union." Those who are devoted to republican principles of self-government cherish the spirit of federalism. The great teaching of *The Federalist*, to paraphrase Diamond, is that federalism is the better way of organizing "popular systems of civil government" (Cooke 1961, 51–52). The authors of *The Federalist* chose an appropriate name for their work.

Many political scientists ignore Madison's qualification of "proper structure" in reading this passage. They refer only to an "extended republic." The concluding sentence is then viewed as less than honest political rhetoric.

THE ARGUMENT IN ESSAY 39 OF *THE FEDERALIST*: USING THE LANGUAGE OF THE OPPOSITION

In essay 39 of *The Federalist*, Madison initially addresses the question of whether "the general form and aspect" of the proposed government are "strictly republican." In doing so, he presumes that no other form is "reconcilable with the genius of the people of America; with the fundamental principles of the revolution; or with that honorable determination, which animates every votary of freedom, to rest all our political experiments on the capacity of mankind for self-government" (Cooke 1961, 250). Republican principles of self-government presumably should apply to all political experiments undertaken by the American people.

Having concluded his initial argument by answering his own question in the affirmative, Madison addresses the contention of critics that the new government ought not only to conform to republican principles but with equal care to preserve "the *federal* form, which regards the union as a *confederacy* of sovereign States." These critics argue that the new government is "a *national* government, which regards the union as a *consolidation* of the States" (ibid., 253, emphasis in original). It should be emphasized that Madison is here referring to the "*federal* form" that regards the union as a confederacy of *sovereign* states. Here he accepts the defining characteristics that pertain generally to the sovereignty (supremacy) of states where there is a government of sovereign states, no internal administration, and equal suffrage of members.

In the next paragraph, Madison clarifies his analytical task: "Without enquiring into the accuracy of the distinction on which the objection is founded," he says, "it will be necessary to a just estimate of its force, first to ascertain the real character of the government in question." He plans to rely upon the definition used by those who regard the union as a confederacy of sovereign states, and he will do so "without enquiring into the accuracy of the distinction" (ibid., 253). Apparently, Madison shares Hamilton's concern about the lack of logical coherence in referring to a *government* of sovereign states ("a distinction, more subtle than accurate"). In the analysis that follows, he again, three paragraphs later, reminds the reader that the terms "federal" and "national" are being used "as these terms are understood by the objectors" (ibid., 254). In total, we have three statements about the special meaning that is to be attached to the language used in essay 39.

In his analysis, Madison first considers the basis of the new Constitution as being derived from the assent and ratification of the people in each state. In this sense, it is a "federal" rather than a "national" act. Further, the Constitution must be ratified by the unanimous consent of the several states. Each state is considered to be a sovereign body and is "only to be bound by its own voluntary act" (ibid.). This is consistent with the "federal" character of the Constitution.

In dealing with the ordinary powers of government, Madison characterizes the House of Representatives as "national" in character and the Senate as "federal." The election of the president through the electoral college, where the votes are allocated to states by a compound ratio, gives the presidency a mixed character. Since the proposed government is designed to act in relation to individuals, it can be conceived as "national" in character. But with regard to the extent of its powers, the idea of a national government involves "an indefinite supremacy over all persons and things, so far as they are objects of lawful Government." The proposed government in this relationship "cannot be deemed a *national* one; since its jurisdiction extends to certain enumerated objects only, and leaves to the several States a residuary and inviolable sovereignty over all other objects" (ibid., 256, emphasis in original).

In concluding this assessment where he is using the terms "federal" and "national" as "understood by the objectors" (ibid., 254), Madison indicates that "the proposed Constitution therefore is in strictness neither a national nor a federal constitution; but a composition of both" (ibid., 257). He leaves unaddressed "the accuracy of the distinction on which the objection is founded" (ibid., 253) and thus does not address the nature of a "proper federal system" (essay 51) in essay 39 of *The Federalist* (Cooke 1961, 352).

Explicit in Madison's argument, but repeatedly ignored by readers, is a distinction between a limited national government and a unitary national government of unlimited sovereignty (supremacy). In the latter sense, the proposed government "cannot be deemed a national one." A limited national government is entirely compatible with states independently exercising "a residuary and inviolable sovereignty over all other objects" (ibid., 256) not assigned by the Constitution to the limited national government.

We might infer, then, that the concurrent exercise of authority by a limited national government and by states exercising a limited "sovereignty" (i.e., authority to make laws) represents an essential characteristic of a "proper federal system."

Whether the federal principle might be extended to apply to the organization of local governments with reference to states and to other communities of nation-states in the world is an issue not addressed in *The Federalist*. Such, however, may be the implications of Madison's concluding paragraph in essay 51:

> It is no less certain than it is important, notwithstanding the contrary opinions which have been entertained, that the larger the society, provided it lie within a practicable sphere, the more duly capable it will be of self-government. And happily for the *republican cause*, the practicable sphere may be carried to a very great extent, by a judicious modification and mixture of the *federal principle*. [Ibid., 353, emphasis in original]

If the reference to "the larger the society" implies both "the extent and proper structure" mentioned in essay 10, then we might have here an indefinite extension of the federal principle. So long as principles of limited government and constitutional rule are accepted as the basis for organizing all units of government, "the practicable sphere" for applying the federal principle might be "carried to a very great extent." But we should not delude ourselves into thinking that an association of sovereign states, like the

United Nations, conforms to a "proper federal system." This was the type of issue being addressed in 1787 and 1788.

THE ARGUMENT IN ESSAYS 15 AND 16 OF *THE FEDERALIST*: CONCEPTUAL CLARIFICATION

Essay 9 ends with reference to the erroneous theory upon which traditional conceptions of confederation had been based. In essays 15 and 16, Hamilton returns to that consideration. In doing so, he indicates that although there is general recognition of defects in "our national system," its usefulness "is destroyed by a strenuous opposition to a remedy, upon the only principles, that can give it a chance of success." There is a fundamental contradiction in that position:

> They seem still to aim at things repugnant and irreconcilable—at an augmentation of Federal authority without a diminution of State authority—at sovereignty in the Union and complete independence in the members. They still in fine seem to cherish with blind devotion the political monster of an *imperium in imperio*. [Ibid., 93]

Hamilton is saying that unlimited sovereignty cannot exist in states and still augment the exercise of governmental authority by the Union. It makes no sense to refer to an empire within an empire, a government of governments, or a sovereign of sovereigns. The term "sovereignty," meaning supremacy, implies that sovereigns rule over subjects, not other sovereigns. By contrast, Hamilton recognizes that

> there is nothing absurd or impracticable in the idea of a league or alliance between independent nations, for certain defined purposes precisely stated in a treaty; regulating all the details of time, place, circumstance and quantity; leaving nothing to future discretion; and depending for its execution on the good faith of the parties. [Ibid., 94]

In such arrangements, independent nations retain complete sovereignty; the alliance can be unilaterally broken. But considerations of peace and justice cannot be built upon arrangements that depend upon the voluntary actions of all parties: peace and justice depend upon a capacity to make binding commitments.

The concept of government implies something more than an agreement depending upon the good faith of each of the parties:

> Government implies the making of laws. It is essential to the idea of a law, that it be attended with a sanction; or, in other words, a penalty or punishment for disobedience. If there be no penalty annexed to disobedience, the resolutions or commands which pretend to be laws will in fact amount to nothing more than advice or recommendation. [Ibid., 95]

Laws, to be effective, must be enforceable. Laws cannot be enforced if those who are subject to law must first consent to their enforcement; human societies must relax a rule of unanimity. The idea of government requires something other than the "complete independence in the members" (ibid., 93). On theoretical grounds, the traditional defining characteristics of a confederation do not stand as valid because they do not meet the minimally necessary condition for a government to exist. When people pretend that a confederation, as traditionally defined, is a government, they are deceiving themselves.

In pursuing his analysis, Hamilton identifies "the great and radical vice in the construction of the existing Confederation" with "the principle of LEGISLATION for STATES or GOVERNMENTS, in their CORPORATE or COLLECTIVE CAPACITIES and as contradistinguished from the INDIVIDUALS of whom they consist" (ibid.). Penalties for the enforcement of laws can be inflicted in two ways. One is by courts and ministers of justice where the law is applied to individuals. The other is to have recourse to collective sanctions applied to collectivities as such. Hamilton suggests that the application of collective sanctions requires recourse to a coercion of arms: justice cannot be done when sanctions are applied to collectivities as such. It is this

issue that lay at the core of his diagnosis of the failure of confederation and why he thought that fundamental errors in the conception of confederation called for "an alteration in the first
principles and main pillars of the fabric" in the design of a federal
system of government.

If we attempt sympathetically to understand what it is here
that is of such crucial concern to Hamilton, we can try to imagine what happens when collectivities, as such, are made the object of sanctions for the breach of some rule of law. If a sanction
is applied to a collectivity, as such, distinction cannot be made
between innocent bystanders and wrongdoers. If we take the
structure of a private-for-profit corporation and impose a sanction upon the corporation as such, what is it that happens? A
corporation cannot be arrested and confined to prison. A fine
can be levied against a corporation. That fine can be paid from
the corporate treasury. The treasury derives either from invest-
ments made by shareholders or from revenue paid by customers.
The burden for the payment then accrues to shareholders or
customers or both. Yet neither shareholders nor customers may
be culpable of a criminal offense against the law. The application
of collective sanctions may have left those culpable for a crime
immune from punishment and placed the burden for collective
sanctions upon innocent bystanders. The corporate status of a
collectivity, indeed, may shield wrongdoers with a screen of immunity. Justice cannot be done under such circumstances; injus-
tices may be compounded.

Hamilton concludes that, if the Union is to exercise the authority of government, "we must resolve to incorporate into our
plan those ingredients which may be considered as forming the
characteristic difference between a league and a government; we
must extend the authority of the union to the persons of the citizens—the only proper objects of government" (Cooke 1961, 95).
In essay 16 of *The Federalist* the basic rudiments of a federal solution are indicated in the following statement:

> [I]f it be possible at any rate to construct a Foederal government
> capable of regulating the common concerns and preserving the

general tranquility, it must be founded, as to the objects committed to its care, upon the reverse of the principle contended for by the opponents of the proposed constitution. It must carry its agency to the persons of the citizens. It must stand in need of no intermediate legislations; but must itself be empowered to employ the arm of the ordinary magistrate to execute its own resolutions. The majesty of the national authority must be manifested through the medium of the Courts of Justice. The government of the Union, like that of each State, must be able to address itself immediately to the hopes and fears of individuals; and to attract to its support those passions, which have the strongest influence upon the human heart. It must in short, possess all the means and have a right to resort to all the methods of executing the powers, with which it is entrusted, that are possessed and exercised by the government of the particular States. [Ibid., 102–3]

A federal arrangement implies multiple units of government having concurrent jurisdiction. The national government is one of limited jurisdiction but with general competence to govern within that jurisdiction. The states also exercise a limited jurisdiction, with general competence to govern within that jurisdiction. In turn, each set of governments is governed by principles of constitutional law.

The conceptual innovation being introduced in the design of a federal system of government is the concurrent operation of a system of compound republics, each of which reaches to persons and citizens. Citizens function collectively, taking decisions of a constitutional nature in establishing the terms and conditions of government; and individually, in exercising the basic prerogatives of persons possessing constitutional rights that are correlated with limits upon governmental authority. This change in conceptualizing the place of individuals in concurrent republics altered the basic fabric in the design of American federal systems of government.

CONCLUSION

Hamilton and Madison recognize that a proper federal system involves concurrent jurisdiction on the part of a limited national government and limited state governments that independently exercise concurrent jurisdiction with reference to individuals. The limits are specified by reference to the provisions of the U.S. Constitution and the various state constitutions. Those specifically assigned to the Union represent the powers of a limited national government. The residual powers are reserved to the states. This arrangement is consistent with Diamond's statement of modern definitions of the "essential federal characteristic" as involving a division of supreme authority "between member states and a central government, each having the final say regarding matters belonging to its sphere" (Diamond 1961, 22), with the essential qualification that governments, as such, are not supreme. But Diamond neglects the place of constitutional decision making in the American system of governance. His statement of a corollary of his definition, that "there are three kinds of government—confederal, federal, and unitary (national)" (ibid.), would not have been accepted by Hamilton and probably not by Madison. Hamilton would have considered what Diamond refers to as a confederal (confederate) government to not be a government at all.

In attempting to eliminate reference to what he considers a logical absurdity, Hamilton variously uses the terms "confederation," "confederacy," and "federal" to refer to a system of government that has concurrent units of government. Hamilton also uses the term "consolidation" as applying to the organization of the Union as a single limited structure of government without implying that the states are thereby eliminated as independent units of government. The consolidation occurs only in relation to national interests; the separate existence of each state is maintained with reference to local affairs.

Diamond is thus correct in saying that the authors of *The Federalist* use the terms "confederation" and "federal" roughly as synonyms. They usually distinguish what they consider to be the proper meaning of these terms from the erroneous meaning by appropriate textual modifiers. But ambiguities inevitably occur. The defining characteristics that Diamond accepts as representing the true meaning of confederation and federal are rejected, explicitly and vigorously, by Hamilton as logical absurdities. They do not meet the essential defining characteristics of a government, so it makes no sense to use them to refer to a type of government.

The authors of *The Federalist* would also have disagreed that national governments are identical with unitary governments. Unitary national governments exercise an unlimited sovereignty. Thus a limited national government is consistent with principles of federal organization; an unlimited national government is inconsistent with principles of federal organization. The end of federalism occurs when a national government usurps the prerogatives of other units of government and exercises unlimited authority over all persons and things. Again, ambiguity arises because the authors of *The Federalist* do not always use the term "limited national government" in referring to the proposed government to be organized under the new Constitution. Unfortunately, they variously use the terms "general," "federal," and "national" in referring to that government.

Diamond argues in rebuttal that a federal system is not necessary for such a distribution of authority to subordinate units of government. A system of decentralized authority within a unitary nation-state could also yield substantial independence for local authorities within a system of local self-government. He points to the English system of local self-government as an example.

Such a possibility might be theoretically valid as long as one assumes that those who exercise complete sovereignty have a benevolent interest in maintaining republican institutions of local self-government. But to make that presumption would be "to forget," as Hamilton says, "that men are ambitious, vindictive and rapacious" (Cooke 1961, 28). Madison, indeed, argues that representative institutions will give access to a better-qualified personnel as the size of a republic increases. But he also argues that size is correlated with oligarchical tendencies in large deliberative assemblies. Hamilton, too, alludes to the passions that drive those who exercise leadership positions:

> Men of this class, whether the favourites of a king or of a people, have in too many instances abused the confidence they possessed; and assuming the pretext of some public motive, have

not scrupled to sacrifice the national tranquility to personal advantage, or personal gratification. [Ibid., 29]

Americans, in their efforts to cope with the problems of oppression and tyranny, used processes of constitutional decision making to formulate constitutions as rules of law that apply to the organization and conduct of government itself. Why should the American people have simply surrendered unlimited sovereignty to a national government and relied upon its goodwill to create appropriate republican institutions of local self-government? The logic of the American solution was otherwise. Americans, instead, relied upon their capacity to covenant with one another about the terms and conditions of government so that they might have a system of government organized in accordance with principles and forms of their own choosing. The whole process remains viable only so long as the rules of constitutional law can be enforced against those who exercise the prerogatives of government. A federal system depends upon the maintenance of limits to the prerogatives of governments. The possibility of maintaining effective limits upon these prerogatives is severely limited when a democratic society cannot have reference to well-established processes of constitutional choice.

Faith in a single government monopolizing sovereign authority is not consistent with the maintenance of republican institutions of local self-government. American experience with machine politics and boss rule in the nineteenth century contributed to the emasculation of local self-government. A prolonged state constitutional struggle was necessary before the authority of state legislatures could be effectively restrained and adequate provisions could be made for home rule and local control over local affairs. Twentieth-century "reform" of English local government has so transformed local government that substantial doubt exists about its self-governing character. To point to the possibility of decentralization is an unsatisfactory substitute for a constitutional system of rule based upon federal principles for the concurrent exercise of governmental authority.

While I have argued that *The Federalist*'s position on federalism is much more defensible than Diamond suggests, we should, at the same time, recognize that there are serious ambiguities and difficulties inherent in some of the arguments offered by Hamilton and Madison. First, there is insufficient emphasis upon the nearly unique place of constitutional decision making in the proposed American system of government and on the relationship of constitutional decision making to the organization and maintenance of a federal system. Americans of the time were so deeply immersed in processes of constitutional decision making that they simply took its rationale for granted; they felt they did not need to expound a theory of constitutional choice. It is only in the twentieth century, after having ridiculed the formality of constitutions, that we find it necessary to be reminded of the central importance of a theory of constitutional choice for understanding and designing political systems. It would, however, have been helpful if Americans had expounded their theory of constitutional choice as carefully as Thomas Hobbes expounded his theory of sovereignty.

Second, obvious confusion arises from ambiguities in the use of such terms as "confederation," "federal," "national," "state," "consolidation," "democracy," "republic," and many others in *The Federalist*. These can usually be resolved if the reader employs an appropriate understanding of political theory. But the critical question is, What is an appropriate understanding of political theory? Diamond obviously uses a different understanding of political theory from the one I have used. What Hamilton called a general theory of limited constitutions is the proper theory for construing the meaning of American federalism.

Unfortunately, we tend to see what we look for. Until we open ourselves to the possibility of different ways of conceptualizing our experience, we cannot be critical of the language we use: The sun does not rise, the earth spins; yet we as human beings have the aesthetic experience of observing sunrises knowing that what we experience is an interesting illusion worthy of aesthetic appreciation. Governments are not supreme when their authority is limited by rules of constitutional law and processes that make those rules effective in the conduct of public affairs. The illusion of an omniscient observer, who presumes that "the government" is an omnicompetent problem-solver, may have an aesthetic appeal for some; but it is a most dangerous illusion.

Third, the use of the term "sovereignty" probably contributes needless confusion to *The Federalist* and to all subsequent discussions about the American system of government. Sovereignty often refers to the exercise of supreme authority. There are those, including Hobbes, who would argue that the exercise of supreme authority cannot be limited. Hobbes would argue, as Hamilton did with reference to confederation, that to speak of limiting sovereignty, in the sense of supremacy, is a logical absurdity. Others, like Tocqueville, use the term "sovereignty" to mean the right to make laws. This carries quite different implications in a democratic society that distinguishes legislative processes pertaining to fundamental laws (that is, constitutions) from those applicable to ordinary laws enacted by "governments."

The concepts of limited national sovereignty and limited state sovereignty require one to raise the question of who imposes the limits. This requires one to have reference to constitutions and to processes of constitutional decision making. If we view people acting collectively as exercising ultimate constitutional authority, can we then view the people as being sovereign? They make laws establishing the terms and conditions of government. One might then refer to a federal system as one that involves popular sovereignty. But then we become concerned with the question of which people are acting in what contexts. It can all make sense only so long as there is general agreement among people about what they mean. This drives us back to the covenantal nature of constitutions, the metaphysical and moral grounds that inform processes of constitutional choice, and the language that is used to articulate a theory of constitutional choice.

The American experiments in constitutional choice can best be understood if we abandon reference to a theory of sovereignty as the exercise of supreme authority and refer instead to a theory of constitutional choice. The basic question in constituting a government is not one of assigning unlimited and undivided authority to some sovereign entity that has the last say and rules over a society. Instead, the task is one of allocating and distributing authority so that rules of constitutional law can specify both capabilities and limits that apply to citizens and governmental officials alike in the governance of society. A system is devised whereby citizens can enforce the limits of law upon officials (as subjects of law) no less than officials acting upon citizens (as subjects of law).

The task of devising a system of government based upon a theory of constitutional choice is well formulated by Madison in essay 51 of *The Federalist.*

> This policy of supplying by opposite and rival interests, the defect of better motives, might be traced through the whole system of human affairs, private as well as public. We see it particularly displayed in all the subordinate distributions of power; where the constant aim is to divide and arrange the several offices in such a manner as that each may be a check on the other: that the private interest of every individual may be a sentinel over the public rights. These inventions of prudence cannot be less requisite in the distribution of the supreme powers of the State. [Cooke 1961, 349]

Where interests are arrayed against interests, there must exist processes for articulating contending interests and reaching decisions with regard to matters under contention. These are prerogatives to be exercised by people in the choice of elected officials and in making decisions of a constitutional nature. The way that people exercise their prerogatives in using a constitutional system of government will determine whether the limits of constitutional law are effectively maintained. Hamilton recognizes that the nature and extent of powers specified in a constitution can have only a limited effect: they are words on paper. He goes on to observe:

> Every thing beyond this, must be left to the prudence and firmness of the people; who, as they will hold the scales in their own hands, it is to be hoped, will always take care to preserve the constitutional equilibrium between the General and the State Governments. [Ibid., 198]

This principle applies to all constitutional constraints. They depend upon the "prudence and firmness of the people." Constitutional equilibria with reference to a federal system, checks and balances internal to any unit of government, and the constitutional rights of individuals with reference to governments all depend upon "the prudence and firmness of the people" for their maintenance. But it is the way in which interests are designed to check one another that provides the processes by which people become informed and are thus rendered capable of making decisions.

Alexis de Tocqueville, in two notations entered in his notebook on December 28 and 29, 1831 ([Mayer] 1959, 247–48), recognized the close connection between constitutional principles and enlightened citizenship in the operation of those principles:

> It is an axiom of American public law that every power must be given full authority in its own sphere which must be defined in a way that prevents it [the power] stepping beyond it [its sphere]: that is a great principle, and worth thinking about.

> This much can be stated, that it is only a very enlightened people that could invent the federal constitution of the United States, and that only a very enlightened people and one peculiarly accustomed to the representative system, could make such a complicated machinery work, and know how to maintain the different powers within their own spheres, powers which, without this continual care, would not fail to come into violent collision. The constitution of the United States is an admirable work, nevertheless one may believe that its founders would not have succeeded, had not the previous 150 years given the different States of the Union the *taste for, and practice of, provincial governments*, and if a high civilization had not at the same time put them in a *position to maintain a strong, though limited, central government*. The federal constitution of the United States seems to me the best, perhaps the only, arrangement that would allow the establishment of a vast republic, and yet to imitate it is absolutely impracticable without the preexisting conditions of which I was speaking above. [Tocqueville's emphasis]

A theory of constitutional choice enables us to understand how a democratic system of government may be constituted so that people can be said to govern. A general theory of limited constitutions can be reiterated in organizing multiple units of government to derive a theory of federalism. Principles of constitutional choice can then be applied to all political experiment. Relatively simple solutions can be reiterated to derive more complex solutions under conditions in which citizens function as both rulers and subjects of law. By contrast, the traditional theory of sovereignty presumes that some one body exercises supreme authority. Such a presumption is incompatible with the existence of a democratic society of continental proportions.

Perhaps it is enough to recognize that *The Federalist* makes a major contribution toward a theory of constitutional rule and federalism, which in turn is a major contribution to democratic traditions of self-government. It is a theory of concurrent, compound republics that enables democratic societies to reach out to continental proportions. We are the ones who bear the burden of advancing beyond what was done in the late 1780s. Yet to do so requires critical attention to the language we use. Otherwise our effort to move forward may be to step backward. We ignore the hazards of life when we neglect what others have learned before us.

FIVE

GARCIA, THE ECLIPSE OF FEDERALISM, AND THE CENTRAL-GOVERNMENT TRAP

The United States Supreme Court rendered a decision in *Garcia* v. *San Antonio Metropolitan Transit Authority* (105 S.Ct. 1005; 1985) on February 19, 1985. At issue was the question of whether the wage and hour provisions of the Fair Labor Standards Act applied to employees of the transit authority or whether the transit authority as an instrumentality of a state was immune from Federal[1] regulation under the Commerce Clause of the U.S. Constitution granting authority to the Congress to regulate commerce "among the several states." The majority opinion, prepared by Justice Harry A. Blackmun, held that the Fair Labor Standards Act applied to the transit authority.

The essential thrust of this decision is not unlike many other decisions regarding the application of national legislation to instrumentalities of state and local government. What is different is that this decision became an occasion for the justices of the Supreme Court to review the Commerce Clause in light of the Necessary and Proper Clause and the Tenth Amendment powers "reserved to the states respectively, or to the people." Justice Blackmun, speaking for the Court, could find no criterion that could be used to place discrete limits upon the substantive powers that establish the scope of Federal authority under the U.S. Constitution. The language assigning the Congress power to regulate commerce among the several states has been extended to include whatever affects or is affected by interstate commerce. So long as that interpretation of the Commerce Clause is used, the powers of the Congress potentially apply, so far as I can understand, to any and all aspects of American society.

In light of these circumstances, Justice Blackmun concluded that the framers of the U.S. Constitution "chose to rely on a federal system in which restraints on [F]ederal power over the states inhered principally in the workings of the National Government itself, rather than in discrete limitations upon the objects of [F]ederal authority. State sovereignty interests, then, are more properly protected by procedural safeguards inherent in the structure of the [F]ederal system than by judicially created limitations on [F]ederal powers" (105 S.Ct. 1018; 1985).

Specific limitations upon the authority of Congress and upon the states as reflected in the first eight amendments and the Thirteenth, Fourteenth, and Fifteenth Amendments would presumably be subject to adjudication. Otherwise, Justice Blackmun can be construed as advancing an argument that the scope of substantive powers of the national government are not subject to adjudication in establishing limits to national authority. Rather, such limits are properly protected by the "federal" structure of the national government, which includes reference to states in establishing modes of election, patterns of representation, and membership in Congress, and in electing the president. The way these structures work in the political process is presumed to yield an appropriate set of safeguards. The states and localities can rely upon the structures and procedures of the national government to safeguard their interests. The courts need not and cannot construe limits with reference to the substantive powers of the national government.

Whether *Garcia* becomes only a minor case in American constitutional jurisprudence will depend upon how it is construed. So long as the conceptualizations of law and the workings of government that have prevailed in the twentieth century are relied upon, the case is of minor importance, deserving recognition only as a footnote in the continuing centralization and nationalization of the American system of government. If, however, the general theory of limited constitutions originally used to design the American federal system of government were relied upon, *Garcia* would be seen as a case in which the Supreme Court took an explicitly articulated step toward abandoning constitutional jurisdiction with reference to the substantive powers of the national government.

These ambiguities arise from nineteenth and twentieth-century traditions of facade smashing that became an important mode of interpretation in the study of law and government.[2] The task of the analyst was to understand the "realities" of power in forming winning coalitions rather than to be diverted by the formalities and pageantries that form the facade of governments. Constitutions came to be viewed as formalisms that decorated the facade of politics and concealed fundamental realities. Similarly, theories used to conceptualize and design the structures and processes of government were viewed as "literary theories" and "paper pictures" that had no effective relationship to political realities (Wilson [1885] 1956, 31). Facade smashing became indispensable to legal and political realists. What self-respecting scholar would embrace the study of facades when the fundamental task of science is to understand the reality of power relationships?

There is, however, a basic question whether human beings, to some significant degree, create their own social realities. If they do, then human societies can be viewed as artifactual in nature. Conceptions used to characterize and to create patterns of power relationships may then be elements of fundamental importance for understanding social realities. An artifact requires reference to the conceptions, intentions, and skills used by those who fashion it, even when those artifacts are consciously ordered patterns of human relationships. Human creations require an account of human cognition, intentionality, and technical processes if the realm of the artifactual is to be understood. Such conceptions are fundamental to the use of law to achieve patterns of order and change in modern societies. Can such principles also be applied to systems of governance, or are all governments essentially oligarchies where some rule over others?

If we used the method of the cultural sciences instead of the method of the natural sciences relied upon by the legal and political realists, we would seek to understand how concepts are used to design institutions of government as human artifacts. We might then come to understand how theory is used to specify relations between conditions and consequences in such a way that some potentials might be realized and others foreclosed. Any artifact also has the potential for functioning as an instrument or as a tool. The design concept may be faulty and the instrument may not work in the way that it was expected to work. But such a judgment requires knowledgeable understanding of how the instrument was intended to be used—its capabilities as well as its limitations.

From this point of view, a constitution might be viewed as crudely equivalent to a set of drawings or blueprints specifying essential structural features that establish the terms and conditions of government. Explanations of how a design is expected to work provide us with basic concepts in the theory of design (V. Ostrom 1980; V. Ostrom 1987, chs. 1, 4, 9). Constitutions need not be dismissed as mere formalisms, and the theories used in their design need not be treated as "literary theories" or "paper pictures." Rather, they provide the essential ingredient for understanding how a system of government is intended to work.

If human beings are to establish governments and to govern by reflection and choice, it becomes necessary to specify the conceptions that are used to inform human decisions, actions, and judgments. In what follows I shall, first, examine how the Blackmun doctrine applies to Madison's analysis in essay 39 of *The Federalist*, which closely parallels Blackmun's argument. There are basic puzzles in fashioning Madison's conjectures into a definitive and plausible legal doctrine in support of Blackmun's argument. In a second section, I shall briefly refer to the tie between electoral arrangements, modes of representation, and collective decisions to indicate the tenuous relationship between voting and what something called "government" does. These processes do not determine results; at best, they place constraints upon the oligarchical tendencies inherent in all structures of government. These problems, in turn, pertain to a larger issue about the structure of government and the rule of law, which I shall consider in the third section. A further question then arises about what happens when the different instrumentalities of the national government are free to reach their own mutual oligarchical accommodations in the conduct of something called "government." The thesis I shall advance is that the pursuit of opportunities under such circumstances is likely to yield what I refer to as the central-government trap. People create traps for themselves when they seriously constrain their available options without intending consciously to do so. Finally, in the last section, I shall press the analysis to yield some implications about the future of American society.

THE BLACKMUN DOCTRINE AND MADISON'S CONJECTURE IN ESSAY 39 OF *THE FEDERALIST*

The Blackmun doctrine about the place of "federal" features in the constitution of the American national government closely parallels an extended analysis made by James Madison in essay 39 of *The Federalist*. Blackmun asserted that the framers of the U.S. Constitution chose to rely upon a federal system designed so that the restraints on national powers over the states would turn principally upon the workings of the national government. If this assertion is to be plausible, the only source, of which I am aware, for such an argument among the framers is Madison's essay 39. Madison's analysis has been used by some scholars as an authoritative statement of "true" definitions for distinguishing such terms as "federal" and "national." But, as I have already indicated in Chapter 4, there are reasons to dispute this argument.

Essays 37–51 of *The Federalist* constitute the core of Madison's analysis of those general features of the U.S. Constitution that apply both to its federal structure and to a general theory of limited constitutions. Essay 37 addresses general problems of cognition and epistemology. Essay 38 addresses the principal objections that had been made both to the general theory of design and to particular features of the U.S. Constitution. Among the objections were those that pertained to the standing of states and to the standing of individuals.

Those objections point to the most fundamental theoretical issue raised about the basic structural modifications made in the U.S. Constitution in contrast to the Articles of Confederation. The issue had been posed by Hamilton in essay 9 of *The Federalist*, critically addressed in essays 15 and 16, and further elaborated in essays 17–22. The nub of the issue is whether governments can govern other governments as collectivities, or whether the structures and processes of government must relate to the standing of individuals as persons and citizens. Hamilton's analysis leads him to the conclusion that conceptualizing a government of governments is an absurdity because law cannot be made effective and justice cannot be done under circumstances where governments (collectivities) are the objects of collective action by another government.

The question to be addressed in essay 39 is the extent to which the proposed constitution also "ought, with equal care, to have preserved the *federal* form which regards the union as a *Confederacy* of sovereign states" (Hamilton, Jay, and Madison [1788] n.d., 246, Madison's emphasis) in addition to adhering to republican forms of organization in the government of the Union. Here, Madison is taking "*federal* form" as that associated with a confederacy of "*sovereign* states" (my emphasis). He proposes in the next paragraph to examine the extent to which the proposed government conforms to this conception of federal form "without inquiring into the accuracy of the distinction on which the objection is founded" (ibid.). In other words, Madison proposes to use the opposition's own language and conceptualizations to conduct an analysis of the extent to which the proposed Constitution meets their objections; he does not propose to inquire into the issue—the absurdity of a government of governments—that is the focal point of Hamilton's analysis in essays 15 and 16.

That analysis is consistent with the Blackmun doctrine that the internal constitution of the national government takes account of "federal form," especially in the constitution of the Senate, the apportionment of representatives to states in the House of Representatives, and the allocation of votes in the electoral college by a compound ratio that gives the presidency a constitutionally mixed character. Whether these structural conditions are sufficient to safeguard state and local interests is not an issue addressed by Madison because he presumes that the national government is a substantively limited national government subject to the constraint of explicitly delegated powers. Blackmun's argument is that "the Framers chose to rely upon a federal system" in which the restraints upon national authority with reference to the states would operate principally through procedures that derived from the "federal form" of the national government rather than through the language used in the Constitution. In view of the hypothetical nature of Madison's analysis, where he questions the "accuracy" of the conceptualizations used in his analysis of the "federal form" of the national government, that argument does not withstand critical scrutiny.

Moreover, Madison categorically says that in the "extent" of its powers, the proposed national government is "federal, not national" (Hamilton, Jay, and Madison [1788] n.d., 250). Madison's argument in essay 39 of *The Federalist* thus explicitly includes reference to the limited extent of national powers, enumerated in the text of the Constitution, as one of the attributes of "federal form." These issues were more fully elaborated in Chapter 4.

A further issue is raised as to how "words on paper" can be expected somehow to preserve a "federal form" within the workings of the national government, maintaining the constitutional integrity of a national government as such, if they cannot be acted upon to limit the national government's substantive powers. This issue turns, in part, upon the extent to which electoral arrangements and modes of representation *determine* in some precise way what governments do.

ELECTORAL ARRANGEMENTS, MODES OF REPRESENTATION, AND COLLECTIVE DECISIONS

Elections are of basic importance in a democratic society, but the link between voting and what governments do is a tenuous one. Political experience under state constitutions in the nineteenth century is sufficient to indicate that intermediate patterns of organization having to do with political parties and how they come to function pose a basic puzzle about the viability of democratic societies. Broad suffrage in democratic elections is insufficient by itself to safeguard the interests of people in the decisions made by governments. This problem is explored by Madison in essay 51 of *The Federalist*, when he calls for "auxiliary precautions" (Hamilton, Jay, and Madison [1788] n.d., 337–38). It was also considered by Tocqueville in chapter 15 of *Democracy in America*, on the unlimited power of the majority. Among modern authors, Moisei Ostrogorski, in the second volume of his *Democracy and the Organization of Political Parties* ([1902] 1964), has treated it extensively.

Coalitions are organized to enable some who function in collective decision processes to prevail over others in the taking of collective decisions. Under a plurality voting rule, those who muster the larger vote determine the decision. If societies were constituted only on the principle that plurality winners prevail, then we might anticipate tightly disciplined coalitions to predominate.

Domination of the institutions of government by tightly organized political coalitions operating as political machines and run by "bosses" cannot be ameliorated by recourse to electoral processes as such. Reform movements in the nineteenth century sought to throw the rascals out and to elect good men to public office, but the reformers were confronted with the same structural problems and coalitional politics in reelecting reform slates. Reformers faded like morning glories when confronted with the long-term task of maintaining successful reform coalitions (Riordon 1963).

These problems were eventually resolved and brought within tolerable limits by *constitutional* changes, mainly in state constitutions. A variety of new measures altered electoral arrangements, instituting direct primary elections in which any maverick could challenge a candidate slated by a machine for a place on the general-election ballot. Extensive limitations were also placed on state legislative authority, as when local communities were guaranteed rights of local self-government and authority to formulate their own home-rule charters.

Electoral arrangements and modes of representation, as such, are insufficient to *determine* collective decisions. The organization of political parties and coalitions that form slates, win elections, and operate as teams in legislative bodies, also has constitutional significance. The opportunity for political bosses to gain dominance over electoral processes is strongly reinforced by the oligarchical tendencies in large legislative bodies. There is no assurance that the procedural safeguards inherent in the "federal form" of the national government will guarantee that party leadership will take proper account of constituents' interests.

Since the Congress is authorized under the U.S. Constitution to make and alter regulations pertaining to the times, places, and manner of holding elections for senators and representatives, except as to the place of choosing senators (that is, they must be chosen from states), there is little to constrain the modification of electoral processes by congressional authority. Changes enacted by the Congress can yield coalitional structures quite different from those that now derive from diverse state constitutional and statutory provisions. The "federal form" of the national government, as such, is not a sufficient basis for determining the place of a national government in a federal system of governance. Blackmun confuses federal form with the eclipse of federalism.

THE STRUCTURE OF GOVERNMENT
AND THE RULE OF LAW

Systems of government are potentially operable under many different conditions. One condition is to rely primarily upon fear and use the instruments of power to clobber anyone who steps out of line or fails to show proper submissiveness to power holders. Fear is enhanced by unpredictability, and despotic regimes can make a virtue of arbitrariness whenever submissiveness is lacking. Although relationships in such societies are ordered by rules, they lack a reliable standard of conduct other than submissive obedience, and it is doubtful if they can properly be characterized as having a rule of law that is publicly knowable and applied in nonarbitrary ways.

The maintenance of a rule of law depends upon distinguishing the processes of law making and law adjudicating from the processes of law enforcing. The executive instrumentalities that collect taxes, spend money, maintain public facilities and services, and control instrumentalities of coercion in a society constitute an essential core in any system of government, whether democratic or not. To make a distinction between the structures and processes of legislation and executive processes implies that executive instrumentalities can be bound by publicly knowable rules of law. Under these rules, standards are set that apply *alike* to executive and judicial officials in their rule-enforcing, rule-adjudicating functions, and to individuals in their rule-following functions. When the application of criminal sanctions requires that an accused be entitled to a trial in a court of law, the application of executive sanctions is held in abeyance until an independent judgment is rendered by an impartial judiciary. Arbitrary regimes render judgment with a bullet in the back of the head.

Executive instrumentalities can be made to face both legislatively and judicially established limits before sanctions can be applied. This is why it is said that freedom depends upon a rule of law. The operation of distinguishable processes of law making and law adjudicating apart from law enforcing means that standards can be created that are publicly knowable, and allow for the performance of officials to be subject to a public assessment by citizens who have access to legal and judicial processes.

Where a rule of law can be said to exist, the institutions of government are subject to distinguishable structures and processes that pertain to law making, law enforcing, and law adjudicating. Members in any one political community adhering to a rule of law thus rely upon multiple agencies to discharge rulership prerogatives. Where distinguishable structures and processes of rulership exist, there is a specialization of functions accompanying a division of labor that implies a distribution of authority among them. How these structures and processes are both differentiated and linked to one another in a more general process of governance is subject to considerable variation in different systems of governance. The existence of distinguishable legislative, executive, and judicial structures and processes means that authority has been distributed among different structures. Some degree of separation of powers exists in all societies that maintain a rule of law.[3]

In the American system of government, the development of constitutional decision making and the formulation of constitutions as fundamental law have been accompanied by explicit constitutional formulations pertaining to the organization of legislative, executive, and judicial instrumentalities of government. These assignments of authority are the subject of the first three articles of the U.S. Constitution. The assignment of authority to each instrumentality is, in turn, subject to correlative limits inherent in the exercise of authority by the other instrumentalities of government. By avoiding an explicit doctrine of supremacy, except for the supremacy of law, the American constitutional formulation does not violate the basic maxim that no one individual, or no one body of individuals, is a fit judge of his, her, or its own cause in relation to the interests of others. This rule must be violated by any constitution having recourse to a single supreme authority. Such a breach of a basic maxim of justice is consistent with the prior observation that a supreme sovereign, as the source of law, is above the law, cannot be held accountable to law, and therefore stands beyond the reach of law in relation to the rest of society.

The general theory of limited constitutions, as applied in the American system of governance, presumes that residual authority resides in the constitutional authority of the people in each state to establish the terms and conditions of government that apply to each state and to the system of governance within each state. The U.S. Constitution was conceived not as a general and full grant of governmental (plenary) authority but as one that is subject to an explicit delegation of limited authority. The basic structure of state constitutions also places limits upon the lawmaking authority of state legislatures. Authority not proscribed, however, is presumed to be within the realm of state legislative prerogatives. State constitutions abound with limits upon legislatures, including those bearing upon provisions for local self-government. Viewed as a system of constitutional contracts, the structure of state constitutions and the U.S. Constitution are based upon different but complementary assumptions, relating to the basic core and nexus of authority relationships. The core is found in the state constitutions; the federal connections are found in the U.S. Constitution and in local charters as these relate to that core of authority "reserved," in the words of the Tenth Amendment, "to the states respectively, or to the people."

A general theory of limited constitutions also implies, as Hamilton argues in essay 78 of *The Federalist*, that acts of a legislature contrary to the provisions of a constitution cannot be given standing as law by a judiciary in deciding cases that arise in such circumstances. A constitution is intended to be fundamental law binding upon the basic exercise of governmental authority:

> No legislative act, therefore, contrary to the Constitution, can be valid. To deny this, would be to affirm, that the deputy is greater than his principal; that the servant is above his master; that the representatives of the people are superior to the people themselves; that men acting by virtue of powers, may do not only what those powers authorize, but what they forbid. [Hamilton, Jay, and Madison (1788) n.d., 507]

Hamilton asserts that it is "the *courts* [that] were designed to be an intermediate body between the *people* and the *legislature*, in order, among other things, to keep the latter within the limits assigned to their authority" (my emphasis). In support of this assertion, he argues:

> The interpretation of law is the proper and peculiar province of the courts. A constitution is, in fact, and must be regarded by judges, as a fundamental law. It therefore belongs to them to ascertain its meaning, as well as the meaning of any particular act proceeding from the legislative body. If there should happen to be an irreconcilable variance between the two, that which has the superior obligation and validity ought, of course, to be pre-

ferred, or, in other words the Constitution ought to be preferred to the statute, the intention of the *people* to the intention
of their agents. [Ibid., 506, my emphasis]

Hamilton derives these arguments from a general theory of limited constitutions, not from particular provisions in the U.S.
Constitution.

The standing of fundamental law in governing the processes
of government interposes an additional form of jurisprudence beyond that contemplated in either civil (common) law or criminal
law. Constitutional law turns upon the valid exercise of governmental authority. A governmental act that is invalid has no legal
standing. Officials have no entitlement to act contrary to fundamental law, and if an injury were caused while an official was acting contrary to fundamental law, that official, in accordance with
the principles of a general theory of limited constitutions, would
be individually liable as an ordinary person for a redress of that
injury. Individuals cannot act in an official capacity when they act
beyond the scope of their authority. If they do so, they stand accountable and liable as ordinary citizens.

The crux of the decision in *Garcia* arises from the circumstance that the U.S. Constitution as a legal document presumes
that a limited and explicit delegation of authority was being specified by its framers in light of a presumption of residual authority
residing with the people of the several states. The presumption of
a limited delegation contains very few specifications of what is
forbidden. Most such constraints in the U.S. Constitution have
been added by amendments. But this should not mean that persons knowledgeable about a general theory of limited constitutions cannot construe a "constitutional contract," so to speak, in
light of the explicit language of the framers. If the constitutional
contract needs to be revised, there are stipulated procedures for
doing so: it is a governable contract (Williamson 1985).

The authority to regulate "commerce . . . among the several
states" was, for example, not conceived to be equivalent to all commerce. Power to provide for the "general welfare *of the United States*"
(my emphasis) was not conceived as an authorization to appropriate

and spend national funds for any and all purposes. A "necessary and proper" clause does not justify any expediency. A necessary condition implies necessity: an objective or purpose cannot be yielded in the absence of a necessary condition. A "proper" condition implies standards pertaining to normative distinctions between right and wrong, to justice, equality, and liberty.

The extension of the phrase "commerce . . . among the several states" to include "anything that affects or is affected by" interstate commerce is not subject to limitation, as Justice Blackmun recognizes. *Garcia* might have been an occasion for questioning the appropriateness of a standard that extended the scope of the Commerce Clause without limit, as it might have been to reconsider whether "anything that affects or is affected by" some relationship or grant of power is a proper way to construe meaning in constitutional jurisprudence. "Anything which affects or is affected by" some grant of power is a much less stringent requirement than "necessary and proper."

The Blackmun doctrine takes the position that the substantive grants of powers (that is, what is authorized) cannot be limited except where prohibitions (what is forbidden) are stated explicitly. There are relatively few such prohibitions that pertain to the exercise of prerogatives by the legislative, executive, and judicial instrumentalities of government in the U.S. Constitution. The Constitution, exclusive of amendments, does not specify the standards that are applicable to a valid rule of law except to prohibit bills of attainder, ex post facto laws, and a few similar provisions. It is a general theory of limited constitutions that must be relied upon if we are to understand the relationships of the diverse instrumentalities of the national government either to a rule of law or to a federal system of governance.

THE CENTRAL-GOVERNMENT TRAP

In the absence of specific constitutional prohibitions, what patterns can be expected to occur in the exercise of governmental authority by the instrumentalities of the national government when those instrumentalities are free to determine among themselves the scope of their own authority? A positive analysis is needed to respond to this question. I shall pursue such an analysis to indicate the consequences that are likely to follow. The analysis is conjectural. The conjectures seek to clarify implications that would follow from the Blackmun doctrine and its abandonment of the limits inherent in a general theory of limited constitutions.

I will begin by assuming that all human beings are endowed with virtually unlimited imaginations and with seriously limited capabilities. Rich imaginations fuel large aspirations, but any one individual acting alone can achieve relatively little. We attempt to compensate for this disparity by taking advantage of the capabilities of others afforded by the institutional arrangements that exist or can be created through recourse to systems of rule-ordered relationships in a society. Those who exercise the prerogatives of government are also subject to the human condition of rich imaginations and limited capabilities. We can expect human beings to be always striving, testing limits in light of their own essential interests, and then puzzling about the discrepancy between aspirations and what is achieved.

Law is one way for achieving some degree of order while permitting choice among human beings. Rules of law are a means of transforming all potential acts into those that are prohibited (forbidden), permitted, and required. So long as norms (that is, the criteria for distinguishing what is forbidden, permitted, or required) can be used to order human relationships, sufficient predictability can be achieved by excluding some possibilities and requiring some possibilities while permitting others. The range of opportunity, the degree of openness, and the latitudes of freedom enjoyed by individuals, voluntary associations, and diverse units of government in a federal system are a function of what is permitted, in contrast to what is either prohibited or required.

Law can variously liberate or bind, as in a trap; it depends upon how the domains of the prohibited, permitted, and required are proportioned. If unlimited latitude of authority applies to those who exercise the prerogatives of government, it is reasonable to expect simultaneous tendencies to extend authority and to

shirk responsibilities. Aspiration fueled by rich imaginations leads
to more extended commitments followed by an inability to meet
those commitments. This is a perennial problem that applies to all
human beings. We can expect that problem to manifest itself in
the discharge of legislative, executive, and judicial prerogatives in
any system of government. The critical issue bears upon what degree of operable constraint places limits upon the exercise of governmental authority.

Legislation as positive morality. With congressional and judicial
relaxation of constitutional standards that apply both to what the
Congress may do and to how it may be done, we see a very substantial extension of national legislative authority to more and
more exigencies of life in American society. But this process is accompanied by less and less attention to the qualitative character of
legislation. Instead of establishing adequate standards that authorize executive action and simultaneously place limits upon the exercise of executive prerogative, modern legislation has increasingly
taken the form of pronouncing a public goal, granting authority
to some executive instrumentality to achieve that goal, and assigning to that executive instrumentality authority to formulate the
"necessary" rules and regulations. Fundamental rule-making authority is transferred to the executive.

Several problems arise in the use of such methods in processes
of governance. First, goals are specified in highly moralistic termi-
nology that often obfuscates the task of achieving them. Legislation takes on more the characteristic of positive morality than
positive law, and legislators are likely to trap themselves into a position where critical discussion in a legislative process appears to
oppose moral virtue. Under such circumstances, due deliberation
is sacrificed to the celebration of virtue. Anyone calling attention
to the moral hazards that may be involved is presumed to be mor-
ally offensive.

Second, goals expressed as positive morality can be viewed as
values to be maximized. Happiness, justice, welfare, health, safety,
a normal life for the handicapped, the preservation of life, pure
water, clean air, and so on, all become values to be maximized

without due consideration of the costs entailed. If those costs could be confined to monetary ones, the resulting escalation of government expenditures would be serious enough. A willingness to spend any amount of money or effort to prolong lives, for example, can entail extraordinary costs. If we now view all nonmonetary values in a way that justifies maximum effort to realize each one, we confront circumstances that defy rational choice. This concept of maximizing a multitude of different values also applies to the way that rules and regulations are formulated, leaving people with contradictory requirements: equal protection of the law, for example, comes to mean arbitrary assignments of children to schools.

Third, the transfer of rule-making authority to executive instrumentalities means that law is no longer formulated by those who face constituents with reference to public matters that acquire their publicness within specifiable communities of relationships (that is, with consent of the governed). Professional criteria become paramount, reinforcing tendencies toward the maximization of particular values, the rent-seeking propensities of professionals, and a view that implementation as conceived by enforcers should prevail in relation to those who are subject to the rules and regulations. The looseness of legislative standards, efforts to maximize multiple values, and the professional biases of administrative rule makers and enforcers yield a view of the essential aspect of rules, among professional administrators, as pertaining to their mandatory quality. The areas of law pertaining to what is prohibited and what is required are expanded at the cost of what is permitted. Individuals find themselves in circumstances where they can exercise less and less latitude in the governance of their own affairs and are increasingly bound by rules that yield absurd, contradictory requirements. Law is equated with command, and the governance of society is increasingly viewed as a command-and-control problem.

Fourth, when legislation becomes positive morality instead of positive law, less attention is given to the way in which patterns of human social interaction and the structures of opportunities often yield counterintentional or counterintuitive consequences. A specification of goals, other than to indicate intentionality, is insufficient in establishing rule-ordered relationships. One needs to know first, what counterintentional or counterintuitive relationships are operable, and then how to proceed in light of those relationships instead of assuming that naive statements of objectives can be made operable. The formula of "one person, one vote" plus majority rule, for example, is an insufficient basis for constituting government in a democratic society. It is more likely to yield majority tyranny and democratic despotism. The constitution of the U.S. Senate grossly violates that rule. In like fashion, principles of bureaucratic administration will not of themselves suffice to yield a rational legal order, as Max Weber presumed, but can be expected to yield loss of control, distortion of information, goal displacement, and corruption, as the aggregate size of governmental administration increases (V. Ostrom 1989, 58–63). The art of legislation and the critical knowledge necessary for effective legislation is instead abandoned to preoccupation with glittering generalities and to recurrent problems having to do with money matters, attending to constituency complaints, and seeking reelection.

Finally, the conceptualization of legislation in terms of competing moral imperatives no longer leaves any ground for establishing a principle of fiscal equivalence in which identifiable communities of potential beneficiaries bear the costs of collective action. Taxes are sanitized by passing them through the Internal Revenue Service, and members of the Congress function not as trustees spending their constituents' moneys for national public services and facilities but as brokers competing with one another to get as much as they can for their constituents and themselves from the national treasury. Fiscal realities are replaced by fiscal illusions, as moral imperatives replace positive law, and as executive instrumentalities are instructed to maximize a multitude of different values by mandatory rule.

Executive reorganization. Similar transformations are occurring in the executive, where authority is being increasingly transferred to the office of the president. Reorganization efforts, since the Brownlow Commission of 1937, have viewed the presidency as the command-and-control center of government, exercising a unity of command over a hierarchically ordered bureaucratic structure in which a command relationship reaches from the president to the most subordinate individuals in the national administration. Furthermore, the Administrative Reorganization Act presumes that relationships internal to the executive can be reconstituted on the basis of reorganization plans formulated by the president and given the force of law. The rule-making authority that Congress assigns to a particular administrative instrumentality of the national government is thus subject to reassignment by the president in the form of reorganization plans that have the force of law.

These reorganization plans may take the form of transferring subordinate, administrative responsibility to the president, as was done in the plan that created the Office of Management and Budget in 1970. The president is then in a position to issue instructions as he sees fit without further notice. The exercise of executive authority is thus increasingly subject to executive privilege where standards applicable to executive performance are privy to the executive establishment.

This same reorganization plan included provision for the organization of a Domestic Council in the office of the president subject to the same legal presumption that the president may direct as he sees fit. The language in the explanatory documentation indicates that the Domestic Council is the body to decide "what Government should do" (U.S. Codes, 1970: III, 6, 316). The term "Government" in this context is identified with the executive establishment, and the decision about what "Government" should do is internal to the executive. The presumption is that legislative standards have become sufficiently loose to allow for the effective decisions about public policy to be taken within the councils of the executive, as the president may from time to time direct.

The span-of-control problem is such that any extended command structure will be subject both to a loss of information and

to a loss of control without regard to the superior-subordinate status of officials in a hierarchy of command. Highly centralized
command systems resolve this problem by developing redundant
structures that attempt to extend the reach of a chief executive
with regard to both command and intelligence functions. The reorganization plan for the Office of Management and Budget, for
example, anticipates the creation of Washington-based coordina-
tors to extend the reach of the president to subordinate levels of
the national bureaucracy and to relationships with state and local
government agencies in different regions of the United States.
Typically, inspectorates and secret police agencies provide independent channels to overcome the loss of information characteristic of extended bureaucratic structures. The so-called plumber's
unit organized in the office of the president during the Nixon
presidency was such an effort to ascertain where "leaks" were occurring in bureaucratic "pipelines."

During the Nixon presidency efforts were also made to impound funds appropriated by the Congress, efforts consistent
with the presumption that decisions about what "Government"
should do are to be taken by the executive. In one of the rare Supreme Court decisions in recent decades pertaining to constitutional limits and the separation of powers, such impoundments
were held to exceed the powers of the president. Recently, Congress has considered vesting the president with discretionary authority to impound funds so as to bring expenditures within
predetermined deficit targets. The logic of the Blackmun doctrine, which assumes that the structural features of congressional
organization are a sufficient safeguard in establishing constitu-
tionality, would allow for such an affirmative conveyance of legislative authority to the executive. Congress would then be free to
make "appropriations," but those "appropriations" would need to
have no essential bearing upon patterns of public expenditures.
Control over the public purse would, so to speak, pass to executive
instrumentalities subject to the direction of the president.

The president is increasingly being viewed as the sole executive exercising a unity of command over all executive instrumentalities of government. These instrumentalities increasingly

exercise legislative functions formulating rules for the ordering of relationships in American society. The imposition of "civil penalties" for the violation of rules implies that the prosecutory and adjudicatory functions of the executive are being expanded as well. With the erosion of constitutional limits, presidential government can be easily transformed into an autocracy. This is what happens when people view "the government" as a universal problem-solver.

Mandatory judicial remedies. Transformations of a comparable magnitude are also occurring in the Federal judiciary. The focal point in this transformation pertains to those provisions of the U.S. Constitution that contain specific prohibitions upon the exercise of governmental authority, especially with reference to the Fourteenth Amendment and to the first eight amendments. The key provision in the Fourteenth Amendment is the following:

> No state shall make or enforce any law which shall abridge the privileges and immunities of citizens of the United States; nor shall any state deprive any person of life, liberty, or property without due process of law; nor deny to any person within its jurisdiction the equal protection of the law.

This provision is usually presumed to encompass the First Amendment, which begins: "Congress shall make no law. . . . " Its provisions are extended to the states and instrumentalities of the states, including local units of government, as well as to the national government. Similar applications occur with reference to many of the other first eight amendments to the U.S. Constitution.

The earlier presumption in constitutional jurisprudence was that an act of an official body beyond its constitutional competence did not have legal standing and was therefore null and void. The potential immunity of an official arises only from lawful action. Beginning with the school desegregation cases, the Federal courts have gone beyond the earlier forms of relief holding an offending statute or regulation to be invalid, and without legal force, to a mandatory form of relief requiring a positive program of actions to remove the offending practice and substitute a conforming remedy. Furthermore, remedies are presumed to be available for racial segregation as a de facto wrong. Affirmatively mandated programs to desegregate schools have been the subject of numerous court orders.

A variety of difficulties arise under these conceptions of the judicial process. First, the granting of a remedy for a de facto wrong does not establish a de jure link with regard to the proximate source of the wrong. Segregation in schools may arise as a consequence of specific school policies or regulations that have the effect of yielding segregation. These might appropriately be held null and void. It is also possible for segregation to occur in schools as a consequence of the discriminatory policies and practices of those who function as realtors in a realty market. Granting a remedy that orders the desegregation of schools by busing students from one school to another to achieve racial balance does not address the de jure source of a wrong if that wrong arose from the collusive practices of realtors. It is possible for schools to be innocent bystanders with regard to offenses over which they had no control and for which they are ordered to provide remedies.

These circumstances yield a second but closely related issue that is fundamental to the problem being addressed by Alexander Hamilton in essays 15 and 16 of *The Federalist*. Hamilton considered the application of legislation to units of government in their corporate or collective capacity to be a fundamental conceptual error that precludes justice from being done. Collective sanctions apply to all members of a collectivity; yet not all members of a collectivity may have offended. Collective sanctions thus apply indiscriminately to innocent bystanders and offenders alike. In such circumstances, Hamilton argues, justice cannot be done.

The mandatory remedies applied to school districts in desegregation cases and to other instrumentalities of state and local governments in other cases offend against the basic principle advanced by Hamilton. It was this principle that required a basic reformulation of the framework for the fundamental law incorporated in the U.S. Constitution in contrast to the Articles of Confederation. This principle required a new structure necessitating "an alteration in the first principles and main pillars of the fabric" (Hamilton, Jay, and Madison [1788] n.d., 89). Applying desegregation decrees to school districts as collectivities, rather than to school officials (or others) as individuals, means that collective sanctions are being applied, and that those who are subject to the sanctions may be innocent bystanders upon whom costs are being imposed without regard to their standing as individuals. People, under such circumstances, find themselves trapped in unreasonable situations that are somehow, but ambiguously, related to basic social values of fundamental importance.

A third difficulty arises in applying mandatory remedies to collectivities such as school districts, other units of local government, and instrumentalities of state government. Court decrees take on the task of formulating policies, establishing programs, and modifying institutional structures in particular units of government. In setting policies, establishing programs, and modifying institutional structures, courts are assuming legislative, executive, and constitutional prerogatives that properly reside with legislative bodies, executive instrumentalities, or with people as constitutional decision makers. These court orders are subject to enforcement through contempt proceedings. Judges in such circumstances function as rule makers, rule enforcers, and rule adjudicators in the application of judicial decrees to collectivities. They violate the basic maxim of justice that no one is a fit judge of his or her own cause in relation to the interests of others. There is no easily accessible remedy when the Federal judiciary becomes a primary offender in usurping the legislative, executive, and constitutional prerogatives of state and local units of government and of the communities of people who are involved.

A further difficulty arises when courts construe constitutional limits to be equivalent to positive national legislation. Ambiguities about what is forbidden, permitted, and required are resolved in the direction of expanding the domain of the forbidden and required at the cost of constraining the domain of the permitted. The effect is to unduly constrain the discretion of public instrumentalities of state and local government and to yield a uniform application of legal standards for the nation as a whole. A standard such as equal protection of the laws is increasingly construed with reference to uniform national standards of equality. Standards that apply to the decisions of a particular collectivity, with reference to the application of its particular statutory enactments or ordinances to people within its jurisdiction, are downplayed. Yet equal protection of the law is a standard that might be met by each collectivity and nevertheless yield considerable diversity across collectivities. The concept of the supremacy of law does not presuppose that the general corpus of a uniform code of law applies to the United States as a whole.

The concept of self-governing society organized within the framework of a federal system of government implies that constitutional limits apply to the exercise of discretion within the different units of government, but that discretion in terms of what is permitted under law need not be squeezed out either by prohibitions or mandated requirements. A rule of law may allow for diversity rather than requiring uniformity throughout the whole structure of a society.

The insufficiency of mutual accommodations. Given the tendencies to usurp authority and shirk responsibilities that have characterized the mutual accommodations reached by instrumentalities of the American national government, what conclusions can we reach? Without some fundamental form of constitutional jurisprudence and constitutional decision making to limit the proper exercise of legislative, executive, and judicial processes in a national government, we can expect serious manifestations of institutional weaknesses and institutional failures to occur in the operation of the national government. There is no ground for believing that these weaknesses and failures will be self-correcting. "Checks and balances" do not work without recurrent attention to constitutional choice; they are insufficient to maintain a constitutional system. The many possibilities for error may interact with one another to amplify error, creating a system of rules that entrap, rather than facilitate the pursuit of mutually productive opportunities.

One such possibility is the assumption that failures derive from evil men rather than in the basic way that institutions are structured. Changes in personnel or changes in leadership are assumed to be the key factor. The issue is addressed as a matter of *will* rather than one of critical understanding and awareness of the problems involved in the nature and constitution of order. More rules are fabricated as a means of outlawing this or that evil without having made a critical diagnosis of the sources of evils. People find themselves snared in traps of their own making.

If we leave the structure of government to be worked out by the mutual accommodations reached among the legislative, executive, and judicial instrumentalities of the national government; if we permit dominant coalitions to pursue whatever opportunities become available; then we are relying primarily upon the exigencies of chance to prevail in the governance of society. Constitutional considerations are abandoned to calculations that presume that winning coalitions can and should prevail. These coalitions may be joined by state and local officials who trade their constitutional responsibilities for funds from the national treasury. Federal principles in a system of constitutional government are abandoned to the wheeling and dealing that is necessary to fashion winning coalitions and raid the national treasury.

As such processes come to prevail, we can expect a commensurate erosion in the rule of law and a decline in respect for law. The scope of individual discretion will be increasingly narrowed by the mandatory requirements of poorly conceived rules and regulations. The presumption that each one of us is first one's own governor, responsible for the conduct of one's own affairs and knowing how to relate oneself to other individuals in accordance with reasonable norms, will increasingly be abandoned for the presumption that most people prefer to avoid moral responsibility.

Before long, people will increasingly find themselves in circumstances where reasonable options no longer prevail and will begin a search for options that afford ways out of their difficulties. Temptation strategies may become the best available option, including the temptation to go "underground," to avoid the mandatory requirement of rules, or to gain the acquiescence of others, including officials, in ignoring the application of troublesome rules. The United States is moving on the same course that Argentina has already taken.

Tocqueville, in *The Old Regime and the French Revolution*, reports that a uniform code of law, which applied to diverse material, environmental, and cultural circumstances, yielded accommodations by which a primary function of the French bureaucracy came to be that of waiving the rule of law. Citizens came to look upon laws as arbitrary obstacles for which one should be entitled to a waiver in his or her particular circumstances (Tocqueville [1856] 1955, 67–68). Indeed, whenever they become obstacles to what people view as reasonable courses of action, it is but another step to where laws become "traps for money," as Hobbes characterized unnecessary laws ([1651] 1960, 228). Thus an erosion of law can be expected to yield pervasive patterns of corruption in any highly centralized political regime.

We have now examined four types of political transformation: increasing centralization of authority in the national government; increasing erosion of legislative standards; increasing centralization of executive authority; and an increasing arbitrariness in the exercise of judicial authority. As these occur in a society, illusions of power can be expected to give way to increasing immobility. Centralized regimes relying upon mandatory prescriptions that constrain discretion on the part of individuals are often accompanied by processes of psychological detachment, social disengagement, and loss of initiative on the part of those who seek to minimize their individual costs of entrapment. The dynamic of individual initiatives and leadership on behalf of multitudinous efforts in a society can be throttled by the numerous impediments created by restrictive rules and regulations. Individuals can adopt free-riding, or easy-riding, strategies of letting others attempt to cope with the burdens of collective action while they seek escape through disengagement and mind-altering experiences. This yields social immobility.

We then face a puzzling problem where those who aspire to active political leadership find that the only way to break the shackles of immobility and provoke movement in a society is by calling for moral crusades. In such circumstances, the way for national leadership to mobilize increased participation among members of that society is to do so through a *mass movement* that makes a strong moral appeal to each individual. Mass movements organized as moral crusades are situations that provoke the worst tensions through disparities between unlimited imaginations and limited capabilities. We observe these tendencies in calls for a war on poverty or for crusades that are the "moral equivalent of war." Wars in democratic societies are obsessive struggles in which all other conditions of life are subordinated to the requirements of warfare. Moral crusades are likely to have a similarly obsessive nature: all other facets of life are subordinated to the overriding considerations of the crusade. Such circumstances can be immensely disruptive for the multifaceted character of life in free, productive societies.

Much more may be at stake than an erosion of the rule of law. Appeals to moral crusades, while occasionally an important stimulant to collective action in democratic societies, pose serious threats to the survival of democratic institutions. Every system of totalitarian government has arisen in the call for a crusade or a revolutionary struggle that is the moral equivalent of war. As Hobbes observed, the death of democracy occurs when people acquiesce in the usurpation of authority by those leaders who demand that their authority be unlimited (Hobbes [1642] 1949, 91–93).

The tendencies that I have taken into account, and the implications that I see, need to be viewed with caution. If people rely upon the exigencies of historical accident—the pulling and hauling of social forces—and personal caprice to achieve mutual accommodations among the legislative, executive, and judicial instrumentalities of government, they can become shackled in ways that are appropriately referred to as a "central-government trap." The trap is of our own making, and it is easy to levy an accusation that the source of evil is "the government." The Blackmun doctrine can only strengthen and reinforce that trap.

Instead, we need to look at ourselves in the mirror of life and reconsider our situation. In the absence of understanding, the central-government trap can work to tighten its grip, but there *are* options, and they need to be explored. The requirements of self-governing societies need not depend upon states to rule over societies. The problems of a constitutional order, which we face today, are no more difficult than the problems involved in the institutions of slavery and of machine politics and boss rule. We cannot assume, however, that American society is somehow immune to despotism just because we are Americans and so presumably occupy some peculiar place in human destiny. If something exists somewhere, it can exist anywhere in human societies if the appropriate conditions are allowed to arise. Moral crusaders who are ruthless in overriding opposition and in subordinating all other values to their overriding moral cause can create despotic regimes anywhere. They will use theories of design to create systems of government that are capable of overriding opposition and dominating the exercise of authority. Struggles for power, far from the reach of ordinary people in the normal exigencies of life, will lead to the erosion of constitutional limits unless people are critically concerned about the maintenance of those limits.

THE LIMITS OF "FEDERAL FORM"

Much of the treatment of structures and processes of government, devoid as it is of reference to the relevant political communities, is analogous to treating a head devoid of a body. The point of Hamilton's analysis in essays 15 and 16 of *The Federalist* is that reference to other units of government, as such, is insufficient in the constitution of a federal system of government; the nexus of relationships must instead be extended to the persons of individuals. But this does not mean reference to individuals alone. Rather, the nexus between a limited national government and individuals also requires reference to the political nexus of individuals to instrumentalities of state government within each state, to the nexus of individuals to other units of local government within each state, and to the nexus of other associated relationships that constitute the social infrastructure. Each nexus of associated relationships must be taken into account in considering the relationships of structures and processes of government in the political

community that is the United States of America. That community, as I have pointed out elsewhere, is a highly compounded republic, not a simple republic governed by a single ultimate center
of authority (V. Ostrom 1987).

The elements of so-called federal form that are built into the
structure of the national government constitute a way of taking
into account the configuration of relationships that make up the
American political community as it is relevant to the governance
of national affairs. Members of Congress, in performing legislative functions, will reflect some sensitivity to constituency relationships as these pertain to national affairs. To assume that
these "federal forms" are both necessary and sufficient to take
account of local and state "interests" is implausible for at least
three reasons.

First, structural conditions pertaining to electoral arrangements and modes of representation do not determine outcomes
in circumstances governed by plurality voting and collective
choice. The character of coalitional politics and the forms that
party coalitions take have substantial independence as intermediate processes in their own right. It is the openness of governmental structures to diverse coalitional strategies that led
Madison to generalize that any and all exercises of public authority "may be misapplied and abused" (Hamilton, Jay, and
Madison [1788] n.d., 260).

Rules, including the rules of fundamental law embodied in
constitutions, operate in a configurational way rather than in a
linear, causally determined way. Rules of a configurational nature
are articulated in ways that bound the latitudes of discretion on
more than one dimension. Rules for authorizing collective action
need then to be viewed in relation to the potential veto capabilities of an executive, or of a citizen seeking to enjoin the implementation of legislation as well as to other rules, represented by an
"equal protection" clause, that constrain majority coalitions from
acting to benefit a majority by taking away from a minority. Instead, general rules should have equal application in relation to
the relevant community of people implicated. The domain of discretion is established by both rules that authorize and rules that

limit. Voting rules, veto rules, equal application rules, and due process rules operate in configurational ways (E. Ostrom, 1986).

Second, the exigencies of collective choice apply not only to relationships among individuals in a political community but to the structure of opportunities that become available to people within the material and environing conditions of the world in which they live. The "country" that is pertinent to the United States as a national political community is different from the "country" that is pertinent to the peoples of Hawaii, Alaska, Florida, or Minnesota as political communities. The conditions of life in each countryside vary such that architectural standards, for example, appropriate to Alaska or to Minnesota are not likely to be appropriate to Hawaii and Florida. Similar principles pertain to the variability of the material and environing conditions that apply to Los Angeles, San Francisco, New Orleans, Minneapolis, or Chicago. A uniform code of laws applicable to semitropical and semiarctic regions, or to arid and humid regions, to identify only two climatic variables, would be likely to yield limits to discretion that become traps for one or another community of people in these diverse circumstances. People everywhere are likely to have water problems, but the water problems of New Orleans are quite different from the water problems of Los Angeles. Similar problems need not be common problems. The water problems of both Los Angeles and New Orleans may be affected by river systems that are interstate in character. But the way that those river systems affect the material conditions of life varies significantly between the Mississippi valley and the Colorado basin.

A federal structure permits cognizance of the diverse national, regional, and local communities of interests without presuming that national interests override all other communities of interest. The modes of representation used in constituting the Congress are inappropriate for taking collective decisions that bear upon the community of interests that people in Alaska share in relation to the material and environmental conditions of the Alaskan countryside. Representatives from Arizona, California, Hawaii, Louisiana, Florida, and a multitude of other environs are now taking decisions about environmental circumstances for which they have little understanding or sympathy.

Third, the capacity of people to function in larger political communities may depend critically upon the knowledge and skills that these same people acquire in smaller political communities. What people can learn about democratic processes of governance in their local communities may thus be an essential foundation for acquiring an understanding of the counterintentional and counterintuitive character of political relationships, and of learning how to relate to other human beings in the presence of disagreement and conflict. These are difficult lessons for each and every person to learn, but learning them is the only way to avoid naiveté and come to appreciate the complex process of conflict resolution, in which due deliberation affords alternatives to mutually destructive confrontations.

Those who continue to assume that the national government, because of its "federal form," is competent to determine all matters that pertain to the governance of American society have fallen into two errors: that of neglecting the limited capabilities of those occupying positions of national authority; and that of considering citizens to be "more than kings and less than men" (Tocqueville [1835] 1945, 2: 231), so that they are presumed to be competent to select their national rulers, but incompetent to govern their own local affairs. The "federal form" of the national government is no substitute for a federal system of governance.

The *Garcia* decision, then, leaves American citizens in a puzzling circumstance. Its implicit rejection of the general theory of limited constitutions, a theory whereby the whole system of fundamental law is connected with a core that has reference to state constitutional formulations, leaves us in a position where we either have to abandon constitutional government or reformulate the U.S. Constitution. Moreover, to build such limitations successfully into the U.S. Constitution would require substantial redundancy and endless detail. In fashioning new constitutional arrangements, we would again face the eternal problem of whether words on paper will suffice to achieve constitutional limitations. The answer is no. We cannot avoid the strange puzzle that is inherent in all language. Except where proper names are used, words are but names for classes of events. The symbols (words) in any language thus operate in a one-many relationship. There comes a point where all use of language depends upon a tacit understanding about the meaning of language, that is, about the referents for the use of words and how those words and their referents fit into more general configurations of meaning and relationships (Polanyi 1962). No one can draft a meaningful legal instrument without a shared common understanding of what words mean. This is why the theory used to construe meaning is of such fundamental importance in the constitution of democratic systems of governance.

If we are unwilling to stipulate the theory we are using, or to say how different conceptualizations about the nature and constitution of order in human societies are articulated in both an explanatory and a juridical language, our words lose their meaning. People talk, but they do not know what they are talking about.

The problem of communication can be resolved only when people come to appreciate that different conceptualizations can apply to the design and creation of different systems of governance. We can assume that there are common features to rule-ordered relationships in all human societies, but those features cannot be understood so long as political discourse focuses upon disembodied heads, upon governments apart from citizens and the place of citizens in a system of constitutional rule. Democratic societies must always be cognizant of the rulership prerogatives of citizens. Unless citizens can hold officials accountable so that they perform within the bounds of fundamental law, democratic societies cannot maintain control over their systems of governance. When people no longer maintain limits upon the exercise of governmental prerogatives and no longer hold their officials accountable to fundamental law, democracy no longer exists and autocracy prevails. This, however, does not prevent people from meaninglessly chattering about "democracy."

The fundamental condition for avoiding the central-government trap is to have mutual respect for each other's freedom, to rest all political experiments on the capacity of mankind for self-government, and never to view oneself as the master of others. Human beings can learn to discipline their imaginations through due deliberation and reflection. They can also learn to enhance their capabilities through working with others, to appreciate that counterintentional and counterintuitive relationships can trap people in counterproductive relationships, and to reflect upon the exigencies of conflict situations as a means of liberating themselves from such traps and reestablishing mutually productive communities of relationships. This is what it means to live in a self-governing society. Those who view themselves as political masters are trapped in a vicious form of servitude that denies them access to what it means to be free.

My referent in this essay has been the general theory of limited constitutions as formulated by Alexander Hamilton and James Madison in *The Federalist* (V. Ostrom 1987). This is a theory that was ridiculed by Jeremy Bentham in his extended note on the nature of law ([1823] 1948). John Austin ([1832] 1955) referred to constitutional law as positive morality, not positive law. Frank Goodnow (1990) considered constitutions to be meaningless formalities. Woodrow Wilson ([1885] 1956) viewed what I regard as general theory of limited constitutions as "literary theories" and "paper pictures."

Twentieth-century legal and political realists have assumed that law is command and that collective action in a society depends upon a unity of command. The basic axiom in this theory, when stated (as by Wilson) in the negative form, is that "the more authority is divided the more irresponsible it becomes" (ibid., 77). This view must be juxtaposed with Hobbes's basic analysis that a unitary sovereign is the source of law, above the law, and not accountable to law. If Hobbes is correct, Wilson is wrong. In the modern mode of analysis, fragmentation of authority and overlapping jurisdictions are viewed as major sources of institutional failure in the American system of government. Yet authority must be fragmented (that is, differentiated) if there is to be either a rule of law or constitutional government. Overlapping jurisdictions are necessary features in federal systems of governance. We cannot straighten out our own thinking by presuming to be omniscient observers. *Garcia* requires us to rethink the foundations of our legal and political sciences before we can assess where we are and what might be done in an experiment that is going awry.

III

SOME EMERGENT PATTERNS OF ORDER

Constitutional rule necessarily implies fragmentation of authority in any one unit of government. Federal systems of government necessarily imply overlapping jurisdictions. How the American federal system works necessarily depends upon the emergence of patterns of order in interorganizational and intergovernmental relationships. The operational characteristics of federal systems of governance turn upon emergent patterns of order and how they work at the interpersonal, interorganizational, and intergovernmental levels of operation. The burden upon students of federalism, then, is to understand how overlapping jurisdictions and fragmentation of authority yield emergent patterns of order that are at least as consistent with standards of liberty, justice, and general welfare among persons of equal standing as the patterns that can be achieved where unitary states rule over societies.

Chapter 6 explains how overlapping jurisdictions and fragmentation of authority can be conceptualized as a polycentric political system that, in metropolitan areas, is constitutive of a system of governance. What emerges is a way of organizing a public economy and a system of governance that allows for competitive option and offers the promise of better performance than can be achieved by an overarching form of monopoly control. Chapter 7 is an effort to contribute to a theory of goods and explain the emergence of public economies as distinguished from market economies in a federal system of governance. Chapter 8 is concerned with the emergence of an open public realm in the American federal system that is constitutive of public opinion, civic knowledge, and a culture of inquiry. This open public realm accrues in the context of interpersonal, interorganizational, and intergovernmental relationships. Chapter 9 addresses polycentricity as the set of structural conditions that are conducive to the emergence of new patterns of order in human societies. The American federal system is conceived as a structural framework that facilitates contestation and innovation to yield emergent patterns of order that might apply to "the whole system of human affairs, private as well as public."

SIX

THE ORGANIZATION OF GOVERNMENT IN METROPOLITAN AREAS: A THEORETICAL INQUIRY

Vincent Ostrom, Charles M. Tiebout, and Robert Warren

The "problem of metropolitan government" is a phrase often used in characterizing the difficulties supposed to arise because a metropolitan region is a legal nonentity. From this point of view, the people of a metropolitan region have no general instrumentality of government available to deal directly with the range of problems that they share in common. Rather, there is a multiplicity of federal and state governmental agencies, counties, cities, and special districts that govern within a metropolitan region.

This view assumes that the multiplicity of political units in a metropolitan area is essentially a pathological phenomenon. The diagnosis asserts that there are too many governments and not enough government. The symptoms are described as "duplication of functions" and "overlapping jurisdictions." Autonomous units of government, acting in their own behalf, are considered incapable of resolving the diverse problems of the wider metropolitan community. The political topography of the metropolis is called a "crazy-quilt pattern" and its organization is said to be an "organized chaos." The prescription is reorganization into larger units, reorganization that supposedly will provide "a general metropolitan framework" for gathering up the various functions of government. A political system with a single dominant center for making decisions is viewed as the ideal model for the organization of metropolitan government. "Gargantua" is one name for it.[1]

The assumption that each unit of local government acts independently without regard for other public interests in the metropolitan community has only a limited validity. The traditional pattern of government in a metropolitan area, with its multiplicity of political jurisdictions, may more appropriately be conceived as a *polycentric political system*.[2] "Polycentric" connotes many centers of decision making that are formally independent of each other. Whether they actually function independently, or instead constitute an interdependent system of relations, is an empirical question in particular cases. To the extent that they take each other into account in competitive relationships, enter into various contractual and cooperative undertakings, or have recourse to mediating mechanisms to resolve conflicts, the various political jurisdictions in a metropolitan area may function in a coherent manner with consistent and predictable patterns of interacting behavior. To the extent that this is so, they may be said to function as a "system."

The study of government in metropolitan areas conceived as a polycentric political system should precede any judgment that it is pathological. Both the structure and the behavior of the system need analysis before any reasonable estimate can be made of its performance in dealing with the various public problems arising in a metropolitan community. Better analysis of how a metropolitan area is governed can lead in turn to more appropriate measures of reorganization and reform.[3]

This essay is an initial effort to explore some of the potentialities of a polycentric political system in providing for the government of metropolitan areas. We view the "business" of governments in metropolitan areas as providing "public goods and services." The first section of the paper will examine the special character of these public goods and services. We shall then turn to an analysis of the problems of scale in constituting public organizations that provide them. Such a discussion seems relevant to the analysis of any political structure in a metropolitan area, and equally applicable to Gargantua or to a polycentric political system. A brief reference will then be made to the problems of public organization in Gargantua. Finally, patterns of organization in a polycentric political system will be analyzed with particular regard to the experience of the Los Angeles metropolitan area.

THE NATURE OF PUBLIC GOODS AND SERVICES

The conditions giving rise to public rather than private provision of certain goods and services are examined in this section. Three views of these conditions can usefully be distinguished: (1) public goods arise from efforts to control indirect consequences, externalities, or spillover effects; (2) goods are provided publicly because they cannot be packaged; and (3) public goods consist of the maintenance of preferred states of community affairs.

The control of indirect consequences as public goods. It was John Dewey who, some years ago, stated that "the line between private and public is to be drawn on the basis of the extent and scope of the consequences of acts which are so important as to need control whether by inhibition or by promotion" (1927, 15). This basic criterion has become the one traditionally offered. The indirect consequences of a transaction, which affect others than those directly concerned, can also be described as "externalities" or "spillover effects." Those indirectly affected are viewed as being external to the immediate transaction. Some externalities are of a favorable or beneficial nature; others are adverse or detrimental.

Favorable externalities can frequently be recaptured by the economic unit that creates them. The builder of a large supermarket, for example, may create externalities for the location of a nearby drugstore. If the builder of the supermarket also controls the adjacent land, he can capture the externalities accruing to the drugstore through higher rents or by common ownership of the two enterprises. From the builder's point of view, he has "internalized" the externalities (Krutilla and Eckstein 1958, 69ff.).[4]

Where favorable externalities cannot be internalized by private parties, a sufficient mechanism to proceed may be lacking, and public agencies may be called upon to provide a good or service. A privately owned park, even with an admission charge, may not be able to cover costs. If the externalities in the form of the dollar value of a better neighborhood could be captured, such a park might be profitable.

Unfavorable spillovers or externalities are another matter. The management of a refinery that belches out smoke has little incentive to install costly equipment to eliminate the smoke. Control or internalization of diseconomies usually falls upon public agencies. A function of government, then, is to internalize the externalities—positive and negative—for those goods that the producers and consumers are unable or unwilling to internalize for themselves, and this process of internalization is identified with "public goods."

Not all public goods are of the same scale. Scale implies both the geographic domain and the intensity or weight of the externality. A playground creates externalities that are neighborhood-wide in scope, while national defense activities benefit a whole nation—and affect many outside it. Thus to each public good there corresponds some "public." The public, in Dewey's formula, "consists of all those who are affected by the indirect consequences of transactions to such an extent that it is deemed necessary to have those consequences systematically provided for" (1927, 15–16). We shall return to the concept of the public when we come to consider the criteria of scale appropriate to public organizations.

Packageability. Public goods and services and, in turn, the functions of governments in metropolitan areas can also be distinguished from private goods by a criterion commonly used by economists. A private good must be "packageable," that is, susceptible of being differentiated as a commodity or service, before it can be readily purchased and sold in the private market. Those who do not pay for a private good can then be excluded from enjoying its benefits. This notion is formulated by economists as the "exclusion principle" (Musgrave 1959, esp. ch. 1). In contrast with Dewey's formulation of the nature of public goods, the exclusion principle focuses attention on the practicability of denying benefits. National defense, for example, will not be provided by private firms because, among other reasons, the citizen who did not pay would still enjoy the benefits. Furthermore, if citizens understate their preferences for defense—as by failing to build bomb shelters in times of war—on the assumption that it will be paid for by others, the result will be an inadequate provision for defense.

Most municipal public goods such as fire and police protection, or the abatement of air pollution, are not easily packageable, either; they cannot be sold only to those individuals who are willing to pay (Tiebout 1956). This suggests two problems for public organizations.

First, private goods, because they are easily packageable, are readily subject to measurement and quantification. Public goods, by contrast, are generally not so measurable. If more police are added to the force, output will presumably increase. But how much it will increase is a question without an exact answer. Moreover, when factors of production can be quantified in measurable units of output, the production process can be subject to more rigorous controls. A more rational pricing policy is also possible. With quantifiable data about both input and output, any production process can be analyzed and the performance of different modes of production can be compared for their efficiency. Rational control over the production and provision of public goods and services therefore depends, among other things, upon the development of effective standards of measurement; this applies as much to the allocation of joint costs as to that of joint benefits.

A second, closely related, problem arises in the assessment of costs upon persons who can benefit without paying directly for the good. Only public agencies with their taxing powers can seek to apportion the costs of public goods among the various beneficiaries. The scale criterion of political representation, discussed below, takes account of how this difference between private and public goods affects the organization of public agencies.

Public goods as the maintenance of preferred states of community affairs. The exclusion principle provides a criterion for distinguishing most public goods from private; but it does not, as commonly stated, clarify or specify the conditions that determine the patterns of organization in a public economy. However, by viewing public goods as "the maintenance of preferred states of community affairs," we may introduce a modified concept of packageability, one that is amenable to some measurement and quantification, and that therefore may be more helpful in clarifying criteria for the organization of public services in metropolitan areas. The modification consists in extending the exclusion principle from an individual consumer to all the inhabitants of an area within designated boundaries.

The concept can be illustrated on a small scale in the operation of a household heating system that uses conveniently measurable units of inputs. The household temperature it maintains is a joint benefit to the family, and a marginal change in family size will have no material effect upon the costs of maintaining this public good for the family. Yet, since the family good derived from it is effectively confined to the household, outsiders are excluded and there are no substantial spillover effects or externalities for them. The family good is not a public good in the larger community. Household heating, then, is treated as a private good in most communities. Similarly, a public good on a neighborhood or community scale can be viewed as "packaged" within appropriate boundaries so that others outside the boundaries may be excluded from its use. In this way, in some communities adjacent to New York City, for example, the use of parks and beaches is restricted to local residents whose taxes presumably support these recreation facilities.

Wherever this is practicable, the analogy of a household as a "package" for an atmosphere with a controlled temperature may be generalized and applied to the maintenance of a desired state of affairs within particular local government boundaries. Just as the temperature and the cost of heating can be measured, so it may be possible to develop direct or closely approximate measures both of a given state of community affairs resulting from the production of many public goods and services and also of the costs of furnishing them. An air pollution abatement program, for example, may be measured by an index of quantities of various pollutants found in air samples. Given costs of abatement, some preferred tolerance levels may then be specified.

Similarly, any community has a "fire loss potential," defined as the losses to be expected if no provision for fire protection is made. The difference between this potential and the actual fire losses is then the output or "production" of the fire protection service, and the net fire loss can be termed the "state of affairs" in that community with respect to fire losses. Fire protection, of course, does not eliminate but only reduces fire losses. Any effort at complete elimination would probably be so expensive that the costs would greatly exceed the benefits. The "preferred" state of affairs is some optimal level of performance where benefits exceed costs. The provision of a community fire department as a public good can thus be viewed as the maintenance of a preferred state of affairs in fire protection for that community, and the benefits can ordinarily be confined to its residents.

Police protection can be regarded in the same way. The traffic patrol, for example, operates to optimize the flow of traffic while reducing the losses to property and injury to persons. Even if perfect control were possible, the costs would be so great that the preferred state of affairs in police protection would be something less.

It must be acknowledged, however, that in the case of police protection and many other public services—in contrast, say, with garbage collection or air pollution abatement—the performance level or net payoff is much more difficult to measure and to quantify. Proximate measures such as the gross number of arrests for different types of offenses per month or per 10,000 population annually have little meaning unless considered in relation to various conditions existing in the community. Decision-makers consequently may be forced, for want of better measurements, to assume that the preferred state of affairs is defined as a balance between the demands for public services and the complaints from taxpayers.

While the output of a public good may not be packaged, this does not of course mean that its material inputs cannot be. The preferred state of affairs produced by mosquito spraying, for example, is enjoyed by the whole community, while spraying supplies and equipment are readily packageable. Mosquito spraying, that is to say, can be produced by a private vendor under contract to a public agency.

This illustrates an important point, that the *production* of goods and services needs to be distinguished from their *provision* at public expense. Government provision need not involve public production; indeed, at some stage in the sequence from raw materials to finished products virtually every public good, not itself a natural resource, is of private origin. It follows that a public agency by contractual arrangements with private firms—or with other public agencies—can provide the local community with public services without going into the business of producing them itself.

When the desired performance level or the net payoff can be specified by a measurable index, an element of rigor can be introduced to assure substantial production controls in providing a public good, even where the production itself is the function of a separate agency or entrepreneur. The producer can be held accountable for maintaining affairs within certain tolerances, and the agency responsible for providing the service can ascertain the adequacy of performance. Advances in the measurement and quantification of performance levels in a public economy will consequently permit much greater flexibility in the patterns of organization.

If Dewey's definition of the public (1927, 4–5) is extended to include "events" generally rather than being limited to "acts" or to "transactions" among actors, his formulation is consistent with the conception of public goods as the maintenance of preferred states of affairs.[5] Public control seeks to internalize those events, viewed as consequences that impinge directly and indirectly upon diverse elements in a community, in such a way that adverse consequences will be inhibited and favorable consequences will be promoted.

In the final analysis, distinctions between private and public goods cannot be as sharply made in the world of human experience as this analysis might imply. In part, the technical character of specific goods influences the degree of differentiation or isolability that characterizes their distribution and utilization. Vegetables and landscapes cannot be handled in the same way. Many private goods have spillover effects such that other members of the community bear some portion of the benefits and losses, whatever the degree of public regulation. In every large community most people philosophically accept some of the costs of bigness—air pollution, traffic congestion, noise, and a variety of inconveniences—on the assumption that these are inevitable concomitants of the benefits that derive from living in a metropolis.

SCALE PROBLEMS IN PUBLIC ORGANIZATION

If we view the boundaries of a local unit of government as the "package" in which its public goods are provided, so that those outside the boundaries are excluded from their use, we may say that where a public good is adequately packaged within appropriate boundaries, it has been successfully internalized.[6] Where externalities spill over upon neighboring communities, the public good has not been fully internalized.

In designing the appropriate "package" for the production and provision of public goods several criteria should be considered. Among these are control, efficiency, political representation, and self-determination. Needless to say, they are sometimes in conflict.

The criterion of control. The first standard applicable to the scale of public organization for the production of public services requires that the boundary conditions of a political jurisdiction include the relevant set of events to be controlled.[7] Events are not uniformly distributed in space; rather, they occur as sets under conditions such that their boundaries can be defined with more or less precision. Rivers flow in watershed basins, for example. Patterns of social interaction are also differentially distributed in space, and boundaries can generally be defined for them too. In other words, all phenomena can be described in relation to specifiable boundary conditions, and the criterion of control requires that these be taken into account in determining the scale of a public organization. Otherwise, the public agency is disabled in regulating a set of events in order to realize some preferred state of affairs. If the boundaries cannot be suitably adjusted, the likely result is a transfer of the governmental function to a unit scaled to meet the criterion of control more adequately.

Pasadena, for example, is subject to severe smog attacks, but the city's boundary conditions do not cover an area sufficient to assure effective control of the meteorological and social space that constitutes the "smogisphere" of southern California. None of the separate cities of southern California, in fact, can encompass the problem. Instead, county air pollution control districts were organized for the Los Angeles metropolitan community. The failure even of counties to adequately meet the criterion of effective control has led the California state government to assume an increasingly important role in smog control.

The criterion of efficiency. The most efficient solution would require the modification of boundary conditions so as to assure a producer of public goods and services the most favorable economy of scale, as well as effective control. Two streams with different hydrologic characteristics, for example, might be effectively controlled separately; but if they are managed together, the potentialities of one may complement the other. This has certainly been the case with Los Angeles's joint management of the Owens and Los Angeles rivers. One has been made the tributary of the other through the three-hundred-mile Los Angeles Aqueduct, which skirts the Sierra. Joint management permits a greater joint payoff in recreational facilities and in water and power production.

Other factors, such as technological developments and the skill or proficiency of a labor force, can bear upon efficiency as a criterion of the scale of organization needed. If machinery for painting center stripes on city streets can be efficiently used only on a large scale, then special arrangements may be required to enable several small cities to procure such a service jointly. The same may apply to using uncommon and expensive professional skills;

and it accounts for the fact that mental institutions and prisons are apt to be state rather than municipal undertakings.

The criterion of political representation. Another criterion for the scale of public organization requires that the appropriate political interests be included within its decision-making arrangements. The direct participants in a transaction are apt to negotiate only their own interests, leaving the indirect consequences or spillover effects to impinge upon others. Third-party interests may be ignored. Public organizations seek to take account of third-party effects by internalizing the various interests involved in their rendering of public decisions and in their control of public affairs. In determining the set of interests that are to be internalized within the organization, it is important to specify the boundary or scale conditions of any political jurisdiction.

Three elements of scale require consideration here. The *scale of formal organization* indicates the size of the governmental unit that provides a public good. The *public*, as noted above, consists of those who are affected by its provision. The *political community* can be defined as those who are actually taken into account in deciding whether and how to provide the good. Those who are affected by such a decision may be different from those who influence its making. An ideal solution, assuming criteria of responsibility and accountability consonant with democratic theory, would require that these three boundaries be coterminous. Where in fact the boundary conditions differ, scale problems arise.

If both the direct and indirect beneficiaries of a public transaction are included within the domain of a public organization, the means are in principle available for assessing the cost of public control upon the beneficiaries. Except where a redistribution of income is sought as a matter of public policy, an efficient allocation of economic resources is enhanced by the capacity to charge the costs of providing public goods and services to the beneficiaries.[8]

The public implicated in different sets of transactions varies in scale with each set: the relevant public for one set may be confined to a neighborhood, whereas for another it may be most of the population of the globe. Between these two extremes lie a vast number of potential scales. Given certain levels of information, technology, and communication, and certain patterns of identification, a scheme might be imagined that had an appropriate scale of public organization for each different public good. As these conditions and circumstances change, the scale of the public for any set of transactions should be altered correspondingly. If it is not, what then?

Where the political community does not contain the whole public, some interests may be disregarded. A city, for instance, may decide to discharge its sewage below its boundaries, and the affected public there may have no voice in the decision. On the other hand, where the political community contains the whole public and, in addition, people unaffected by a particular transaction, the unaffected are given a voice when none may be desired. Capricious actions can result. The total political community in a city of three million population may not be an appropriate decision-making mechanism in planning a local playground.

Nevertheless, the statement that a government is "too large [or too small] to deal with a problem" often overlooks the possibility that the scale of the public and the political community need not coincide with that of the formal boundaries of a public organization. Informal arrangements between public organizations may create a political community large enough to deal with any particular public's problem. Similarly, a public organization may also be able to constitute political communities within its boundaries to deal with problems that affect only a subset of the population. It would be a mistake to conclude that public organizations are of an inappropriate size until the informal mechanisms that might permit larger or smaller political communities have been investigated.

Seen in relation to the political community, the scale of formal public organizations merely specifies their formal boundaries. Since the feasible number of governmental units is limited when compared to the number of public goods to be provided, a one-to-one mapping of the public, the political community, and the formal public organization is impracticable. Moreover, the relevant publics change. Even if, at one time, formal public organizations, political communities, and the publics were coterminous, over time they would become dislocated. As a result, public organizations may (1) reconstitute themselves; (2) voluntarily cooperate; or, failing cooperation, (3) turn to other levels of government in a quest for an appropriate fit among the interests affecting and affected by public transactions.

The criterion of local self-determination. The criteria of effective control, of efficiency, and of the inclusion of appropriate political interests can be formulated on general theoretical grounds. Their application, however, depends upon the particular institutions empowered to decide questions of scale. The conditions attending the organization of local governments in the United States usually require that these criteria be subordinated to considerations of self-determination—that is, controlled by the decisions of the citizenry in the local community.

The patterns of local self-determination manifest in incorporation proceedings usually require a petition of local citizens to institute the proceedings and an affirmative vote of the local electorate to approve. Commitments to local consent and local control may also involve substantial home rule in determining which interests of the community its local officials will attend to, and how these officials will be organized and held responsible for their discharge of public functions.

Local self-government of municipal affairs assumes that public goods can be successfully internalized. Presumably, the purely "municipal" affairs of a local jurisdiction do not create problems for other political communities. Where internalization is not possible, and where control consequently cannot be maintained, the local unit of government becomes another "interest" group in quest of public goods or potential public goods that spill over upon others beyond its borders.

The choice of local public services implicit in any system of self-government in a metropolis presumes that substantial variety will exist in patterns of public organization and in the public goods provided among the different local communities. Patterns of local autonomy and home rule constitute substantial commitments to a polycentric system.

PUBLIC ORGANIZATION IN GARGANTUA

Since all patterns of organization are less than perfectly efficient, responsive, or representative, some consideration should be given to the problem of organizing for different types of public services in Gargantua. This brief discussion will only touch on the theoretical considerations involved in organizing diverse public services in the big system, in contrast to organizing them in a polycentric political system.

Gargantua unquestionably provides an appropriate scale of organization for many huge public services. In Gargantua, the provision of harbor and airport facilities, mass transit, sanitary facilities, and imported water supplies may be appropriately organized. By definition, Gargantua should best be able to deal with metropolitan-wide problems at the metropolitan level.

However, Gargantua with its single dominant center of decision making is apt to become a victim of the complexity of its own hierarchical or bureaucratic structure. Its complex channels of communication may make its administration unresponsive to many of the more localized public interests in the community. The costs of maintaining control in Gargantua's public economy may be so great that its production of public goods becomes grossly inefficient.

Gargantua, as a result, may become insensitive and clumsy in meeting the demands of local citizens for the public goods they desire in their daily life. Two to three years may be required to secure street or sidewalk improvements, for example, even where local residents bear the cost. Modifications in traffic control at a local intersection may take an unconscionable amount of time. Some decision-makers will be more successful in pursuing their interests than others. The lack of effective organization for these others may result in policies with highly predictable biases. Bureaucratic unresponsiveness in Gargantua may produce frustration and cynicism on the part of the local citizen who finds no point of access for remedying local problems of a public character. Municipal reform may become simply a matter of "throwing the rascals out." The citizen may not have access to sufficient information to render an informed judgment at the polls. Lack of effective communication in the large public organization may indeed lead to the eclipse of the public and to the blight of the community.

The problem of Gargantua, then, is to recognize the variety of smaller sets of publics that may exist within its boundaries. Many of the interests of smaller publics might be properly negotiated within the confines of a smaller political community without requiring the attention of centralized decision-makers concerned with the big system. This task of recognizing the smaller publics is a problem of "field" or "area" organization. The persistence of bureaucratic unresponsiveness in the big system, however, indicates it is not easily resolved. Large-scale, metropolitan-wide organization is unquestionably appropriate for a limited number of public services, but it is not the most appropriate scale of organization for the provision of all public services required in a metropolis.

PUBLIC ORGANIZATION IN A
POLYCENTRIC POLITICAL SYSTEM

No a priori judgment can be made about the adequacy of a polycentric system of government as against the single jurisdiction. The multiplicity of interests in various public goods sought by people in a metropolitan region can be handled only in the context of many different organizational levels. The polycentric system is confronted with the problem of realizing the needs of wider community interests or publics beyond the functional or territorial bounds of each of the formal entities within the broader metropolitan region. The single jurisdiction, in turn, confronts the problem of recognizing and organizing the various subsidiary sets of interests within the big system. It is doubtful that suboptimization in Gargantua is any easier to accomplish than supraoptimization in a polycentric political system.

The performance of a polycentric political system can only be understood and evaluated by reference to the patterns of cooperation, competition, and conflict that may exist among its various units. When joint activities produce a greater return to all parties concerned, cooperative arrangements pose no difficulty if the appropriate set of public interests is adequately represented among the negotiators. A contractual arrangement will suffice. As a result, this discussion of the behavior of a polycentric political system will focus upon the more difficult problems of competition, of conflict and its resolution. If a polycentric political system can resolve conflict and maintain competition within appropriate bounds, it can be a viable arrangement for dealing with a variety of public problems in a metropolitan area.[9]

Competition. Where the provision of public goods and services has been successfully internalized within a public jurisdiction, there are, by definition, no substantial spillover effects. In such circumstances there need be no detrimental consequences from competition in the municipal services economy. Patterns of competition among producers of public services in a metropolitan area, just as among firms in the market, may produce substantial benefits by inducing self-regulating tendencies. The result may be pressure for the more efficient solution in the operation of the whole system.

Variety in service levels among various independent local government agencies within a larger metropolitan community may also give rise to a quasi-market choice for local residents, permitting them to select the particular community in the metropolitan area that most closely approximates the public service levels they desire. Public service agencies may then be forced to compete over the service levels offered in relation to the taxes charged. Such competition, however, would only be appropriate for those public goods that are adequately internalized within the boundaries of a given political jurisdiction.

Conditions amenable to competition normally exist among local units of government where a number of units are located in close proximity to each other, and where information about each other's performance is publicly available. Information can lead to comparison and comparison can lead to pressure for performances to approximate the operations of the more efficient units. Where more than one public jurisdiction is capable of rendering service in a single area, further competitive tendencies may develop. The separation of the *provision* of public goods and services from their *production* opens up the greatest possibility of redefining economic functions in a public economy. Public control can be maintained in relation to performance criteria in the provision of services, while an increasing amount of competition can be allowed to develop among the agencies that produce them.

With the incorporation of the city of Lakewood in 1954, Los Angeles County, for example, expanded its system of contracting for the production of municipal services to a point approaching quasi-market conditions. Newly incorporated cities, operating under the so-called Lakewood Plan, contract with the county or other appropriate agencies to produce the general range of municipal services needed in the local community. Each city contracts for municipal services for the city as a whole. Services beyond the general level of performance by county administration in unincorporated areas are subject to negotiation for most service functions. Each city also has the option of producing municipal services for itself. Private contractors, too, have undertaken such services as street sweeping, engineering, street maintenance and repair, and related public works. Some contracts have been negotiated with neighboring cities. As the number of vendors increases, competition brings pressures toward greater responsiveness and efficiency.

By separating the production from the provision of public goods it may be possible to differentiate, unitize, and measure the production while continuing to provide undifferentiated public goods to the citizen-consumer. Thus Los Angeles County has, under the Lakewood Plan, unitized the production of police services into packages, each consisting of a police car on continuous patrol with associated auxiliary services. A price is placed on this police-car-on-continuous-patrol package, and a municipality may contract for police service on that basis. Within the local community, police service is still provided as a public good for the community as a whole.

Problems of scale arising from possible conflicts between criteria of production and criteria of political representation may be effectively resolved in this way. Efficient scales of organization for the production of different public goods may be quite independent of the scales required to recognize appropriate publics for their consumption of public goods and services. But competition among vendors may allow the most efficient organization to be utilized in the production, while an entirely different community of interest and scale of organization controls the provision of services in a local community.

The separation of production from provision may also turn local governments into the equivalents of associations of consumers. While Sidney and Beatrice Webb (1922, 437ff.) viewed local governments in this way, the dominance of production criteria in American municipal administration has largely led to the subordination of consumer interests. However, cities organized to provide the local citizenry with public services produced by other agencies may be expected to give consumer interests stronger representation. Among the so-called Lakewood Plan cities in Los Angeles County, for example, the local chief administrative officer has increasingly become a spokesman or bargainer for consumer interests at the local level.

In this role, the chief administrative officer is similar to a buyer in a large corporation. Recognizing that the greater the number of vendors of public services, the greater the competition, the local chief administrative officer may seek to expand the number of his potential suppliers. As competition increases, vendors become more sensitive to the consumer demands they negotiate.

The production of public goods under the contract system in Los Angeles County has also placed considerable pressure upon the county administration to become more responsive to the public service clientele organized through their local cities. Important changes in operating procedures and organizational arrangements have been introduced into the county's administration of police protection, fire protection, library services, street maintenance, building inspection, and engineering services in order to increase efficiency and responsiveness.

Under these conditions, a polycentric political system can be viable in supplying a variety of public goods with many different

scales of organization and in providing reasonably efficient arrangements for the production and consumption of public goods.
With the development of quasi-market conditions in production,
much of the flexibility and responsiveness of market organization
can be realized in a public economy.

Several difficulties in the regulation of a competitive public
economy can be anticipated. Whether prices and costs can be economically allocated depends on whether municipal services can be
effectively measured. Since the preferred states of affairs in a community cannot be converted to a single scale of values, such as the
dollar profits of a private enterprise, it will be more difficult to
sustain an objective competitive relationship in a public economy.
Although costs of contract services from different vendors of a
public good may be the same, objective standards for determining
the value of the benefits are needed, and may be hard to come by;
otherwise the latitude of discretion available to the negotiators
may limit the competitive vitality of the system and shift the competition to side-payments.

Without careful control of cost allocations and pricing arrangements, funds from noncompetitive welfare functions might
be used to subsidize the more competitive service areas. In Los
Angeles County, close scrutiny of cost accounting practices and
pricing policies by the grand jury has helped to prevent funds
from being so transferred.

Any long-term reliance upon quasi-market mechanisms in the
production of public goods and services will no doubt require
more of such careful scrutiny, control, and regulation than has
been applied toward maintaining the competitive structure of the
private market economy. Indeed, the measurement of cost and
output performance may become an essential public function if
continued reliance is placed primarily upon a polycentric system
in the government of metropolitan areas.

Reliance upon outside vendors to produce public services may
also reduce the degree of local political control. The employee is subject to the control of the vendor and not directly to the control of the
municipality. In contrast to the more immediate lines of responsibility and communication between local municipal employees and city

officials, reliance upon vendors to provide municipal services may also restrict the quality and quantity of information about community affairs that is provided to the city's decision-makers. Such a constraint on information might reduce the degree of their control over public affairs.

This discussion merely indicates some of the considerations to be examined in analyzing the effects of competitive arrangements for providing public services in a metropolitan area. As long as the particular contracting agencies encompass the appropriate sets of public interests, no absolute impediment to competition need exist. With appropriate public control, such arrangements may afford great flexibility in taking advantage of economies of scale. At the same time, they may allow substantial diversity to the particular demands of the immediate communities.

Conflict and conflict resolution. More difficult problems for a polycentric political system are created when the provision of public goods cannot be confined to the boundaries of the existing units of government. These situations, since they involve serious spillover effects, are apt to provoke conflict between the various units in the system. Arrangements must be available for the resolution of such conflicts if a polycentric political system is to solve its problems. Otherwise, competition and conflict are apt to become acute.

No community, on its own initiative, has much incentive to assume the full costs of controlling adverse consequences that are shared by a wider public. The competitive disadvantage of enforcing pollution abatement regulations, for example, against individuals and firms within a single community, when competitors in neighboring communities are not required to bear such costs, leads each community to excuse its failure to act by the failure of other similarly situated communities to act. In a polycentric system this is especially serious where many of the public "goods" involve the costly abatement of public nuisances.

Concerted action by the various units of government in a metropolitan area is easier to organize when costs and benefits are fairly uniformly distributed throughout the area. By way of example, this has been done under contractual agreements for mutual aid to assure the mobilization of greater fire-fighting capability in case of serious conflagrations. The random and unpredictable nature of such fires causes them to be treated as a uniform risk that might occur to any community in the larger metropolitan area.

Similar considerations apply to efforts to control mosquito infestations or air pollution. Leagues of cities, chambers of commerce, and other civic associations have frequently become the agencies for negotiating legislative proposals for the creation of mosquito abatement districts, air pollution control districts, and the like.

More difficult problems for the polycentric political system arise when the benefits and the costs are not uniformly distributed. Communities may differ in their perception of the benefits they receive from the provision of a common public good. In turn, a community may be unwilling to "pay its fair share" for providing that good simply because its demands for provision are less than those in neighboring communities. These situations call for effective governmental mechanisms that can internalize the problem. If necessary, sanctions must be available for the enforcement of decisions.

The conflicting claims of municipal water supply systems pumping water from the same underground basins in southern California, for example, have uniformly been resolved by recourse to legal action in the state courts. The courts have thereby become the primary authorities for resolving conflicts among water supply agencies in southern California; and their decisions have come to provide many of the basic policies of water administration in the southern California metropolitan region. The state's judiciary has played a comparable role in conflicts among other local government agencies in such diverse fields as public health, incorporation and annexation proceedings, law enforcement, and urban planning.

The heavy reliance upon courts for the resolution of conflicts among local units of government unquestionably reflects an effort to minimize the risks of external control by a superior decision-maker. Court decisions are taken on a case-by-case basis. The adversaries usually define the issues and consequently limit the areas of judicial discretion. This method also minimizes the degree of control exercised following a judgment. California courts, in particular, have accepted the basic doctrines of home rule and are thus favorably disposed to the interests of local units of government in dealing with problems of municipal affairs.

The example of municipal water administration may be pursued further, to illustrate other decision-making arrangements and their consequences (for additional detail, see V. Ostrom 1953, especially chs. 3, 6, and 7).

While litigation may be an appropriate means for resolving conflicts over a given water supply, local water administrators in southern California have long recognized that no lawsuit ever produced any additional water. Organization for the importation of new water supplies is now seen as the only means for solving the long-term problem.

Los Angeles built the first major aqueduct to import water into the area on its own initiative. This water supply was used to force adjoining areas to annex or consolidate to the City of Los Angeles if they wished to gain access to the new supply. The condition for the provision of water required adjoining areas to sacrifice their identities as separate political communities. To get that one public good they were forced to give up other public goods. This provoked sufficient opposition to block any new developments that were not based upon consent and cooperation. The mechanisms for the resolution of subsequent conflicts were required to take on new forms.

The importation of Colorado River water was later undertaken by a coalition of communities in southern California formed through the agency of the southern section of the League of California Cities. The league afforded a neutral ground for negotiating the common interests of Los Angeles and the other cities in the metropolitan area that shared common water problems. After satisfactory arrangements had been negotiated, including provision for the formation of a new metropolitan water district and endorsement of the Boulder Canyon project, a Boulder Dam Association was formed to realize these objectives. In due course a new agency, the Metropolitan Water District of Southern California, was formed; and the Colorado River aqueduct was constructed and put into operation by this new district.

More recently, the Southern California Water Coordinating Conference, meeting under the auspices of the Los Angeles Chamber of Commerce, has been the agency for negotiating regional interests in the development of the California Water Program. The Metropolitan Water District was not able to represent areas in southern California that did not belong to that district; and the rise of a variety of special municipal water districts precluded the League of California Cities, which represents cities only, from again serving as the agency for the negotiation of metropolitan interests in municipal water supply.

These illustrations suggest that a variety of informal arrangements may be available for negotiating basic policies among local government agencies in a metropolitan area. Such arrangements are vital in negotiating common interests among them. The larger public is taken into account in an informally constituted political community. These arrangements work effectively only so long as substantial unanimity can be reached, for formal implementation of such decisions must be ratified by each of the appropriate official agencies, which include the state government when changes in state law or administrative policies are involved.

Higher levels of government may also be invoked in seeking the resolution of conflict among local governments in metropolitan areas. Again recourse is sought to a more inclusive political community. Under these circumstances, conflict tends to centralize decision making and control. The danger is that the more inclusive political community will not give appropriate recognition to the particular public interests at issue, and will tend to inject a variety of other interests into settlements of local controversies.

Appeal to central authorities runs the risk of placing greater control over local metropolitan affairs with agencies such as the state legislature, while at the same time reducing the capability of local governments for dealing with their problems in the local context. Sensitivity over the maintenance of local control may produce great pressure for the subordination of differences while

conflicting parties seek a common position approximating unanimity. A substantial investment in informal negotiating and decision-making arrangements can be justified from the perspective
of the local authorities if such arrangements can prevent the loss
of local autonomy to higher levels of government.

Ironically but logically, both this effort to avoid recourse to
conflict, and the consequent centralization of decision making,
tend to reduce the local autonomy or degree of independence exercised by the local governing boards. Pressure for agreement on a
common approach to some metropolitan problem limits the
choices available to any particular local government. However, the
range of choice here may still be greater than what would result
from a settlement reached by a central authority. Negotiation
among independent agencies allows the use of a veto against any
unacceptable position. Agreement must be negotiated within the
limits of the various veto positions if the alternative of recourse to
an external authority at a higher level of political jurisdiction is to
be avoided.

To minimize the costs of conflict to their power positions, administrators of local government agencies in metropolitan areas
have tended to develop an extensive system of communication
about each other's experience and to negotiate standards of performance applicable to various types of public services. Professional
administrative standards may thus operate to constrain the variety
of experience in local government agencies. Information about areas
of difference and of potential conflict tends to be repressed under
these conditions. The negotiations about common problems
through informal agencies are apt to be conducted in secrecy, and
careful control may be developed over sensitive information.

These pressures to avoid the costs of conflict and seek agreement about metropolitan problems reflect the importance to local
governments of resolving general public problems by negotiation
at the local level. To the extent that these pressures are effective,
the patterns of local government in a metropolitan area can only
be understood by attention to the variety of formal and informal
arrangements that may exist for settling areawide problems.

Contrary to frequent assertions about the lack of a "metropolitan framework" for dealing with metropolitan problems, most metropolitan areas have a very rich and intricate "framework" for negotiating, adjudicating, and deciding questions that affect their diverse public interests. Much more careful attention needs to be given to the study of this framework.

SEVEN

PUBLIC GOODS AND PUBLIC CHOICES: THE EMERGENCE OF PUBLIC ECONOMIES AND INDUSTRY STRUCTURES

Vincent Ostrom and Elinor Ostrom

Until recently, the private sector and the public sector have been viewed as two mutually exclusive parts of the economy. The private sector is generally viewed as organized through market transactions. The public sector is generally viewed as being organized only through governmental institutions where services are delivered through a system of public administration. Coordination in the private sector is attained by the market system that governs economic relationships through competitive buying and selling. Coordination in the public sector presumably is attained, by contrast, through a bureaucratic system in which superiors control subordinates in an integrated command structure that holds each public employee accountable to a chief executive as an elective public official (Kaufmann, Majone, and Ostrom 1986, 129–38).

During the last two or three decades, traditional presumptions about public-sector organization have been subject to serious challenge. Economists studying public-sector investment and expenditure decisions have observed that institutions designed to overcome problems of market failure often manifest serious deficiencies of their own. Market failures are not necessarily corrected by recourse to public-sector solutions. Public bureaucracies are themselves subject to serious problems of institutional weakness and failure.

Highly federalized systems of government with many different governmental units allow for the emergence of public economies where diverse organizations, private as well as public, perform complementary roles in the production and use or consumption of public goods and services.[1] A public economy need not be an exclusive government monopoly. It can be a mixed economy with substantial private participation in the delivery of public services. Such a possibility offers important prospects for overcoming some public-sector inefficiencies and providing citizen-taxpayers with better services for their tax dollars.

Public economies, however, are quite different from market economies. A private entrepreneur who decides to engage in the delivery of a public service by relying upon traditional market mechanisms is destined to failure. He must instead understand the logic of a public economy and learn to pursue his opportunities within those constraints. The *private* delivery of *public* services is a different ballgame from the *private* delivery of *private* goods and services.

In clarifying the logic of a public economy in a highly federalized system of government, we shall first consider the nature of public goods as distinguished from private goods. We shall then explore the organizational possibilities for the public sector, including the development of marketlike arrangements. Such arrangements suggest an industry approach to public services, an approach with implications for public administration quite different from management and control through an overarching public bureaucracy.

THE NATURE OF PUBLIC GOODS

People have long been aware that the nature of goods has a bearing upon human welfare. Aristotle, for example, observed that

"that which is common to the greatest number has the least care bestowed upon it" (*Politics* Bk. II, ch. 3, 1261, tr. Benjamin Jowett). Within recent decades an extensive literature has developed on the characteristics that distinguish public or collective goods from private or individual goods.[2] In this discussion, we shall consider exclusion, on the one hand, and jointness of use or consumption, on the other, as two essential characteristics in distinguishing between private and public goods. We shall also examine basic differences in measurement and degree of choice that have a significant bearing upon the organization of public services. Implications will then be drawn about some inherent problems of organizing economic relationships that involve public goods in contrast to market economies with private goods.

Exclusion. Exclusion has long been identified as a necessary characteristic for goods and services to be supplied under market conditions. Exclusion occurs when potential users can be denied goods or services unless they meet the terms and conditions of the vendor. If both agree, goods or services are supplied at a price. A quid pro quo exchange occurs: the buyer acquires the good and the seller acquires the value specified.

Where exclusion is infeasible, anyone can derive benefits from the good so long as nature or the efforts of others supply it. The air we breathe can be viewed as a good supplied by nature, so exclusion is difficult to attain. A view of a building—whether seen as a "good" or a "bad"—is supplied by the efforts of others and is not subject to exclusion in normal circumstances. Air, noise, and water pollution are "bads" that an individual cannot exclude or avoid except at a cost; conversely, an individual cannot be excluded from enjoying the benefits when pollution levels are reduced.

Jointness of use or consumption. Another attribute of public goods or services pertains to jointness of use or consumption. No jointness of consumption exists when consumption by one person precludes its use or consumption by another person. In that case consumption is completely subtractible. A slice of bread consumed by one person is not available for consumption by another;

it is subtracted from the total that was originally available. A good having *no* jointness of consumption and with which exclusion *is* feasible is defined as a purely private good. Jointness of consumption, on the other hand, implies that the use or enjoyment of a good by one person does not foreclose its use or enjoyment by others; despite its use by one person, it remains available for use by others in undiminished quantity and quality. A weather forecast is an example of a joint consumption good.

Few, if any, joint consumption goods are perfectly nonsubtractible. The use and enjoyment of gravity as a force that firmly keeps our feet on the ground may illustrate the case of perfect nonsubtractibility, but most joint consumption goods are instead subject to partial subtractibility. At certain thresholds of supply, one person's use of a good subtracts in part from its use and enjoyment by others. Congestion begins to occur. Each further increase in use impairs the use of the good for each other person in the community of users. Highways, for example, become subject to congestion when the addition of more users causes delays and inconveniences for others. Fire protection, another joint consumption good, may deteriorate when a fire service experiences a higher rate of demand than it was designed to meet. Such goods are then subject to degradation or erosion in their quality unless supply is modified to meet the new demand.

Both exclusion and jointness of consumption are characteristics that vary in degree rather than being all-or-none characteristics. The two extreme cases of jointness of consumption—complete subtractibility and complete nonsubtractibility—give logical clarity in distinguishing purely private from purely public goods. Whenever use by one user subtracts *in part* from the use and enjoyment of a good by other users we have partial subtractibility. In the same way we can think of exclusion as applying in degrees. A walled city can attain a high degree of exclusion by controlling admission to those who wish to reside, enter, and do business within the city. Even in the unwalled city, jurisdictional boundaries may be a way to distinguish between residents and nonresidents where some public goods and services exist primarily for the joint benefit of persons living within those boundaries. A weak form of partial exclusion may exist in such circumstances.

Exclusion and jointness of consumption are independent attributes. Both characteristics can be arrayed in relation to one another. The jointness characteristic can be arrayed into two classes: *alternative uses* that are highly subtractible and *joint uses* that are nonsubtractible. Exclusion can also be arrayed into two classes, in which exclusion is either *feasible* or *infeasible*. Exclusion is technically infeasible where no practical technique exists for either packaging a good or controlling access by a potential user. Exclusion may also be economically infeasible where the costs of exclusion are too high. If these defining characteristics are then arrayed in a simple matrix, four logical types of goods are revealed as indicated in Figure 1.

Market arrangements can be used to deliver either private goods or toll goods, that is, where exclusion is feasible. In the case of toll goods, a price is charged for access or use but the good is enjoyed in common. Special problems arise, as in a theater, where the conduct of one user may detract from the enjoyment of other users. The value of the good depends both upon the quality of the good produced *and* upon the way it is used by others.

In the case of a common-pool resource, exclusion may be infeasible in the sense that many users cannot be denied access. But use by any one user precludes use of some fixed quantity of a good by other users. Each pumper in a groundwater basin, for example, makes a use of water that is alternative to its use by each other pumper. Each fish or ton of fish taken by any one fisherman prevents any other fisherman from taking those same fish. Yet no basis exists for excluding fishermen from access to fish in the ocean. Once appropriated from a natural supply, water can be dealt with as a toll good to be supplied to those who have access to a distribution system; similarly, once taken from the ocean, fish can be dealt with as a private good. Water management problems, typifying common-pool resources, are likely to be subject to market failure, while water distribution problems typifying toll goods are likely to manifest market weaknesses associated with monopoly supply.

FIGURE 1 Types of Goods

	Jointness of Use or Consumption	
Exclusion	Alternative Use	Joint Use
Feasible (Low Cost)	*Private Goods:* Bread, shoes, automobiles, haircuts, books	*Toll Goods:* theaters, nightclubs, telephone service, toll roads, cable TV, electric power, libraries
Infeasible (Costly)	*Common-Pool Resources:* water pumped from a groundwater basin, fish taken from an ocean, crude oil extracted from an oil pool	*Public Goods:* peace and security of a community, national defense, mosquito abatement, air pollution control, fire protection, streets, weather forecasts, public TV

SOURCE: Author.

The range of services rendered by governmental agencies may cover goods and services of every type. The food supplied to school children under surplus commodity programs is an example of government's supplying purely private goods. Most governmental services, however, are of the public good, toll good, or common-pool resource type. These variations may have significant implications for—to take one example—the development of user charges as substitutes for taxes. In this discussion we shall focus more upon the type characterized as public goods because it poses the more difficult problems in the operation of a public economy.

Before pursuing some of the implications that follow from joint consumption in the absence of exclusion, we shall consider two other characteristics of public goods and services, characteristics relating to measurement and degree of choice. Both have important implications for the organization and delivery of public services.

Measurement. Since public goods are difficult to package or unitize they are also difficult to measure. Quantitative measures cannot be calculated like bushels of wheat or tons of steel. Qualitative measures such as the amount of dissolved oxygen in water, victimization rates, speed of response, and traffic delay can be used to measure important characteristics of goods subject to joint consumption, but such measures cannot be aggregated in the same way that gross production can be calculated for a steel factory or for the steel industry as a whole.

The task of measuring performance in the production of public goods will not yield to simple calculations. Performance measurement depends instead upon estimates in which indicators or proxy measures are used as estimates of performance. By means of multiple indicators, weak measures of performance can be developed even though direct measures of output are not feasible. Private goods are easier to measure, account for, and relate to cost-accounting procedures and management controls. Apart from the measurement problem, goods also vary with degrees of choice.

Degree of choice. Where a good is characterized by jointness of consumption and nonexclusion, a user is generally unable to exercise an option and has little choice whether or not to use or consume. The quality of a good or service is available under existing terms and conditions, and one's preference will not materially affect the quality of such a good. Furthermore, individuals may be forced to consume public goods that have a negative value for them. Streets, for example, may become congested thoroughfares restricting the convenience of local residents and shoppers, who are required to cope with the traffic whether they like it or not.

Yet the structure of institutional arrangements may have some effect on the degree of choice that individuals have. Councilmen representing local wards are likely, for example, to be more sensitive to protests by local residents about how streets are used in those wards than councilmen elected at large. Similarly, the use of voucher systems to procure services from alternative vendors of educational services may allow for a much greater degree of choice on the part of individual users. Educational services, however, have less the characteristics of a public good and more the characteristics of a toll good. Other forms of local option might exist in organizing public services.

Table 2 summarizes several of the key characteristics associated with public and private goods.

Some implications for organization. Public goods—defined as goods subject to joint consumption where exclusion is difficult to attain—present serious problems in human organization. If a public good is supplied by nature or the efforts of other individuals, each individual will be free to take advantage of the good since one cannot be excluded from its use or enjoyment. A cost-minimizing individual has an incentive to take advantage of whatever is freely available without paying a price or contributing a proportionate share of the effort to supply a public good. So long as rules of voluntary choice apply, some individuals will have an incentive to *hold out* or act as *free riders*, taking advantage of whatever is freely available. If some are successful in pursuing a holdout strategy, others will have an incentive to follow suit. The likely short-run consequence is that voluntary efforts will *fail* to supply a satisfactory level of public goods. Individuals furthering their own interest will neglect to take sufficient account of the interests of others, and the joint good will inexorably deteriorate.

Market institutions, on the other hand, will fail to supply satisfactory levels of public goods and services. Exclusion is infeasible. Therefore, to supply many public goods and services, it is necessary to have recourse to some form of governmental organization in which sanctions can be used to foreclose the holdout

TABLE 2   Public and Private Goods

Public Goods	Private Goods
Relatively difficult to measure quantity and quality	Relatively easy to measure quantity and quality
Consumed jointly and simultaneously by many people	Can be consumed by only a single person
Difficult to exclude someone who doesn't pay	Easy to exclude someone who doesn't pay
Generally no individual choice to consume or not	Generally individual choice to consume or not
Generally little or no individual choice of kind and quality of goods	Generally individual choice of kind and quality of goods
Payment for goods not closely related to demand or consumption	Payment for goods closely related to demand and consumption
Allocation decisions made primarily by political process	Allocation decisions made primarily by market mechanism

SOURCE: Authors and E. S. Savas. The tables in this chapter were worked out jointly with Savas, editor of the volume in which the essay was originally published.

problem and to compel each individual to pay his or her share of the burden. In small groups, individuals may be successful in keeping account of each other's efforts and applying social coercion so that each person assumes a share of the burden to procure jointly used goods. But large groups are less successful in coping with the provision of public goods shared by a whole community of people. Each individual is more anonymous. Each person's share of the total good may seem insignificantly small. Each can function as a holdout with greater impunity. The possibility of recourse to coercion by levying taxes and preventing holdouts will be more important. This is the reasoning behind Aristotle's contention that the good or property shared in common by "the greatest number has the least care bestowed upon it."

Patterns of organization that can mobilize coercive sanctions are necessary for the operation of a public economy. This is why people seek recourse to governmental institutions. The provision of law and order is simply one of many public goods that are important to the welfare of human societies. Market institutions will fail to supply such goods and services because markets require exclusion, exchange, and voluntary transactions.

But recourse to coercive sanctions and governmental organization does not provide both the necessary and the sufficient conditions for the delivery of public goods and services under relatively optimal conditions. Instruments of coercion can be used to deprive others and make them worse off rather than better off. Governmental institutions permit those who mobilize majority support to impose deprivations upon those in the minority. Governmental institutions can, then, become instruments of tyranny when some individuals dominate the allocation of goods in a society to the detriment of others.

Furthermore, since it is difficult for governmental officials to measure the output of public goods and services, it is also difficult for them to monitor the performance of public employees. Management of public enterprises will be subject to even less effective control than the management of private enterprises, where outputs can be measured in quantifiable units.

Where citizens have little choice about the quality of public services supplied to them, they will also have little incentive to do anything about it. The costs of attempting to do anything are likely to exceed any tangible benefit that they themselves will receive as individuals. As a result, individuals face situations in which anticipated costs exceed anticipated benefits. The rational rule of action in such cases is to forgo the "opportunity" to accrue net losses.

THE ORGANIZATION OF A PUBLIC ECONOMY

The characteristics of nonexclusion, joint consumption, lack of unitization and direct measurability, and a small degree of individual choice pose substantial problems for the organization of a public economy. Recognizing that the world is composed of many different goods and services that have these characteristics, and that such goods come in many different forms, we are confronted with the task of thinking through what patterns of organization might be adequate to accommodate them. Just as we can expect market weakness and failure to occur as a consequence of certain characteristics inherent in a good or service, so, for the same reasons, we can expect problems of institutional weakness and failure in governmental operations.

Furthermore, no solution will work by itself. Markets have important self-regulating or self-governing characteristics; but all market systems depend on nonmarket decision-making arrangements to establish and maintain property rights, to authorize and enforce contracts, and to provide other joint facilities. Such facilities typically include a common medium of exchange, common weights and measures, public roads, and so on, that are used by all market participants.

In considering the organization of a public economy, we shall reason through a number of the problems involved. First, we shall consider some basic elements in a public economy, including some basic assumptions and terms, and characterize the function of collective consumption units and production units. Second, we shall examine certain aspects of public goods that pose special problems in the relationship of collective consumption units to production units in any particular public service industry. Third, we shall examine some opportunities for enhancing efficiency and creating self-regulating tendencies in public economies.

Some basic assumptions and terms. It is useful to consider individuals as the basic unit of analysis, and to assume that goods are scarce and that individuals attach values to goods and services. We can stipulate a decision-making framework that structures opportunities and constraints for individuals to act in relation to one another. Then we can analyze the consequences when people choose strategies to enhance their well-being.

A public good, as defined above, is a good or service subject to joint use or consumption where exclusion is difficult or costly to attain. The essential difficulty in organizing public economies, then, is on the consumption side of economic relationships. Governments, like households, can be viewed first as *collective consumption units*. Once the collective consumption aspects of governmental organization have been identified, we can then turn to the production side. Governmental agencies and private enterprises can also be viewed as potential production units concerned with the supply and delivery of public goods and services. We shall distinguish between these two aspects by referring to "collective consumption units" and "production units." A single unit of government may include both types of organizations within its internal structure. Or a governmental unit operating as a collective consumption unit may contract with another governmental agency or a private enterprise to produce public services for its constituents.

Collective consumption units. In the organization of collective consumption units the holdout problem must be avoided. Arrangements must be made for levying assessments, taxes, or user charges on beneficiaries. Strictly voluntary efforts to supply public goods and services will fail to yield satisfactory results. Authority to levy taxes or assessments or to coerce user charges is necessary to avert holdouts and to supply funds for jointly used goods or services.

Some forms of private organization have the authority to levy compulsory assessments upon members. Home-owners' improvement associations and condominiums may be organized under terms of deed restrictions so that all individuals buying a house in a subdivision or a unit in an apartment complex are required to become and remain members for as long as they continue to own the house or apartment. Bylaws of home-owners' improvement associations or condominiums provide for the election of officers to act on behalf of members and authorize the levy of assessments as the equivalent of a tax for the provision of joint services and facilities. Each property owner voluntarily agrees to pay assessments and be bound by the terms of the bylaws as a part of the purchase contract. With unanimity about the appropriateness of the bylaws and their taxing authority assured, no single resident can function as a holdout and derive benefits from joint endeavors without paying a proportionate share of the costs. When effectively organized, home-owners' improvement associations and condominiums can undertake the provision of police protection services, recreation services, public works, and other efforts for the joint benefit of members. In this respect, they can be viewed as quasi-governmental units.

Where property rights have already been vested and people want to procure services for their joint benefit, the problem of dealing with potential holdouts usually requires some form of governmental organization, established through majority vote as a substitute for the unanimous consent of all property owners or residents. Various forms of municipal corporations and public service districts can be organized under such arrangements. An alternative option sometimes available is to create a special assessment or improvement district within an established unit of government to finance a special service for a particular neighborhood. Each of these public instrumentalities has authority, under the terms of its charter, to exercise governmental prerogatives to tax and to use criminal sanctions to enforce its rules and regulations.

Whereas the income received for providing a private good conveys information about the demand for that good, payment of taxes under threat of coercion indicates only that taxpayers prefer paying taxes to going to jail. Little or no information is revealed about user preferences for goods procured with tax-supported expenditures. As a consequence, alternative mechanisms to prices are needed for articulating and aggregating demands into collective choices that reflect individuals' preferences for a particular quantity and/or quality of public goods or services.

An appropriately constituted collective consumption unit would include within its jurisdictional boundary the relevant beneficiaries who share a common interest in the joint good or service and would exclude those who do not benefit. The unit would be empowered to make operational decisions without requiring unanimity: this is necessary to foreclose holdouts. It would hold a limited monopoly position on the consumption side. It would have authority to exercise coercive sanctions, but it need not meet the criterion sometimes used to define a government, namely, as an agency exercising a monopoly over the legitimate use of force for a society as a whole.

The choice of particular voting rules, expenditures, and levels of service needs to be viewed from a constitutional perspective. What are the likely consequences of such rules if a particular organizational structure is chosen? The set of rules most likely to produce decisions that take account of citizen-consumer interests is the one to be preferred. Citizens are presumed to be the best judges of their own interests. Such rules provide mechanisms for articulating and aggregating demand in the absence of market prices, and for translating demand into decisions about the level of service to be procured.

If action can be taken under a set of decision rules by which the benefits for each individual can be expected to exceed costs, and costs can be fairly proportioned among beneficiaries, each individual will have an incentive to agree to such a form of collective organization, forego holdout strategies, and procure the joint consumption good. Substantial unanimity will exist among the members of such a community to undertake collective action to procure a public good or service.

Production units. A production unit, by contrast, would be one that can aggregate technical factors of production to yield goods and services meeting the requirements of a collective consumption unit. The organization of an appropriate production unit requires a manager who can assume entrepreneurial responsibility for aggregating factors of production and for organizing and monitoring performance of a production team that will supply the appropriate level of a good or service.

A collective consumption unit may supply a public good or service through its own production unit. In that case, the collective consumption unit and the production unit would serve the same population. Yet the constitution of the two units may be essentially separable. The chief executive or city council representing the collective consumption unit, for example, may bargain with managers of production units to secure an appropriate supply and delivery of public goods and services. The headlines in many local newspapers are filled with accounts of such negotiations. They frequently stress the conflict of interest between production units and those who represent the interests of citizens as consumers. Nevertheless, this is a very common pattern of organization, typified by a municipality with its own police, fire, or street maintenance department.

As an alternative to organizing its own production unit, a collective consumption unit might decide to contract with a private vendor to supply a public good or service. In that case, public officials would translate decisions about the quantity or quality of public goods or services into specifications used to secure bids from potential vendors, state the terms and conditions for contractual arrangements, and establish standards for assessing performance. The collective consumption unit would also need to employ its own manager who would function as a purchasing agent, receive service complaints from users, and monitor vendors' performance in delivering services. The collective consumption unit would operate as a "provider" or "arranger" of the service and the private vendor as the "producer" or "supplier."

Organizing the consumption functions in a public economy can, as we have maintained, be distinguished from organizing the production functions. We refer to the one as *provision*; the other as *production*. Some general characteristics of collective consumption units and production units are summarized in Table 3. A variety of municipal services in the United States, including street sweeping, snow removal, solid waste collection and disposal, fire and police protection, engineering services, planning services, and construction of public works, among many others, are in many cases supplied by private vendors.

A third option is to establish standards of service that apply to all residents of a community and leave to each household the decision concerning what private vendor should supply service to that household. Multiple vendors may be franchised or anyone

TABLE 3   Collective Consumption Units and Producer Units

Collective Consumption Unit	Producer Unit
Generally, a government that aggregates and articulates the demands of its constituents	May be a unit of government, a private, profit-making firm, a not-for-profit institution, or a voluntary association
Has coercive power to obtain . funds to pay for public services and to regulate consumption patterns	Aggregates factors of production and produces goods to the specification of a collective consumption unit
Pays producer units for delivering public goods	Receives payment from collective consumption unit for delivering public goods
Receives complaints and monitors performance of production unit	Supplies information to collective consumption unit about costs and production possibilities

SOURCE: Authors and E. S. Savas.

wishing to do business under the terms and conditions specified by the collective consumption unit for such a service may do so. Solid waste collection is a service often supplied under such conditions. Such services are highly individualized, with only a limited degree of joint use or consumption. The limited degree of jointness can be taken care of by applying common standards to all households and vendors.

A fourth option is to collect taxes, assuring that each contributes a proportionate share of the burden, and then make available a voucher to each household so that it can decide among alternative producers and service packages. If applied to educational services, for example, a voucher would be issued for each child or person eligible for them. The decision of the type of school and curriculum to be selected would be left to the family rather than to school authorities. Services amenable to voucher arrangements have characteristics associated with toll goods, consumption of which benefits others as well. The community-at-large benefits from an individual's education in ways that are separable from the benefit derived from it by that individual. Community contributions to each person's education are then justified. If those benefits were to be as great or greater when expenditure decisions are made by the family unit rather than by educational authorities, then a voucher system would be justified. Vouchers have been used for housing (rent supplement vouchers), health services (Medicaid can be considered a form of health voucher), and even for food (food stamps). The last, while usually considered a private good, are like education in that everyone benefits by having no individuals go hungry and become desperate over their own survival.

A fifth possibility is for a collective consumption unit to contract with a production unit that is organized by a different unit of government. Many municipalities acting as collective consumption units contract with other municipalities, or some other unit of government, to supply police, fire protection, water storage and transmission, education, libraries, and a wide range of other public services.

A sixth way of organizing production occurs when a collective consumption unit decides to rely upon its own production unit to supply some components of a service, but upon other consumption and production units to arrange for its other components. Thus its own production unit may draw upon other producers to supply it with factors of production. Or that same unit may serve as a purchasing agent to procure and monitor the delivery of supplemental services. It may even function as a joint producer supplying a mix of services rendered by the joint effort of multiple production teams. Indeed, any given collective consumption unit may rely upon the joint production efforts of several different producers in supplying and delivering a particular bundle of goods and services that are subject to joint consumption. It may also act in cooperation with other joint consumption units that are willing to contribute supplemental funds to procure a particular level of services.

Options for obtaining public services are summarized in Table 4.

TABLE 4   Options for Obtaining Public Services

A government that serves as a collective consumption unit may obtain the desired public goods by	Example
Operating its own production unit	A city with its own fire or police department
Contracting with a private firm	A city that contracts with a private firm for snow removal, street repair, or traffic light maintenance
Establishing standards of service and leaving it up to each consumer to select a private vendor and to purchase service	A city that licenses taxis to provide service, refuse collection firms to remove trash
Issuing vouchers to families and permitting them to purchase service from any authorized supplier	A jurisdiction that issues food stamps, rent vouchers, or education vouchers, or operates a medicaid program
Contracting with another government unit	A city that purchases tax assessment and collection services from a county government unit, sewage treatment from a special sanitary district, and special vocational education services from a school board in an adjacent city

continued on next page

TABLE 4 *continued*

Public goods obtained by	Example
Producing some services with its own unit, and purchasing other services from other jurisdictions and from private firms	A city with its own police patrol force, which purchases laboratory services from the county sheriff, joins with several adjacent communities to pay for a joint dispatching service, and pays a private ambulance firm to provide emergency medical transportation

SOURCE: Authors and E. S. Savas.

Public service industries. As soon as we begin to array some of the options for organizing collective consumption units and production units, a wide variety of possibilities becomes apparent. Such a system may have large numbers of autonomous units of government and multiple levels of government with substantial degrees of overlap. Many private enterprises and voluntary associations may function as integral parts of such a public economy. Separation of powers within each unit of government may exist to a degree where all decision-makers are constrained by enforceable legal or constitutional limits upon their authority. Each citizen participates in multiple consumption units organized around diverse communities of interest and is served by an array of different public and private producing units supplying any particular bundle of public goods or services.

In such circumstances, each citizen is served not by "the government" but by a variety of different *public service industries*. Each public service industry is composed of the collective consumption units serving as providers and of production units serving as suppliers of some types of closely related public goods or services that are jointly consumed by discrete communities of individuals.

We can then think of the public sector in a federal system with many units and agencies of government as being composed of many public service industries including the police industry, the education industry, the water industry, the fire protection industry, the welfare industry, the health services industry, the transportation industry, and so on. The governmental component in some industries, such as the police industry, will be proportionately larger than in others, such as the health services or the transportation industry. But most public service industries will have important private components.

Each industry, moreover, will be characterized by distinctive production technologies and types of services rendered. These facilitate coordination of operational arrangements within an industry and allow for substantial independence between industries. The water industry, for example, is based upon technologies that facilitate collaboration among many agencies operating at different levels of government and among both public and private interests. These technologies in the water industry are easily distinguishable from the ones in the police industry or the education industry. The water industry serving any particular area will normally include such large-scale water production agencies as the U.S. Corps of Engineers, which operates dams and large water storage facilities; intermediate producers like metropolitan water districts and county water authorities, which operate large aqueducts and intermediate storage facilities; and municipal water departments, water service districts, mutual water companies, or private water utility companies that operate terminal storage facilities and retail distribution systems. The quality and cost of water delivered at the tap and the facilities available for recreation, navigation, flood control, and related uses will depend upon the joint operation of many different governments, agencies, and firms functioning in a water industry.

A functional view of a federal system of government considers the way that such diverse collective consumption and production units work together. They do so in multiorganizational arrangements that constitute public economies in which coordination is achieved by cooperative arrangements among the competitive alternatives that are available. There need be no overarching bureaucratic structure to achieve coordination. The chaos that some presume to exist often reveals, on closer examination, a highly productive public economy that has many of the characteristics of a market economy, one in which many different units of government serve as collective consumption units acting on behalf of diverse communities of people.

Such systems of multiorganizational relationships function in an institutionally rich structure of rule-ordered relationships for which many of the operational policies are worked out in both formal contractual arrangements and informal contractual understandings. The standard organizational milieu for discussing problems of mutual interest, keeping informed about related developments, and anticipating potential conflicts occurs in voluntary associations that themselves may be formally organized. Even with limited staff they are able to organize information, inquire about developments of mutual interest, keep records, and monitor developments in other jurisdictions.

Policy considerations that occur in overlapping jurisdictions are of importance, and information about those developments, as well as suggestions about how those policies might appropriately be shaped, is worthy of mutual consideration. Where unresolved conflicts arise, adjudication in equity courts may be a way of avoiding a recalcitrant holdout in the search for an equitable solution. The whole structure is a richly nested configuration of rule-ordered relationships, partially exemplified by the array of contracts, memoranda, court decisions, and statutory and constitutional provisions to be found in a two-volume collection titled *Central Valley Project Documents* (U.S. Cong. 1956, 1957). This is but a portion of what might be viewed as the law of the California water industry.

In any such structure of relationships, public policies emerge rather than being "decided" or "implemented" as though the exercise of public authority were exclusively a matter of command and control. Arbitrary commands are contestable, and those who assume responsibility for rendering services and contributing to a public way of life in democratic communities must learn how to live with themselves and other people in the community with whom they work. Relationships go well when they are conducted in mutually respectful and productive ways. They go miserably when they are strongly coerced.

SOME PROBLEMS OF CONSUMPTION AND PRODUCTION IN PUBLIC SERVICE INDUSTRIES

The special characteristics of public goods generate a number of difficulties that affect relationships within public service industries. These difficulties especially create problems in the relationship of collective consumption units with production units. Marketing arrangements in the private sector usually involve financial arrangements as an incidental feature of each transaction. The public sector, by contrast, usually disassociates financial arrangements from service delivery. This disassociation further implies that service delivery may occur without satisfactory information about demand or user preference.

Where jointness of consumption is accompanied by partial subtractibility, special problems may also arise in regulating patterns of use among diverse users. One use or pattern of use may, in the absence of regulation, seriously impair the value of the good or service for other users. Many public services—like some private services—depend critically upon service users to function as essential coproducers. Each of these problems—(1) financing, (2) regulating patterns of use, and (3) coproduction—poses difficulties in the relationship between collective consumption units and production units, and needs to be resolved constructively if public service industries are to give satisfaction.

Finance. In market relationships, the decision to buy any particular good or service automatically entails a consideration of foregone opportunities. The price expressed in money terms is the equivalent of all other goods and services that could be purchased with the same amount of money. A decision to buy a particular good or service reflects a willingness to forego all other opportunities for which that money could have been used. An expression of demand in a market system always includes reference to what is foregone as well as what is purchased.

The articulation of preferences in the public sector often fails to take account of foregone opportunities. The service is available for the taking. Unless collective consumption units are properly constituted to give voice to user preferences, much essential information may be lost in the system. The mode of taxation may have little or no relationship to the service being supplied. Furthermore, individuals may function in many different communities of users. Residents of local neighborhoods may, for example, have different demands for police services involving different communities of interest when they commute from an area of residence to work in a different location.

Because most public goods and services are financed through a process of taxation involving no choice, optimal levels of expenditure are difficult to establish. The provision of public goods can be easily overfinanced or underfinanced. Public officials and professionals may have higher preferences for some public goods than the citizens they serve. Thus they may allocate more tax monies to these services than the citizens being served would allocate if they had an effective voice in the process. Underfinancing can occur where many of the beneficiaries of a public good are not included in the collective consumption units financing the good. Thus they do not help to finance the provision of that good even though they would be willing to help pay their fair share.

Financial arrangements are also the means by which redistribution is accomplished. Many of the proposals for large-scale consolidation of governmental units serving metropolitan areas are based on an assumption that increased equity will result by expanding the tax base. A broader tax base, it is thought, will insure that wealthy suburbanites pay for essential services needed by the poor. No evidence is available to indicate that this actually happens in large cities. Poor neighborhoods receiving "services" that are not tailored to their needs may not be better off when increased resources are allocated to their neighborhood. In large collective consumption units, residents of poor neighborhoods may have even less voice about levels and types of services desired than they do in smaller-sized collective consumption units. Increasing the size of the smallest collective consumption unit to which citizens belong may not help solve problems of redistribution.

The financing of any particular public good or service may require contributions from more than a single collective consumption unit, because beneficiaries from the production of that good may not be isolated in a single unit. Public education, for example, is of primary benefit to the family units whose children are being educated. However, substantial external benefits to others located within the same state and within the nation may accrue as a result of having a good educational system in each locality. The financing of education may best be achieved, then, through a combination of local, state, and national resources. However, the funding of a school system directly from several tax sources may make the school system less sensitive to the diverse interests of the different family units that receive educational services directly. The use of a voucher system for at least a major portion of the financing of public education would increase the relative voice of the family units that would choose the school or schools.

The working out of financial arrangements between collective consumption units and production units is one of the most difficult problems faced by entrepreneurs in a public economy. Without market prices and market transactions, the act of paying for a good generally occurs at a time and place far from the act of using the public good or facility; individual costs are widely separated from individual benefits. Yet a principle of "fiscal equivalence" (Olson 1969)—that those receiving the benefits from a service pay the costs for that service—must apply in the public economy just as it applies in a market economy. Costs must be proportioned to benefits if people are to have any sense of economic reality. Otherwise beneficiaries may assume that public goods are free goods, that money in the public treasury is "the government's money," and that no opportunities are foregone in spending that money. When this happens, the foundations of a democratic society are threatened. The alternative is to adhere as closely as possible to the principle of fiscal equivalence and to proportion taxes as closely as possible to benefits received. Voluntary work and self-help may be another way of bearing the costs of public services.

Where charges can appropriately be levied on individual beneficiaries, user charges or use taxes can substantially alleviate the problems associated with rationing the use of a joint good. Highway construction and maintenance services, highway police patrols, and other services for motorists could, for example, be charged against gasoline taxes rather than other forms of general taxation. User charges or use taxes lead beneficiaries to calculate the cost of a service as against the value of a marginal use. Criminal sanctions need not be the principal means to regulate the use of a public good or service that is freely available to all users, if user charges can more appropriately proportion use to supply.

Regulating patterns of use. The characteristics of partial subtractibility of consumption imply that increased use at any given threshold of supply may impair the value of a good or service for other users. Parks or streets decline in value to each individual user as more users take advantage of available facilities and congestion occurs. Where there are multiple uses, one pattern of use may drive out other patterns. The use of a waterway to discharge wastes, for example, may exclude its use for recreational purposes. As some uses drive out other uses a serious erosion in the qualities of public life can occur (Buchanan 1970).

Jointness of use under conditions of partial subtractibility may require rules for reducing the likelihood of potential conflict among the different uses being made. If rules are to be effective, mechanisms for their enforcement must be available. The delivery of public goods and services under these conditions depends upon the proportioning of supply to demand by way of a system of rules that takes account both of the conditions of supply and the patterns of use. Unless those rules take account of varying patterns of use and of supply conditions in discrete circumstances, they are likely to become serious impediments to joint well-being. Heavy use of city streets for through traffic may, for example, impair their use by local residents in patronizing local businesses and tending to local problems.

Such conditions may require an especially close coordination between production and consumption units. The delivery of service by a producer needs to occur where patterns of use are regulated so as to gain optimal advantage of the services and facilities made available. The construction and maintenance of rural farm-to-farm market roads is not compatible, for example, with their use to transport coal from mines to major transport terminals. Heavy coal hauls will destroy roads that are not constructed and maintained for those loads (Oakerson 1978). Vendors, in such circumstances, are not producing for anonymous buyers; rather, they are supplying a tailor-made service subject to particular terms and conditions of use by discrete communities of users.

The regulation of patterns of use becomes one of the critical consumption functions performed by collective consumption units. This is why authority to enforce rules and regulations by recourse to criminal sanctions is usually assigned to governmental instrumentalities responsible for procuring a public good or service. Collective consumption units must assume primary responsibility for regulating and enforcing patterns of use. Yet those regulations are meaningful only in the light of discrete demand and supply conditions. Modifying supply conditions may alter the regulation and enforcement problems.

Even among governmental agencies, production of a service is frequently separated from regulating and enforcing patterns of use. Agencies responsible for policing the use of streets and highways, for example, are separate from those responsible for constructing and maintaining those streets and roads. Nevertheless, producers in a public economy need to be aware that services subject to joint use involve sensitive problems in proportioning supply to use and in regulating patterns of use. Otherwise, problems of congestion and conflicts among users can lead to the erosion of public services and degradation of community life.

Coproduction. Another problem in proportioning supply to patterns of use arises when users of services also function as essential coproducers. Without the intelligent and motivated efforts of service users, the service may deteriorate into an indifferent product of insignificant value. The quality of an educational product, for example, is critically affected by the productive efforts of students as users of educational services. Unless educational services are delivered under conditions that treat students as essential coproducers, the quality of the product is likely to be of little value. The health of a community depends as much on the informed efforts of individual citizens to maintain good health as it does upon professional personnel in health care institutions. The efforts of citizens to prevent fires and to provide early warning services when fires do break out are essential factors in the supply of fire protection services. The peace and security of a community is produced by the efforts of citizens as well as professional policemen. Collaboration between those who supply a service and those who use a service is essential if most public services are to yield the results desired.

Problems of coproduction arise in all service industries in both the private and public sectors. The private doctor is confronted with the same problem as the public school teacher. When professionals presume to know what is good for people rather than providing them with opportunities to express their own preferences we should not be surprised to find that increasing professionalization of public services is accompanied by a serious erosion in their quality. High expenditures for public services supplied exclusively by highly trained cadres of professional personnel may be a factor contributing to a service paradox: the better services are, as defined by professional criteria, the less satisfied citizens are with those services. An efficient public service delivery system will depend upon service personnel working under conditions where they have incentives to assist citizens in functioning as essential coproducers.

Intelligent and efficient strategies of consumption are as essential to the welfare of human communities as intelligent and efficient strategies of production. Coproduction requires that both go hand in hand to yield optimal results. The organization of a public economy that gives consideration to economies of consumption as well as of production and provides for the coordination of the two is most likely to attain the best results.

OPPORTUNITIES IN PUBLIC SERVICE INDUSTRIES

Where multiple consumption and production units have served communities of people in both procuring and supplying public goods and services, the conventional wisdom has alleged that duplication of function occurs as a consequence of overlapping jurisdictions. Duplication of functions is assumed to be wasteful and inefficient. Presumably, efficiency can be increased by eliminating "duplication of services" and "overlapping jurisdictions." Yet, we know that efficiency can be realized in a market economy only if multiple firms serve the same market. Overlapping service areas and duplicate facilities are necessary conditions for the maintenance of competition in a market economy.

Can we expect similar forces to operate in a public economy? If we can, relationships among the governmental units, public agencies, and private businesses functioning in a public economy can be coordinated through patterns of interorganizational arrangements. Such arrangements, in that case, would manifest market-like characteristics and display both efficiency-inducing and error-correcting behavior. Coordination in the public sector need not, in those circumstances, rely exclusively upon bureaucratic command structures controlled by chief executives. Instead, the structure of interorganizational arrangements may create important economic opportunities and evoke self-regulating tendencies. Some of these opportunities will now be examined.

Proportioning consumption and production possibilities. In a world where goods subject to joint consumption vary from household size to global proportions, the availability of an array of differently sized collective consumption and production units will provide opportunities to realize diverse economies-of-scale. Where heterogeneous preferences for public services exist, advantage can be gained by having relatively small collective consumption units. As long as a collective consumption unit can articulate preferences for its own constituency and has access to a reasonably equitable distribution of income, that unit can specify the mix of services preferred, procure an appropriate supply of those services, and pay for them. In such circumstances, a small collective consumption unit might contract with a large production unit and each might take advantage of diverse scale considerations in both the consumption and production of a public good or service.

It may also happen that the collective consumption unit is large but that efficient production is realized on a smaller scale. The appropriate consumption unit for users of interstate highways in the United States, for example, is probably a national one. This national unit functions as a "provisioner" by developing appropriate specifications and financial arrangements for procuring interstate highway services. However, variability in climatic and geographic conditions over a large continental area are such that the production and maintenance of services can be more efficiently supplied by smaller organizations. Thus, the U.S. Department of Transportation acts as a buyer of interstate highway services from state highway departments and private contractors that act as the principal production units.

The proportioning of diverse consumption and production possibilities in a complex public economy will not occur automatically but requires a conscious pursuit of relative advantages by those involved. An awareness that bigger isn't necessarily better must precede a search for the combinations that generate the highest level of user satisfaction for given expenditures of efforts. Substantial improvements can be made.

Competition, bargaining, and cooperative efforts. If each collective consumption unit has potential access to several production units and is prepared to consider alternative options in arranging for the supply of a public good or service, the relationships between consumption and production units will take on a quasi-market character. The "market" in this case is *not* between producers and *individual* consumers. We would expect such market structures to fail. The quasi market, instead, arises in the relationships among collective consumption units and production units.

If the potential producers include an array of private vendors and public agencies, an opportunity exists for bargaining between consumption and production units to procure public goods or services at least cost. Such an opportunity also creates incentives on the part of the bargaining parties to increase levels of information and to develop indicators of performance. The availability of competitive alternatives facilitates cooperation. Such alternatives are always available in a competitive milieu.

Bargaining may also occur in a noncompetitive situation in which multiple production units may be able to gain a joint benefit by coordinating their actions with one another. Various police agencies may, for example, have mutual aid or joint operating agreements to provide backup services to each other in an emergency. Peak-load capabilities may be maintained by drawing upon reserves in other departments rather than requiring all departments to meet their own separate peak-load demands from their own reserves.

Such joint efforts may be extended to organizing supplemental public or private enterprises to supply a variety of indirect services such as crime laboratories, police training academies, and joint dispatching services. Where high levels of interdependency have developed through cooperative arrangements, collective consumption and production units can be expected to develop routine organizational arrangements to reduce bargaining costs. These arrangements often take the form of voluntary associations, meeting regularly, with officials to set meeting agendas and arrange presentations. Many of these associations may be formally organized with bylaws and membership fees and employ a small permanent secretariat.

Conflict and conflict resolution. If multiple collective consumption and production units are creating significant externalities—some public good in which many units can share—for one another, then cooperative arrangements maintained under a rule of unanimity can always be threatened by the presence of a holdout. In other words, one collectivity may find it advantageous to hold out and enjoy the benefits it can derive from the joint actions of others without assuming its proportionate share of the costs. If some holdouts are successful in their strategy, others will follow suit. Cooperative arrangements will fail, and there will be an erosion in welfare for everyone concerned. The maintenance of a holdout strategy and the impending threat of tragedy may lead some to respond to holdouts with threats or counterthreats. These, unless constrained by the availability of institutions for adjudicating and resolving conflicts, can escalate into violence and warfare.

A highly fragmented political system *without* substantial over-lap among its many jurisdictions is especially vulnerable to this form of institutional failure. Americans refer to this as "balkaniza-tion." With overlapping units of government, conflicts among governments at any one level may be resolved by recourse to the decision-making arrangements that exist at a more inclusive unit of government. Such arrangements are inherent in federal sys-tems. The critical feature is the availability of legal, political, and constitutional remedies to the parties injured as a consequence of negative externalities that are generated by governmental action, such as adversely affecting the property rights of others.

Courts have played an especially important role in resolving conflicts among independent agencies and firms operating in a public economy. They are competent to decide an issue without dominating all channels of control and allocations of resources. In contrast, when a chief executive in an integrated command struc-ture resolves conflicts among his subordinate public agencies, the impact is rarely confined to discrete issues. It is likely to affect future budgetary allocations, career opportunities for public em-ployees, and the organizational status of operating agencies.

In California, where contracting for public services is subject to the greatest competitive pressure, county grand juries have assumed a continuing responsibility for monitoring the operation of intergov-ernmental contracts. Inappropriate use of tax funds by public agen-cies functioning as contract producers would transfer service costs to the public treasury of the producing agency rather than paying for them from the treasury of the benefiting community. Inappro-priate use of tax funds might also amount to subsidizing public producers, which would drive private enterprises out of the business of producing public services even though they might be more efficient at it. Grand juries inquiring into the discharge of public trust by state and local agencies should help maintain the integrity of market-like relationships and encourage competitive pressure.

Without appropriate mechanisms for processing conflicts and monitoring the operation of a public economy, contracting can be used as an instrument for the grossest forms of political corruption. Contracts with firms that are the chosen instruments of political bosses have long been used as a means of milking public treasuries, supplying the coffers of political machines, and creating private fortunes. No system of economic relationships will perform well without appropriate public policies and institutions to enforce these policies.

Conflict arises when someone believes he or she is being harmed by another's action. If the situation is remedied so that no one is harmed, a net improvement in welfare will occur. Thus conflict is as important an indicator of potential economic losses as the red ink on a balance sheet. Mechanisms for conflict resolution contribute to economic welfare when they formulate solutions that right wrongs and restructure arrangements so that either everyone is left better off or no one is harmed or left worse off. But to maintain a system that is open to conflict and conflict resolution, the participating parties in the system must have autonomous legal status with authority to sue and be sued and to take independent decisions in advancing a set of interests. If public economies are to gain the advantage of quasi-market competition and voluntary cooperation, they must be able to maintain arm's-length relationships and have available to them institutions that can adjudicate conflicts among parties with equal standing in law. Adjudication does not occur in the absence of equal legal standing; subordinates obey rather than cooperate.

ALTERNATIVES AND CHOICES

Other ways of organizing public-sector activities are not hard to think of. One possibility is a bureaucratic system of public administration in which all relationships would be coordinated through a command structure culminating in a single center of authority. The public and private sectors would be treated as mutually exclusive; no place would exist for private enterprise in the organization of such a system.

Another possibility is a system in which units of government are collective consumption units whose first order of business is to articulate and aggregate demands for those goods that are subject to joint consumption where exclusion is difficult to attain. Demands are effectively articulated when decisions reflecting user preferences about services are reached and funds are committed. Several options are available for organizing production, including that of contracting with private vendors to produce specified goods or services. Relationships are coordinated among collective consumption and production units by contractual agreements, cooperative arrangements, competitive rivalry, and mechanisms of conflict resolution. In a public economy, no single center of authority is responsible for coordinating all relationships. Market-like mechanisms can develop competitive pressures that tend to generate higher efficiency than can be gained by enterprises organized as exclusive monopolies and managed by elaborate hierarchies of officials.

This new mode of analysis, which applies economic reasoning to nonmarket decision making, should be used to reconsider the basic structure of a public economy in a federal system of government characterized by overlapping jurisdictions and fragmentation of authority. Changes that offer the prospect of advancing the net well-being of everyone concerned should be experimented with as being economically justified. In this mode of analysis the exercise of political power is economically justified only when benefits exceed costs; and is not justified as a means for the powerful to benefit themselves at the cost of the powerless. The critical factor here is to begin with the nature of the goods involved, in terms of exclusion, partial subtractibility, and measurability. To the extent that such characteristics exist, elements of public choice, in increasing degrees, can be introduced.

If the community of beneficiaries can be identified, then a principle of fiscal equivalence can be relied upon to design a unit of government as a collective consumption unit. In this way, it is the beneficiaries who bear the cost, exercise the dominant voice in determining the quantity and/or quality of service to be made available, and function as coproducers in achieving the desired results. Wherever user charges or use taxes can be established, they can be applied to give users a sense of reality about the costs inherent in alternative choices.

The particular forms of organization to use in establishing collective consumption units—consumer cooperatives, municipal corporations, public service districts, or other forms of governmental organization—are choices that can be taken by the relevant community of people so long as they bear the costs of the service. The community of beneficiaries can, so long as they bear the costs, also be assigned substantial constitutional authority to establish and modify the terms and conditions that apply to the future governance of any particular collective consumption unit.

The selection of appropriate arrangements for the supply and delivery of a public service is open to several potential options. The wider the range of these options, the greater the degree of competitive pressure that will exist in any particular public service industry. It is precisely this competitive pressure that offers prospects for the best performance, both in the sense of being responsive to user demands and in that of minimizing costs in doing so. In a well-developed public economy, many collective consumption units may find advisable a mixed strategy in which they rely, in part, upon their own production agencies but maintain extensive contractual arrangements with private enterprises and other public agencies.

Competitive pressures are the key factor in maintaining the viability of a democratic system of public administration. Substantial incentives will exist among established businesses and governmental agencies to protect their own interests by restricting the entry of competitive alternatives. If such efforts are successful, competitive rivalry loses its capacity to enhance efficiency and deteriorates into collusive efforts by some to gain dominance over others. This risk is carried to the greatest extreme in the case of a fully integrated monopoly solution. The traditional principles of public administration imply monopoly organization applied to the entire public sector. Private enterprises, as producers of public goods and services, can significantly improve the efficiency of the public sector so long as competitive pressures can be openly and publicly maintained. The emergence of public economies with complexly structured competitive public service industries is one of the important sources of institutional innovation to be achieved in the American federal system of government. Competition facilitates voluntary cooperation.

EIGHT

RES PUBLICA: THE EMERGENCE OF
PUBLIC OPINION, CIVIC KNOWLEDGE,
AND A CULTURE OF INQUIRY

The term *res publica* is the source of a puzzle. It is the Latin from which the term "republic" derives. *Res* means thing and *res publica* seemingly refers to the public thing. Following the tradition of James Madison in essay 10 of *The Federalist*, "republican" government can be conceived as representative government. But an anomaly remains about the association between republican government conceived as representative government and something that might be referred to as "the public thing." The two concepts do not fit in a congruent way. Puzzles about the meaning of terms sometimes reveal underlying problems pertaining to the conceptualization of meaning rather than simple problems of definition. Publicness also implies openness. Is there, then, an essential association between representativeness and openness in the constitution of order in the American federal system?

My response to these questions upon reflection is in the affirmative. I have come to allude to "the public thing" as "an open public realm," aware that "open" and "public" are redundant. The term "public" is also associated with the jurisdiction of "governments." This is the meaning sometimes implied by "the public sector": the governmental domain. The association of "public" with the jurisdiction of "governments" may lead to an incorrect association. When I use the term "open public realm," I am pointing to a realm that is outside the jurisdiction of governments as such. It is a nongovernmental realm that is an essential feature in understanding the American federal system. That nongovernmental realm is not a private realm. What emerge from the workings of the open public realm are many features pertaining to the operation of a democratic society: public opinion, civic knowledge, and a culture of inquiry. Representativeness acquires its meaning as it interrelates processes for expressing thoughts and feelings with processes of collective choice and collective action.

In this essay, I shall first consider some reflections about the meaning of the term "republic." Second, I shall attempt to indicate some of the features that are constitutive of an open public realm. Third, I shall reflect upon the properties that emerge from the workings of institutions in the open public realm and their importance to American federalism.

THE MEANING OF REPUBLIC (*RES PUBLICA*)

In the concluding section of the last chapter in volume 1 of *Democracy in America*, Tocqueville addresses himself to the nature of republican institutions in the United States and their durability. He contrasts American and European distinctions. "What is understood by a republican government in the United States," Tocqueville asserts,

> is the slow and quiet action of society upon itself. It is a regular state of things really founded upon the enlightened will of the people. It is a conciliatory government, under which resolutions are allowed to ripen, and in which they are deliberately discussed, and are executed only when mature. The republicans in the United States set a high value on morality, respect reli-

gious beliefs, and acknowledge the existence of rights. They profess to think that a people ought to be moral, religious and temperate in proportion as it is free. What is called the republic in the United States is the tranquil rule of the majority, which, after having had time to examine itself and give proof of its existence, is the common source of all the powers of the state. But the power of the majority itself is not unlimited. Above it in the moral world are humanity, justice and reason; and in the political world, vested rights. The majority recognizes these two barriers, and if it now and then oversteps them, it is because, it has passions and, like them, it is prone to do what is wrong, while it discerns what is right. [(1835) 1945, 1: 416]

To this, Tocqueville contrasts a European conception in which

a republic is not the rule of the majority as has hitherto been thought, but the rule of those who are strenuous partisans of the majority. It is not the people who predominate in this kind of government, but those who know what is good for the people, a happy distinction which allows men to act in the name of nations without consulting them and to claim their gratitude while their rights are being trampled under foot. A republican government, they hold, moreover, is the only one that has the right of doing whatever it chooses and despising what men have hitherto respected, from the highest moral laws to the vulgar rules of common sense. Until our time it has been supposed that despotism was odious, under whatever form it appeared. But it is a discovery of modern days that there are such things as legitimate tyranny and holy injustice, provided they are exercised in the name of the people. [Ibid., 416–17]

Elsewhere, Tocqueville characterizes the French Revolution as being the enemy of both royal and provincial institutions and as manifesting hostility both to despotic power and to checks upon the abuse of despotic power: "[I]ts tendency was both to republicanize and to centralize" (ibid., 96). It republicanized by acting in the name of the people and exercised a monopoly of the authority to govern by acting through centralized instrumentalities of political and administrative control. Such a system has the appeal of simplicity and generality. Complicated systems are repugnant to such an approach, which favors the conception of "a great nation composed of citizens all formed upon one pattern and all governed by a single power" (ibid., 2: 289).

> The very next notion to that of a single and central power which represents itself to the minds of men in the age of equality is the notion of a uniformity of legislation. As every man sees that he differs but little from those about him, he cannot understand why a rule that is applicable to one man should not be equally applicable to all others. Hence the slightest privileges are repugnant to his reason; the faintest dissimilarities in the political institutions of the same people offend him, and uniformity of legislation appears to him to be the first condition of good government. [Ibid.]

Profound puzzles arise from such efforts to republicanize and centralize at the same time. These puzzles are associated with Tocqueville's reference to a democratic despotism involving "an immense and tutelary power" that regards citizens "as more than kings and less than men" (ibid., 318, 319). Such a society, Tocqueville argues, will be characterized by

> an innumerable multitude of men, all equal and alike, incessantly endeavouring to procure the petty and paltry pleasures with which they glut their lives. Each of them, living apart, is a stranger to the fate of the rest; his children and his friends constitute to him the whole of mankind. As for the rest of his fellow citizens he is close to them, but he does not see them; he touches them, but does not feel them; he exists only in himself and for himself alone; and if his kindred still remain to him, he may be said at any rate to have lost his country. [Ibid., 318]

The corollary to the erosion of the bonds of community for structuring the place of government in such a society is described by Tocqueville in the following way:

> Above this race of men stands an immense and tutelary power, which takes upon itself alone to secure their gratification and to

watch over their fate. That power is absolute, minute, regular, provident, and mild. It would be like the authority of a parent if, like that authority, its object was to prepare men for manhood; but it seeks on the contrary to keep them in perpetual childhood; it is well content that the people should rejoice, provided that they think of nothing but rejoicing. For their happiness such a government willingly labors, but it chooses to be the sole agent and the only arbiter of that happiness; it provides for them security, foresees and supplies their necessity, facilitates their pleasures, manages their principal concerns, directs their industry, regulates the descent of property and subdivides their inheritance: what remains but to spare them all the care of thinking and all the trouble of living? [Ibid.]

Tocqueville's allusion to republican government as being the "slow and quiet action of the society on itself" requires us, then, to reconsider what it is that Madison had to say about republican government in essay 10 of *The Federalist*. In presenting his argument there, Madison is preoccupied with the problem of how democratic societies attempt to cope with conflict so that justice can be done, and majority factions are not allowed to prevail over individual rights or minority interests. The potential for majority tyranny was recognized as a fundamental tension in any system of popular (democratic) government. Under majority rule a majority could, under the cloak of law, unjustly oppress and tyrannize others.

In advancing his argument, Madison distinguishes between a pure democracy, where all "citizens assemble and administer the government in person," and a "republic," where government is organized through a "scheme of representation" (Hamilton, Jay, and Madison [1788] n.d., 59). A republican government is thus defined as government by representatives. The core concept in republican government would then be representative government.

For Madison, a scheme of representation ameliorates the tumultuous lack of decorum in a multitude and allows for a more select body to give consideration to relationships between particular interests and the common good. He argues further that "that same advantage which a republic has over a democracy, in controlling the effect of faction, is enjoyed by a large republic over a small republic" (ibid., 61). A more extended republic includes a greater diversity of interests than a more confined republic. A scheme of representation for the more extended republic will allow for a greater detachment on the part of representatives from the immediate interests that fire people's passions.

Alexander Hamilton advances a somewhat similar line of argument in essay 35 of *The Federalist* when he recognizes that people will seek out for their representatives those who make it a practice in life to take account of and represent the interests of others. Lawyers, for example, make it their business to represent and act for others. People who have this experience are required to develop intellectual skills in articulating the interests of others, to consider the implications that follow from those interests and how it may be possible to achieve a mutually agreeable resolution of interests. There are mediating and representing processes of governance in which intermediaries may function as more effective problem-solvers than the principal adversaries themselves.

An argument for an extended republic views the mediating role of a representative legislature to be sufficient to determine what is in the public good. This is the core of the argument advanced by Jeremy Bentham, who presumed that representatives who draw upon resources of goodwill in representing others are capable of knowing the greatest good of the greatest number. The exercise of such authority is the essential condition for good government. The people do not rule in such circumstances. Those who presume to know the greatest good of the greatest number rule in the name of the people. Democracy is not a reality but an illusion: an oligarchy acting in the name of the people. It is the greater diversity of interests and the mediating effect of representative government that enable those who argue on behalf of an extended republic to find a resolution to the problem of majority tyranny.

The key passage in the closing paragraph of Madison's essay, however, refers to both the "*extent*" and "*proper structure*" of the Union as affording a republican remedy to the republican disease of majority tyranny (my emphasis). Even within the confines of essay 10, Madison asserts that "it is vain to say that enlightened statesmen will be able to adjust these clashing interests, and render them sub-servient to the public good. Enlightened statesmen will not always be at the helm" (ibid., 57). Hamilton, in essay 6 of *The Federalist*, argues that men who occupy leading positions in human societies "whether the favorites of a king or of a people have in too many instances abused the confidence they possessed; and assuming the pretext of some public motive, have not scrupled to sacrifice the national tranquillity to personal advantage or personal gratification" (ibid., 28). Both Hamilton and Madison presume that "in every political institution, a power to advance the public happiness in-volves a discretion which can be misapplied and abused" (ibid., 260). The potentials for opportunism, corruption, and exploitation of others pervade governmental institutions.

The "extent" of a republic implies reference to size, and size pertains to both territorial domain and to population. In general discussions of size as a variable that needs to be taken into account in the design of political institutions, both Hamilton and Madi-son are aware that a curvilinear relationship is involved. They do not accept the simple proposition that the greater the extent of a republic the better. In discussing the organization of deliberative assemblies in essay 55 of *The Federalist*, Madison specifically re-jects reliance upon "arithmetical principles in political calcula-tions." In organizing a deliberative assembly that functions as a national legislature, he presumes that sixty or seventy members is better than six or seven. But it does not follow that six or seven hundred would be a better repository of public trust. If extended to six or seven thousand, "the whole reasoning," Madison argues, "ought to be reversed" (ibid., 361).

There is a problem in organizing all deliberative groups: a cabal of a very few may have perverse tendencies, while serious asymmetries arise in the deliberation of large assemblies. Human beings are hard-wired so that only one speaker can be heard and understood at a time. Beyond a very small threshold, deliberative bodies depend upon someone to preside and exercise control over an agenda and maintain ordered deliberations. All democratic as-semblies are, as I argue in Chapter 4, subject to strong oligarchical tendencies that increase with size.

Such patterns are not confined to direct democracies, where all citizens participate in the governing assembly, but apply also to representative assemblies. In representative bodies, Madison argues, two sets of calculations apply. The number of electors needs to be confined so that a representative is knowledgeable of the "local circumstances and lesser interests" of those who are represented. The other calculation pertains to the size of the deliberative assembly itself (Hamilton, Jay, and Madison [1788] n.d., 60). The simple, extended, and populous republic cannot give proper attention to both sets of calculations. A federal system of governance, by contrast, "forms a happy combination in this respect: the great and aggregate interests being referred to the national, the local and particular interests to the State legislature" (ibid.).

Where relationships among variables are of a curvilinear nature and interact in complex configurations, it is not possible to presume that the "*extent*" of a republic can be treated independently of "*proper structure.*" Furthermore, the very large extended republic cannot be organized as a simple republic and take account of the way that particular interests relate to diverse communities of interest. Instead, simple extended republics always confront the condition in which "the countenance of the government may become more democratic, but the soul that animates it will be more oligarchic. The machine will be enlarged but the fewer, and often the more secret, will be the springs by which its motions are directed" (ibid., 382).

We cannot expect a simple command-and-control relationship to work well in an extended republic where electors select representatives to function in a national assembly, and where the national assembly can determine the public good and prescribe rules of law that are to be uniformly enforced throughout a nation as though there were only individuals and a single overarching government. Human artisanship requires the proportioning of too many variables whose relationships with one another are likely to be curvilinear and interactive. Societies cannot rely upon simple command-and-control mechanisms if people are to take best advantage of the opportunities that are available to them. Further, the "encroaching spirit of power" and the "insufficiency of parchment barriers" mean that republican institutions are extraordinarily vulnerable to those who, "assuming the pretext of some public motive, [do] not scruple to sacrifice the national tranquillity to personal advantage or personal gratification" (ibid., 28).

Madison then has reference to the "policy of supplying by opposite and rival interests the defect of better motives" in constituting a federal system of government: "These inventions of prudence cannot be less requisite in the distribution of the supreme powers of the State" (ibid., 337–38). From this basic constitutional principle I conclude that "proper structure" is no less requisite than the "extent" of a republic. I further conclude that it is erroneous to believe that a greater diversity of interests associated with an extended republic, mediated only by representative institutions, is sufficient to resolve the problem of majority tyranny.

These conclusions are reinforced by Hamilton's emphasis upon the importance of a federal system of government in providing a people with a structure of opportunities for choice:

> The people, without exaggeration, may be said to be entirely the masters of their own fate. Power being almost always the rival of power, the general government will at all times stand ready to check the usurpations of the state governments, and these will have the same disposition towards the general government. The people by throwing themselves into either scale, will infallibly make it predominate. If their rights are invaded by either, they can make use of the other as the instrument of redress. How wise will it be in them by cherishing the union [i.e., a federal system of governance] to preserve to themselves an advantage that can never be too highly prized! [Ibid., 174]

The objection can be made that Hamilton's safeguards will yield stalemate and deadlock. In order to understand how people might become masters of their own fate, we need to go beyond institutions of representation, a separation of powers, checks and balances, and federal arrangements and concern ourselves with the constitution of the open public realm. Why is the autonomy of people to function in an open public realm an essential feature of American federalism? People cannot be masters of their own fate in the presence of either preemptive strategies pursued by their representatives or interminable stalemate and deadlock.

THE CONSTITUTION OF THE OPEN
PUBLIC REALM (*RES PUBLICA*)

The constitution of the open public realm should be distinguished from the instrumentalities of government, narrowly construed. How can we elucidate that constitution? Let us begin with those provisions of constitutions that place limits upon the authority of government while correlatively stating the rights reserved to persons or citizens. As the discussion of the theory of American federalism in Chapter 2 indicates, these are usually articulated as "bills of rights" expressed as the inalienable rights of persons or citizens. Their place in constituting the open public realm is the reason why these rights should be conceived as public rights accruing to persons and citizens rather than private rights.

Freedom of speech and press implies authority to communicate with others without interference from the instrumentalities of government that have recourse to the powers of the sword. Limits upon the taking of property and the authority of persons to enter into contractual arrangements with one another enable people to fashion a variety of associated relationships. Contractual provisions are then recognized as having the binding effect of law. This establishes an independent source of law growing from the working arrangements devised by people in ordering their relationships with one another on the basis of mutual agreement or willing consent. Voluntary agreement to contractual arrangements is equivalent to an implicit rule of unanimity among those involved. These working arrangements may become a part of the customs or traditions of the "common law."

The constitution and operational autonomy of the institutions of the civil society thus turn critically upon inalienable rights of persons and citizens, with correlative limits upon the authority of the instrumentalities of government as specified in a limited national constitution, state constitutions, and local charters. Many of the institutions of civil societies, including families, business firms, trade unions, and all voluntary associations, are organized through what amount to governable contracts. Such contracts provide for revision, resolving disputes, and penalties for breaching the rules of association that are enforceable either under the rules of civil procedure or by arbitration. Voluntary associations have an autonomous standing based upon the authority of individuals to contract with one another and to hold property as shares in the assets of that voluntary association. Religious institutions and the press have an autonomous standing based upon freedom of the press and the free exercise of religion. These institutions are also organized through rules of voluntary association.

The constitution of the French republics is based upon different conceptions. As I understand those conceptions, the National Assembly is vested with the sole and exclusive legislative authority. Legislative authority is then exercised in relation to a general code of law—the Code Napoléon. The basic axiomatics of the Code Napoléon, the Civil Code, are grounded in the Declaration of the Rights of Man. The civil law pertains to the exercise of nongovernmental authority; thus civil law is conceptualized as private law subject to adjudication in civil law courts. Contests over the exercise of governmental authority are subject to adjudication through bureaucratic channels by processes established by the Council of State, an administrative court. Administrative law in France subsumes all matters pertaining to governmental authority. No separately identifiable jurisprudence of constitutional law exists in France. The public realm is conceived as pertaining to governmental jurisdiction; the private realm is subject to adjudication under the provisions of civil law by civil law courts.

The theory of American federalism does not recognize a sole and exclusive legislative authority. People exercise fundamental legislative prerogatives in specifying the terms and conditions of government by constitutions formulated and revised through processes of constitutional decision making. Legislative bodies all exercise a limited authority to make and revise statutory law. Persons legislate in relation to one another through their authority to contract with one another. France, too, has a law of contracts, but there is always an effort to rationalize the law of contracts with the Civil Code in which civil law is conceptualized as private law exercised under sole and exclusive legislative authority of the National Assembly. Equivalent features of law fit into differently conceptualized configurations of relationships; code-law jurisprudence is never fully commensurate with common-law jurisprudence; and constitutional law is never fully commensurate with administrative law.

The critical magnitude of these differences, then, is the role of an open public realm that is public by virtue of its openness rather than its identification with instrumentalities of government as such. The autonomy of the open public realm is of basic importance in establishing self-governing capabilities that exist in the society itself. Because of this autonomy, individuals can function first as their own governors and then in establishing a variety of institutional arrangements that function as self-governing arrangements, without prior authorization, licensure, or tutelage by governmental authorities as such. Relationships among autonomous units and agencies of government, as in the organization of public economies, are largely organized by contractual and cooperative arrangements. The interrelationship among autonomous governmental agencies and units of government occurs in the open public realm.

The way in which the open public realm gets linked to institutions of government is of considerable importance in a democratic society. In the American federal system these linkages apply to the multiple units of government and to multiple decision structures within each unit of government. Representation occurs through diverse representatives who act in multiple agency relationships in their discharge of public trusts on behalf of communities of people. For people to represent or be represented implies that they are capable of thinking for themselves, communicating with others, and developing a shared community of understanding of what it means to act on behalf of others. The very act of sorting out legislative, executive, and judicial aspects in the rule-ruler-ruled relationship implies that law itself takes on a publicness when it is formulated in bodies that are independent of those charged with scrutinizing its application and enforcement. The validity of law depends upon the concurrence of legislative, executive, and judicial instrumentalities, not upon the command of a single supreme authority.

To presume that republican government is equivalent to representative government, and that the more extended a republic is the more it will afford "a republican remedy for the diseases most incident to republican government" (Hamilton, Jay, and Madison [1788] n.d., 62), is not a correct inference to be drawn from *The Federalist*. The open public realm is a necessary complement to representative institutions in Madison's search for republican remedies to the diseases most incident to republican governments.

THE OPEN PUBLIC REALM AND THE SCHOOLING OF EXPERIENCE

It is the open public realm and the way it gets linked to the more formalized structures of government that make processes of governance accessible to citizens. The members of legislative bodies (except in town meetings), officers of executive agencies, and judicial magistrates comprise only a small minority of the population in American society. The constitution of the open public realm is where the members of American society experience what it means to live in a democratic society. People learn from their experience in light of the structural conditions that are constituted as instrumentalities of government and the information and knowledge which emerge from engaging in the associated processes of discussion, deliberation, and choice and what it means to act in light of those processes.

The structural conditions implied by the stipulations and rules embodied in a constitution provide at best for a specification of the context—a framework—for formulating, acting upon, enforcing, and determining the proper application of rule-ordered relationships in a society. People need to know what it is that they are doing in these contexts. Discussion, deliberation, and the achievement of resolutions are cognitive processes that inform actions. The context structures; the deliberations at work in structures elucidate information, clarify alternatives, and facilitate inquiry; actions transform, and what is transformed is what emerges.

Efforts to address problematic situations always have a knowledge component. Citizens learn from the way in which institutional arrangements structure their participation in a society and from what that participation means in light of the results to be achieved. Learning from experience in such circumstances implies that all institutional arrangements have an educative character. I refer to this learning from experience as the "schooling of experience" because Tocqueville explicitly refers to three types of experience that serve to school citizens in exercising the prerogatives of government: participation in town meetings, serving as jurors, and creating and participating in voluntary associations. To this we must add the prior place of religion as "the first of their political institutions" even though it has "no direct part in the government of society" (Tocqueville [1835] 1945, 1: 305).

Churches as religious associations function in an open public realm and contribute to the way in which people think about themselves, their relationship to their universe, and how they relate to one another. These presuppositions help to shape a universal consensus that gains expression in what Tocqueville refers to as "the idea of right."

> The idea of right is simply that of virtue introduced into the political world. It is the idea of right that enables men to define anarchy and tyranny, and that taught them how to be independent without arrogance and to obey without servility. The man who submits to violence is debased by his compliance; but when he submits to that right of authority which he acknowledges in a fellow creature, he rises in some measure above the person who gives the command. There are no great men without virtue; and there are no great nations—it may also be added, there would be no society [i.e., "civil" society]—without respect for right; for what is a union of rational and intelligent beings who are held only by force? [Ibid., 1: 244–45]

An idea of right is achieved by applying a method of normative inquiry inherent in the Golden Rule to interdependent relationships with one's equals on an individual-to-individual basis in
dealing with the exigencies of everyday life: "the principle which
the child derives from the possession of his toys is taught to the
man by the objects which he may call his own" (ibid., 245). These
observations anticipate Jean Piaget's *The Moral Judgment of the
Child* ([1932] 1969), where learning how to devise variations in
the rules of games that children play is viewed as the basis for the
development of moral judgments about what distinguishes fairness from unfairness and so right from wrong. Among a free
people, the metaphysical roots of religious teachings pervade the
experiences of everyday life.

An opportunity available to most people is to have some share
in the affairs of a neighborhood community, a village or, among
New Englanders, the township. Self-organizing capabilities exist
at the village level in all societies. With the advance of human
civilization, Tocqueville argues, the more enlightened are apt to be
intolerant of the blunders that are made by the coarser elements of
humanity found in villages; and thus the independence of villages
is apt to be destroyed by those who exercise supreme authority in
a society. Tocqueville, however, sees municipal institutions as the
basic institutions for collective action in a free society because
"town meetings are to liberty what primary schools are to science;
they bring it within the people's reach, they teach men how to use
and how to enjoy it" ([1835] 1945, 1: 61). The governance of the
townships came the closest of any unit of government to being an
open public realm. The basic authority to take collective decisions
resided in a town assembly in which all freeholders were eligible to
participate. The implementation of resolutions of an assembly
was entrusted to a board of selectmen and to a multitude of town
officers assigned specific administrative responsibilities. The selectmen monitored the performance of other elected town officials. Citizens monitored their selectmen, other town officials,
and each other.

Instead of relying upon a hierarchy of superior-subordinate
relationships to achieve accountability among the numerously

elected administrative officials, the American system of township government relied upon the judiciary. An official was held accountable to general standards of law in the discharge of his functions, and citizens could seek recourse to the judiciary to procure the general enforcement of law. An official acting beyond the scope of law was no longer acting in an official capacity, but was liable as an individual potentially culpable of wrongdoing. This link between the exercise of elective authority and judicial power in the discharge of administrative responsibilities revealed to Tocqueville a system of administration that was fundamentally different in its principles of organization from those found in France.

> The courts of justice are the only possible medium between the central power and the administrative bodies; they alone can compel the elected functionary to obey without violating the rights of the electors. The extension of judicial power in the political world ought therefore to be in the exact ratio to the extension of the elective power; if these two institutions do not go hand in hand, the state must fall into anarchy or into servitude. [Ibid., 74]

The distribution of authority into a multitude of hands gains coherence by the way in which the ordinary relationships of life achieve a complementarity with one another as the characteristic features of a community. The government emanates from the governed: "the people was always sovereign in the township" (ibid., 68). In such a system of governance, every individual

> obeys society, not because he is inferior to those who conduct it or because he is less capable than any other of governing himself, but because he acknowledges the utility of an association with his fellow men and he knows that no such association can exist without a regulating force. He is subject in all that concerns the duties of citizens to each other; he is free and responsible to God alone, for all that concerns himself. Hence, arises the maxim, that everyone is the best and sole judge of his own private interest, and that society has no right to control a man's

> actions unless they are prejudicial to the common weal or un-
> less the common weal demands his help. . . . The townships are
> generally subordinate to the state only in those interests [that]
> are common to all of the others. They are independent in all
> that concerns themselves alone. . . . [Ibid., 64–65]

In such circumstances, each individual is first his or her own governor. The town is independent in all that concerns itself alone,
but subject to general laws of the state as these apply across numerous towns. These principles are subject to reiteration as they
apply to the autonomy of each state with regard to its internal
affairs, subject to the general laws of the union as these apply to
the affairs of the several states. A loose hierarchy of law exists in an
open society without a centralized hierarchy of administrative
functionaries. Citizens learn the rudiments of democracy by their
direct participation in the governance of their own local community as essentially an open public realm.

In the constitution of the judiciary, Tocqueville sees the circumstance where the jury "may be regarded as a gratuitous public
school, ever open, in which every juror learns his rights, enters
into daily communication with [those learned in the law] and becomes practically acquainted with the laws" (ibid., 285) from the
conduct of proceedings that are addressed to jurors. The participation of citizens in juries "teaches men to practice equity; every
man learns to judge his neighbors as he would himself be judged"
(ibid., 284). Tocqueville considers citizen participation in juries to
be as important as universal suffrage in the constitution of the
American system of governance (ibid., 283).

The importance of the jury is reinforced by a distinctive feature
of American jurisprudence in which a constitution "governs a legis-
lator as much as a private citizen" (ibid., 101): "all the citizens have
the right of indicting public functionaries before the ordinary tribu-
nals and all of the judges have the power of convicting public officers" (ibid., 103). The exercise of judicial authority also has a
significant autonomy from the way disputes are initiated and the
way the judicial process is articulated through the pleas of the parties to an action in accordance with formal rules of procedure and

evidence. The proceedings are conducted by those learned in the law, but the communication is directed to jurors, who participate in the taking of judicial decisions, in a language that is comprehensible to ordinary citizens.

Since all political questions are likely to be contested as a judicial matter, Tocqueville argues that all parties in American society "are obliged to borrow, in their daily controversies, the ideas, and even the language, peculiar to judicial proceedings." Lawyers "introduce the customs and technicalities of their profession into the management of public affairs." In turn, the jury extends this habit to all elements of society.

> The language of the law thus becomes, in some measure, a vulgar tongue; the spirit of the law, which is produced in the schools and the courts of justice, gradually penetrates beyond their walls into the bosom of society, where it descends to the lowest classes, so that at last the whole people contracts the habits and the tastes of the judicial magistrate. [Ibid., 280]

The mode of judicial inquiry comes to pervade a sense of due process applicable to the way that people address problems and resolve conflicts among themselves.

The third type of experience accessible to every citizen, which Tocqueville views as critical to citizenship in American society, is the experience of forming associations to gain the advantage of joint efforts in accomplishing tasks that individuals cannot accomplish by acting alone.

> Americans of all ages, all conditions, and all dispositions constantly form associations. They have not only commercial and manufacturing companies, in which all take part, but associations of a thousand other kinds, religious, moral, serious, futile, general or restricted, enormous or diminutive. The Americans make associations to give entertainments, to found seminaries, to build inns, to construct churches, to diffuse books, to send missionaries to the antipodes; in this manner they form hospitals, prisons, and schools. . . . Wherever at the head of some new undertaking you see the government in France, or a man

of rank in England, in the United States you will be sure to find an association. [Tocqueville (1840) 1945, 2: 106]

The society is, in effect, an "immense assemblage of associations" (ibid.). The American press is constituted as an implicit assemblage of associations that purveys information and stimulates activity in public affairs.

Americans activate their participation within the institutions of state and national governments by associating themselves together in what Tocqueville refers to as "political associations." People, Tocqueville argues, "cannot belong to these associations for any length of time without finding out how order is maintained among a large number of men and by what contrivances they are made to advance, harmoniously and methodically, to the same object. . . . Political associations may therefore be considered large free schools, where all of the members of the community go to learn the general theory of association" (ibid., 116).

By learning to associate together through covenantal methods to accomplish tasks that cannot be accomplished by acting alone, Tocqueville argues, Americans learn to impose the social virtues upon their conception of self-interest. "Self-interest, rightly understood" turns upon a right understanding of how to take account of the interests of others as one acts in relation to them. This is how Americans ameliorate tendencies toward egoism and individualism in their social activities. The place of the immense assemblages of associations that are constitutive of American society and that activate its system of governance can then be generalized: "In democratic countries the science of association is the mother of science: the progress of all else depends upon the progress it has made" (ibid., 110).

THE EMERGENCE OF PUBLIC OPINION, CIVIC KNOWLEDGE, AND A CULTURE OF INQUIRY

The operation of the open public realm and the way it gets linked to the structures of governmental decision making is the source, then, of a shared community of understanding that a people develops in solving problems cooperatively. This is the foundation for the emergence of public opinion and the spirit of community. These ways of thinking go deeper than simply holding an opinion about how to cope with some contemporary problem. They involve basic presuppositions about human nature, the universe in which life acquires its meaning, and how to relate to one another. The open public realm is where people are continually pressing one another and giving expression to ideas that form a public philosophy: civic knowledge grounded in a civic religion.

If people in a democratic society are to cope with problems that accrue through time, they need to achieve a level of knowledge and civilization where they can address difficulties as problems and conceptualize alternative ways for resolving those problems. Tocqueville suggests that there may be peoples who "are unable to discern the causes of their own wretchedness" and who "fall a sacrifice of the ills of which they are ignorant" ([1835] 1945, 1: 231). A people cannot learn from their experience in such circumstances. Human beings are always prone to error, and it becomes necessary to confront ideas with the results of experience.

If people are to become masters of their own fate, the structures appropriate to a self-governing society need to encompass processes that are capable of maintaining a culture of inquiry and problem solving that has error-correcting potentialities. It is not enough to win elections and put together winning coalitions in diverse decision structures. People need to address the substantive characteristics of practical problems that exist in a world of limiting conditions. Viewed from an experimental perspective, legislative functions are primarily conjectural, attempting to confront the future course of events contingent upon a change of policy. The taking of executive action is operational in characteristics, fitting appropriate actions to specifiable contingencies. In turn, adjudicatory arrangements focus upon the consequences that follow from collective action in assessing the possibility that injuries have been committed. When linked together in an experimental problem-solving mode, the actions taken through diverse decision structures can be viewed as testing the warrantability of the conjectures used to inform the processes of collective decision making. Error-correcting potentials arise in the use of an experimental mode to take collective decisions and to assess the consequences that follow from collective action. Advancement of human knowledge can occur in light of the diverse experimentations that characterize collective action in human societies.

The methodological significance of using an experimental mode for this purpose is reflected in the cumulative effect of contestation, for

> the oftener [a] measure is brought under examination, the greater the diversity of the situation of those who are to examine it, the less must be the danger of those errors which flow from want of due deliberation, or of those missteps which proceed from the contagion of some common passion or interest. [Hamilton, Jay, and Madison (1788) n.d., 477]

An appropriate use of diverse structures offers the prospect of yielding error-correcting potentials that require human beings to go beyond winning elections and putting together winning coalitions. Hamilton's "due deliberation" fosters the conduct of inquiry in an experimental problem-solving mode where the diverse decision structures are appropriately linked to an open public realm. This is why a system of governance characterized by federalism and polycentricity can achieve rationality only by reference to an open public realm as its core.

Any particular society acting upon a limited set of presuppositions and conceptions to constitute a system of order can explore only a limited range of possibilities. Tocqueville's reference to a great experiment to construct society upon a new basis is worthy of critical study for what can be learned from it. But there have been other experiments to construct societies upon other bases, experiments drawing upon conjectures of revolutionary importance. The Russian revolutions of 1917 and the Soviet experiment to construct society upon another basis are efforts of comparable importance. It is as we draw upon diverse experiments to construct societies upon different bases that we can learn from each other's experiences.

An open public realm must, however, be the context in which those who participate in public affairs can draw upon diverse experiences. Life becomes impoverished or enriched in proportion to our capabilities to draw upon the efforts of others to overcome the severe limits that apply to what one can do for oneself when acting alone. But the range of human experiences, with the assemblages of associations that coordinate what each does both for oneself and for others, needs to be sufficiently diverse so that we acquire the learning that can accrue from human institutions.

Alex Weissberg (1952) refers to Soviet society and the Marquis de Custine ([1839] 1989) to the empire of the tzar as "a conspiracy of silence." Each sees this conspiracy as being evoked by the autocratic character of the political regime. Custine suggests its source when he observes that "under an absolute government every indiscretion of speech is equivalent to a crime of high treason" (ibid., 294). When this is so, everyone imposes a tight self-censorship, which is censorship in its most pervasive form. A conspiracy of silence exists. Public opinion and civic knowledge about affairs in a society are repressed. A culture of inquiry cannot develop. One seeks to avoid causing an offense; one does what one is told to do. These principles were as operable under Stalin's autocracy as under the autocracy of any tzar. In his efforts to restructure Soviet society, Gorbachev's call for glasnost—openness—is a recognition of the importance of an open public realm to a society that might reform itself. But for a society long dominated by a conspiracy of silence to develop a critical awareness of alternative possibilities will be a difficult achievement.

Americans face another type of challenge: how to sort out the relevant information to address problematical situations when multitudes of people are clamoring to have their say. The human brain is hard-wired so that each individual can address only one problem at a time. It is difficult to use one's cognitive facilities in both a critical and a constructive way amid the multitudes who scurry for attention. There is no "time" for reflection when everyone demands a say.

If human beings are to be masters of their own fate, they must learn to discern the causes of their own wretchedness, to paraphrase

Tocqueville, and gain access to alternative ways of restructuring order in human societies. This cannot be done when everyone scurries for attention. We can do so only if we take care to think about the troubles of living in highly interdependent patterns of social relationships, patterns where opportunities for "opportunism" and exploitation abound amid possibilities for mutually respectful and productive ways of relating to one another.

We must be able to draw upon the experiences of others if we are to develop a critical awareness of our own experiences and our own limitations, and of the alternatives that are available for the unfolding of human potentials. These conditions can be met only when we can have reference to open, public realms to engage in inquiry about efforts to solve common problems. We learn to govern ourselves and to participate in the vast assemblages of associations that are constitutive of American society as we learn how to relate constructively to one another in an open society. It is not governments that govern; it is citizens who govern. Collective decisions can be transformed into collective actions only when people learn how to coordinate their activities with one another in complementary ways.

NINE

POLYCENTRICITY: THE STRUCTURAL BASIS OF SELF-GOVERNING SYSTEMS

In Chapter 6 it was asserted that traditional patterns of metropolitan government make up a "polycentric political system," in which there exist many decision-making centers, formally independent of each other. To the extent that these political jurisdictions take each other into account in competitive relationships, enter into contractual and cooperative relationships, or turn to central mechanisms to resolve conflicts, they may exhibit coherent, consistent, and predictable patterns of behavior and may be said to function as a "system." These assertions referred to units of government in the context of metropolitan areas. They raise the question of whether general sets of relationships can exist where multiple units, formally independent of one another, can function interdependently as polycentric systems capable of yielding emergent patterns of order. Systems of governance occur wherever complementary arrangements for formulating, using, monitoring, judging, and enforcing rules exist.

If the conditions applicable to polycentric orders can be generalized to apply to all patterns of order in a society, we might then meet the conditions specified by Madison in essay 51 of *The Federalist* where he suggests that "this policy of supplying by opposite and rival interests, the defects of better motives, might be traced through *the whole system of human affairs, private as well as public*" (Hamilton, Jay, and Madison [1788] n.d., 337, my emphasis). If the whole system of human affairs is capable of being organized on principles of polycentricity rather than monocentricity, we could have human societies that no longer depend upon a unity of power to achieve coherence. Such an idea is of radical proportions; but this is what Madison is saying in what I would regard as the single most important assertion about the organizing principle of American federalism to be found in *The Federalist*. This assertion, then, is fully consistent with Tocqueville's observation that American democracy is a self-governing society: "there society governs itself for itself" (Tocqueville [1835] 1945, 1: 57).

If we view a federal society as a covenanting society capable of generating rich assemblages of associations, we would expect to see social units of one sort or another, formally independent but choosing to take each other into account, functioning in mutually accommodating ways to achieve many different patterns of order. How these patterns of order are constituted is, at least in part, an empirical question. In any general system of polycentric order, we would expect particular patterns of polycentricity to be interdependently related to other such patterns.

The appearance of disorder that prevails at the surface, to paraphrase Tocqueville, may upon further inquiry reveal coherent patterns of order. Conversely, the appearances of order that are presumed to exist may be seriously misleading. A bureaucracy, for example, cannot function as the basis for a rational legal order, as Max Weber presumed, when those who exercise the prerogatives of rulership use their discretion to waive the requirements of law. The founder of the Ming dynasty discovered that holding the reins of rulership taut yields oppression, while relaxing them yields corruption (Dardess 1983). The Faustian bargain inherent in the constitution of order in human societies does not allow perfection.

Aspects of polycentricity are likely to arise in all systems of social order because human beings are capable of thinking for themselves and acting in ways that take account of their own interests. When power is used to check power, careful attention should be paid to the way that polycentricity serves as a structural basis for the emergence of actual self-governing arrangements. If such a system is to be extended literally "through the whole system of human affairs," including the "distribution of the supreme powers of the State" (Hamilton, Madison, and Jay [1785] n.d., 338), it is necessary to explore the application of polycentricity to the realm of international affairs as well. When we contemplate how the principles of polycentricity might apply to the whole system of human affairs, we are exploring the fuller implications of the American experiment.

THE CONCEPT OF POLYCENTRICITY

As formulated by Ostrom, Tiebout, and Warren (1961), a polycentric political system would be composed of: (1) many autonomous units formally independent of one another, (2) choosing to act in ways that take account of others, (3) through processes of cooperation, competition, conflict, and conflict resolution. The resolution of conflict need not depend upon "central mechanisms" as stated in that formulation. Noncentral mechanisms for conflict resolution also exist.

It was not until after the essay just cited had been published that I became aware of the prior use of the concept of polycentricity by Michael Polanyi in *The Logic of Liberty* (1951). Polanyi distinguishes between two different methods for organizing social tasks, methods that are constitutive of two different types of social order. One is referred to as a "deliberate" or "directed" social order, coordinated by recourse to an ultimate authority exercising control through a unified command structure. I presume that this type of order is equivalent to Hobbesian sovereignty, in which there is a single ultimate authority exercising a monopoly over rulership prerogatives and the instruments of coercion in a society.

The other type of order for organizing social tasks is identified by Polanyi as "spontaneous" or "polycentric." It is conceptualized as an order where many elements are capable of making mutual adjustments to one another within a general system of rules where each element acts independently of the other elements. Within a set of rules, autonomous decision-makers are free to pursue their own interests subject to the constraint inherent in those particular rules being enforced.

I have difficulty with the use of the term "spontaneous" in the development of social orders. When juxtaposed with the term "deliberate," as it is by Polanyi, the term "spontaneous" implies that a development has occurred without the intention of those involved. I readily recognize that such possibilities may exist. Whether vehicles in meeting one another on the same roadway move to the right or to the left probably derived from experiences in which the rule accrued with significant spontaneity at different places in human history. However, a great deal of deliberateness may be required to establish a federal system of governance where power is used to check power amid opposite and rival interests. A polycentric political system, where rule-ruler-ruled relationships are organized by reference to many autonomous decision structures within each unit of government, requires a good deal of deliberateness in order to function. Anyone who has read Madison's "notes" on the Philadelphia Convention of 1787, not to mention *The Federalist*, will appreciate that formulating the rules for the federal union called the United States of America did not occur spontaneously, nor was it an edict issued by a supreme authority.

As Jean Piaget ([1932] 1969) demonstrates, children at play can, in light of their accumulated experiences and maturation, learn to modify and create games by formulating mutually agreed upon rules that they themselves proceed to enforce. But such capabilities depend upon a sophistication about rule-ordered relationships that must be added to the skills needed for shooting marbles or playing ball.

To expect a democratic society not only to emerge spontaneously, but to modify and sustain itself in the same way, is not plausible in light of the problems of and probable threats to the viability of democratic institutions. I prefer, then, to presume that polycentric systems of order depend upon a good deal of deliberateness in their creation, operation, and maintenance over time.

Yet Polanyi, F. A. Hayek (1973), and others who use the language of "spontaneity" in referring to social orders are emphasizing points that have considerable merit. Such systems depend upon accumulated experience and cannot be laid down by simply putting words on paper, whether in the form of constitutions, statutory enactments, or the edicts of an autocrat. They depend upon people who know what they are doing and have acquired workable standards by which they can measure successes and failures. We can expect more failures than successes to accrue from the type of "spontaneity" that might be associated with trial and error. Liberty and justice are performance criteria that cannot be measured in the same way as net monetary return.

The autonomous character of polycentric systems implies self-organizing capabilities. The many autonomous elements or units seek to order their relationships with one another rather than by reference to some external authority. Self-organizing systems become democratic self-governing systems when those being governed have equal liberty and equal standing in the constitution of an order where rulership prerogatives are subject to effective limits among multiple agents, each exercising a limited public trust. I assume that the rules of such associations are open to public scrutiny, to constrain the organization of unlawful conspiracies.

In a theory of polycentric orders I further assume that individuals are the basic units of analysis. Individuals will occupy positions where decisions are taken on behalf of the interests of others in the exercise of agency and trust relationships. Business firms, units of government, agencies of government, legislative bodies, political parties, courts, and nation-states may also be used as units of analysis having to do with relationships at incremental levels of analysis. Societies then become richly nested assemblages of associations that include the diverse forms of association developed within and among units of government.

Diverse autonomous units can then be subject to analysis in relation to specifiable rules of association. The rules of association within business firms at one level of analysis need then to be explored in relation to the rules of association pertaining to market relationships at another level. But markets, electoral contests, and international relations may involve such different strategic calculations that, when polycentric systems of orders apply through the whole system of human affairs, few predictable inferences can be made regarding units of all types. Most inferences will apply to the relationships of particular types of units functioning in particular forms of polycentric order characterized by particular types of rules and payoff functions. If the whole system of human affairs were subject to systems of polycentric orderings, it would be as though all patterns of order in a society were conceptualized as a series of simultaneous and sequential games. A general system of polycentric ordering, then, would be one where each actor participated in a series of simultaneous and sequential games and where each act had the potential for being construed as a move in simultaneous games. Time out in the play of any one game might be taken to reach resolution of disagreements and conflicts.

We might further anticipate that general systems of polycentric orderings applicable to whole systems of human affairs would take on the characteristics of competitive games: contestability, innovative search for advantage, and convergence toward successful strategies. If the whole system of human affairs were organized in this way, we would expect to see the emergence of a civilization with greater evolutionary potential than can be achieved by those who call for revolutionary change.

THE EMERGENCE OF PATTERNS OF ORDER IN POLYCENTRIC STRUCTURES

In this section I shall consider the patterns of polycentric orderings as these apply to (1) competitive market economies, (2) competitive public economies, (3) scienticfic inquiry, (4) law and adjudicatory arrangements, (5) systems of governance with a separation of powers and checks and balances, and (6) patterns of international order. The challenge is to understand how patterns of polycentricity might extend to the whole system of human affairs.

Competitive market economies. Since Adam Smith's *Wealth of Nations* (1776), competitive market economies have been celebrated as systems of economic order that manifest patterns of polycentricity and significant degrees of spontaneity. Competitive markets are open systems where anyone is free to enter as a trader subject to the condition of conducting exchange relationships by mutual agreement. The ordering of market relationships responds by mutual adjustments to the activity of others. Competition occurs in the exercise of choice among the alternative options available. Exchange is itself a cooperative relationship between particular buyers and sellers.

Voluntary agreement implies that each party to an exchange is left better off by consummating the exchange. Competition implies that those offering a similar product for sale must meet the terms offered by their competitors. The buyer has incentives to take advantage of lower prices for any given quantity or quality of a good. The combination of these circumstances means that no single producer is free to maximize profits. Competition reduces returns to producers and increases returns to consumers.

These results are both counterintentional and counterintuitive. Each producer may seek to maximize profits, but instead his profits will be reduced by the presence of competitive alternatives. Consumer surplus is proportionately increased. It is consumers who benefit from competitive markets. Selfishness in seeking private advantage yields public benefits. It is this relationship that was dramatized in Mandeville's *The Fable of the Bees* ([1714] 1970).

Furthermore, the idiosyncratic pursuit of self-interest yields not chaos but a predictable system of order with tendencies to drive toward an equilibrium of supply and demand at a point where marginal price covers marginal costs. Such a system of relationships offers optimal opportunities for the alleviation of scarcity in human societies. Investment is no longer justified when costs of economic activities exceed benefits, for when they do the net effect is to leave people worse off. The best results are achieved where benefits are equal to or marginally greater than costs. Societies cannot hope to improve upon such conditions given comparable technologies, human skills, levels of knowledge, and access to information.

Given producer motives to maximize profit, incentives exist in any market economy for established producers to collude, restrict entry, reduce competition, and set prices to allow for a more favorable rate of return. To the extent that such strategies are successful, the competitiveness of market systems is reduced. So long as producers can turn to political authorities to fix the terms of trade and enforce cartel agreements among producers, the equilibrating tendencies of market arrangements shift to the advantage of producers and to the disadvantage of consumers. There are conditions where the equilibrating tendencies of an open (free) competitive market economy cannot be maintained and distortions can be expected to occur. A knowledgeable awareness of these conditions is essential to the maintenance of competitive market arrangements as a polycentric order. If courts treat cartel agreements as valid contracts, they are using their prerogatives to impair the competitive viability of a market economy. The viability of any polycentric order depends upon the maintenance of appropriate limits. Such structures are vulnerable to dominance strategies.

Market arrangements work effectively in relation to goods that are subject to exclusion, and are marketable in units that are both measurable and specifiable in equivalent quantities and/or qualities. Markets are facilitated by commensurate institutions pertaining to private property, the enforcement of contracts, the existence of a reliable monetary system as a medium for exchange and as a measure of value, and access to appropriate public infrastructures pertaining to open spaces, roadways, and public utilities.

A competitive market economy contributes to the emergence of public information about the comparative prices of a vast array of goods and services. It is this information that provides participants in market relationships with an awareness of relative advantage that may accrue to entrepreneurial efforts and innovative potentials. It is the accretion of public information that enables each participant successfully to coordinate his or her pursuit of opportunities in relation to others, and to function in a system of order that works by mutual accommodation among the participants.

The contestability of markets offers rewards to those who discover innovative potentials including the use of new ideas, the development of new technologies, and whatever advantage is to be had from local knowledge. The significance of these rewards for innovations is given recognition in patent and copyright laws that allow an innovator to gain monopoly advantage for fixed periods of time because innovations are not easily appropriable as private property. Whenever a competitor gains an advantage from innovative potentials, all other competitors functioning in the same market have an incentive to acquire them. There is, in other words, a convergence toward successful innovations. The most important factors contributing to the success of competitive market economies are their information-generating features and incentives for innovation. Market economies, as Hayek and the Austrian economists have emphasized, appropriately constrained by patent laws, can then be viewed as facilitating processes of discovery and innovation. Appropriate constraining institutions are therefore necessary to the maintenance of competitive market conditions.

Competitive public economies. As we saw in Chapters 6 and 7, competitive *public* economies can emerge in highly federalized systems of government where substantial fragmentation and overlap exists among diverse government units. These latter, in arranging for the provision of public goods and services, function as collective consumption units. The competitive rivalry in public economies cannot be expected to achieve equilibration between marginal cost and marginal price that economists expect from a "perfectly" competitive market economy. We would expect, however, that there would be similar pressures toward enhanced efficiency where diverse communities are organized as collective consumption units, and where competitive alternatives exist among production units. So long as the communities of beneficiaries bear the costs of providing public services and there is an appropriate fit between the nature of the good and the boundaries of the collective consumption unit, we can expect increased sensitivity to benefit-cost calculations so that benefits cover costs. The structures of incentives under these conditions work in the proper direction. Such structures can be expected to yield different results from what would be achieved by supplying public services through a system of public administration organized in the kind of unified command structure characteristic of an integrated public bureaucracy. The more highly federalized a political system, the higher the degree of competitive viability that can be expected to exist in fitting patterns of demand to patterns of supply.

It is in achieving a fit between consumption and production functions that configurations of relationships need to be established among the government units responsible for each. Size economies applicable to the consumption of collective goods and services can function independently of economies-of-scale in transforming factors of production into outputs. To assume that overlapping jurisdictions yield wasteful duplication of services fails to take account of collective consumption functions that need to be organized in public economies as distinguished from market economies. The existence of overlap among collective consumption and production units means that competitive options become available. Contestation is then facilitated in circumstances where increasing information on comparative performance can be expected to emerge, where incentives for innovation occur, and where participants become knowledgeable about the successful and unsuccessful arrangements that become available. Patterns of order are maintained by mutual adjustment among informed participants choosing from among the alternatives that are available to them.

Scientific inquiry. Polanyi's *The Logic of Liberty* (1951) draws heavily upon the organization of scientific communities as manifesting the characteristics of a polycentric order. To engage in the pursuit of scientific inquiry, Polanyi argues, requires that any particular investigator take account of the achievement of others. Whatever it is that becomes problematical is so in light either of some anomaly that arises between a theoretical formulation and the consequences that follow from acting upon it, or of the existence of some alternative way of addressing some problematical situation. An awareness of either of these circumstances depends upon an awareness of the formulations and achievements of others. The merit of any new formulation turns first upon its public reproducibility. The particular formulation and the results achieved, if appropriately formulated and acted upon, are not idiosyncratic to particular human personalities but are presumed to be publicly reproducible by others possessing comparable skills and knowledge.

There are, then, basic presuppositions about the essential coherence of a universal order that enable scholars eventually to resolve puzzles or dilemmas and to choose among competing conjectures. The act of choosing accrues to others in the scientific community. Presumably, some "advantage" must accrue to a new "discovery" as an alternative way of addressing a problematical situation before others can be persuaded by its merit.

This taking account of the work of others and advancing alternative formulations presumes that "the scientific community is held together and all its affairs are peacefully managed through its joint acceptance of the same fundamental scientific beliefs. These beliefs, therefore, may be said to form the constitution of the scientific community and to embody its ultimate sovereign will" (Polanyi 1951, 26). The "sovereign will," in this case, is the concurrence of others in the scientific community rather than some ultimate authority who exercises monopoly control over rulership prerogatives and instruments of coercion. Polanyi explicitly recognizes that a polycentric order among scientific investigators entails normative presuppositions that respect the search for truth, desire justice, and maintain mutual respect and reciprocity in their relationships with one another.

The tensions inherent in the work of the scientific community are, however, exceptionally high because every belief is potentially contestable. Inquiry in the scientific tradition represents, then, a challenge to every form of orthodoxy. Further, there is a danger that scientific investigators may abandon modesty, presume to know the Truth, and create their own form of orthodoxy, while engaging in sweeping rejections of other forms of belief and failing to pursue the merit of the arguments that may be at issue. Dogmas advanced in the name of science are no less dogmatic than other dogmas. Efforts to destroy or silence others is a manifestation of dominance strategies that are repugnant to polycentricity in scientific communities. A repudiation of religion, as such, fails to indicate an appreciation of those who teach that nature is the creation of a transcendent order. The study of nature as God's creation can provide scientific investigators with an appreciation for the existence of an order that gives coherence to all other forms of order. This is consistent with a presumption that a universe exists.

Science as a polycentric order depends, then, upon an autonomous pursuit of inquiry that requires a reciprocal respect for the autonomy of others. Contestability in the realm of ideas is an essential feature of science as such an order. Tensions must necessarily exist in such circumstances, but the reward for participating in contestable arguments in respectful ways is to reap the fruit of tilling the field of knowledge as civilization advances. The civilization advances only when innovations in human knowledge offer others opportunities to achieve net gains in the advancement of human welfare. It is the free professions and the institutions for the transmission of learning to each new generation that provide the essential links between those working at the frontiers of inquiry and the accessibility of knowledge to other members of a society. These institutional arrangements are potentially as open to a polycentric system of order as the scientific community itself. The rules of conduct applicable to these orders may be breached when the modesty appropriate to human fallibility is abandoned for the presupposition that omniscient observers can know what is good for others. Polycentric orders allow others to speak and act for themselves in light of the emergence of new ideas and the accretion of new knowledge.

Law and adjudicatory arrangements. Polanyi conceives of law courts and the larger legal community as forming a polycentric order. The judiciary and members of the legal profession are viewed as participating in processes to elucidate information and articulate contending arguments as means of resolving conflicts and rendering judgments; they do so under conditions where each participant exercises an independence of action in relation to each

other participant, subject to common rules of evidence, procedure, and argumentation.

The possibility of conceptualizing courts and the judicial process as a polycentric order will depend upon the development of
(1) legal concepts and terms that can be known in a public interpersonal context, (2) legal criteria that can be used as a basis for
judgment, and (3) methods of legal reasoning that can be used to
organize thoughts and array evidence for the same purpose. Unless a community of agreement (in other words, substantial consensus) can exist regarding legal concepts, criteria for choice or
judgment, and methods of legal reasoning, there can be no basis
for a polycentric ordering.

A fundamental tension exists between conceptualizing law as
command and law as rules grounded in consensus. When the emphasis is placed upon law as command by those who exercise rulership prerogatives, the correlative relationship on the part of
those who are ruled is to obey and submit to the rule. Where law
is conceptualized as rules grounded in consensus, those subject to
the rules are free to contest how they are formulated and applied.
The point of contestation is to allow for resistance and an opportunity to challenge either the formulation of a rule or its application. It is the emergence, then, of contestation with this end in
view that has been critical in the emergence of an independent
judiciary and the development of rules of procedure that allow for
a polycentric legal order. Harold Berman, in *Law and Revolution*
(1983), provides an account of the origin of Western law with the
papal revolution evoked by the dictate of Pope Gregory VII in
1075, when he was attempting to establish the independence of
the Church from secular authorities in Western Christendom.
The conception of a basic tie between God's law and secular law
served as the basis upon which ecclesiastical authorities could
judge whether the conduct of secular authorities conformed to
religious precepts. A fundamental breach of God's laws and dis-
obedience to the Church in ecclesiastical affairs were grounds for
the excommunication of secular authorities, as church members
from the Church itself. Excommunication was an act of banning
an offender from partaking in the Christian community.

From the time of Pope Gregory VII onward, issues about the proper structure of authority relationships have been contestable in Western Christendom, and it is the persistence of this contestation that has led to the emergence of the systems of law characteristic of Western jurisprudence. The development of the Protestant tradition was an extension of principles of contestation as these applied to the organization of authority relationships in both the ecclesiastical and the secular realms.

The achievement of polycentricity in the function of the judiciary and the maintenance of a rule of law was an important step in the development of Western civilization. The natural response to any offense, unjust deprivation, or threat is to move toward a fight set. Threats or offenses yield a response by counterthreats or counteroffenses (Boulding 1963). Peaceful communication is breached; hostility easily escalates to destructive fighting; and the peace of the community is threatened. The judicial process affords a way, then, to have recourse to intermediaries who seek to do justice, maintain the peace of the community, and search for a constructive resolution of existing conflicts when adversaries are no longer on speaking terms with one another.

The road to justice depends upon suspending judgment and having recourse to a process where the adversaries have their say in mobilizing evidence and advancing arguments bearing upon the matters at issue. The parties are presumed to stand as equals before the bar of the court and are entitled to seek justice through a due process of law. Judges are obliged to do justice by conforming to the requirements of a due process of law. The method of normative inquiry inherent in the Golden Rule is the methodological foundation for principles of equity.

Adherence to principles of polycentricity in the function of the judiciary and in the maintenance of the rule of law is important to the maintenance of polycentricity in other systems of order. Market mechanisms depend upon the existence of property rights, the enforcement of contracts, and the maintenance of a just system of commercial law. This requires a knowledgeable understanding of the appropriate limits that apply to a valid contract. Otherwise, established producers who enter into contracts to form cartels will call upon courts to enforce such contracts against new competitors. Not every contract can be a valid contract—only those that conform to valid principles of polycentric ordering.

Systems of governance. This same principle of polycentricity applies to the scope of judicial authority in systems of governance as polycentric orders. If the whole system of human affairs, including the distribution of rulership functions traditionally ascribed to a sovereign, are subject to principles of polycentric ordering, then any controversies at issue pertaining to those functions must become contestable and justiciable. These in fact are the grounds for the development of a constitutional jurisprudence in the American federal system. A legislature that acts beyond the scope of its constitutional authority is presumed to be acting in circumstances that are without authority, that is, null and void. Such enactments are not entitled to enforcement; they cannot establish the basis for lawful claims, as Alexander Hamilton argued in essay 78 of *The Federalist* and as the U.S. Supreme Court asserted in *Marbury* v. *Madison.*

When the Supreme Court concludes that it has no grounds for establishing limits to the substantive powers assigned by the Constitution to the U.S. Congress, it is drawing limits to the application of the principles of polycentricity that apply to the American federal system of government. Constraining either the jurisdiction of an independent judiciary or limiting the independent standing of that judiciary has a significant bearing, then, upon the degree of polycentricity that can apply through "the whole system of human affairs." It may even result in arbitrary rules becoming uncontestable.

Polycentricity in each unit of government, then, is essential to the maintenance of polycentricity in "the whole system of human affairs." Law acquires a publicness and a justness in proportion as it withstands critical scrutiny under conditions allowing for contestability in diversely structural political processes. Although provisional decisions can be taken by minimum winning coalitions, they can still be contested through diverse political processes that contribute to an understanding of their implications.

In the evolution of Western law, distinctions have long been made between the exercise of legislative, executive, and judicial authority. Such distinctions imply that there is a conceptual basis for distinguishing the different processes applicable to rule-ruler-ruled relationships. Distinguishable legislative, executive, and judicial instrumentalities exist in all Western nations organized through "republican" institutions. The critical controversies have pertained not to the distribution of authority as such, but to the patterns of dominance among the diverse instrumentalities of government. The doctrine of parliamentary supremacy, for instance, implies that parliament as a legislative assembly is supreme. The corollary of such a doctrine is a limitation upon judicial authority placing enactments of parliament beyond judicial scrutiny. Another correlative development in Westminster-type parliamentary systems, a development not consistent with parliamentary supremacy, is that of executive privilege associated with the oaths of secrecy taken by ministers by virtue of their membership in a privy council. This tradition is reinforced by acts to preserve official secrecy. The executive privilege of privy councillors interposes severe limits upon the supremacy of parliaments as representative assemblies while creating opportunities for establishing conspiracies of silence among those who exercise executive prerogatives. The doctrines of parliamentary supremacy and ministerial confidentiality are incompatible. Where an independent judiciary is denied jurisdiction with regard to the exercise of public authority, and its authority is confined to "civil law" as distinguished from "administrative law," even greater opportunities exist to establish conspiracies of silence.

If parliamentary supremacy is to yield responsible government, then a proper accounting must be given to limits upon the judiciary and to the existence of executive privilege. A critical scrutiny of how authority relationships are constituted always needs to take account of opportunities to usurp authority and pervert justice. In much of Latin America, limits upon the creation and maintenance of an independent judiciary create a pattern of executive privilege in which the military presume to be the ultimate guardians of the peace. There, parliamentary supremacy is little more than a pretense that gives way to the privileged standing of the military to assert supreme authority.

When the logic of American federalism, as expounded in Chapter 2, is viewed from the perspective of a system of polycentric ordering, we can begin to understand how fragmentation of authority accompanied by contestation and innovation yields resolutions that achieve consensus among the members of society. There is a search that goes on where people struggle with one another in the way that Jacob struggled with God. Stalemates occur, but those stalemates are indicative of the need to struggle with one another in a search for a better understanding of the way that conflicting interests yield to a community of relationships.

Any such system of polycentric order is, however, vulnerable to the pursuit of strategies in which some will take advantage of opportunities to gain dominance over others. Politicians may have incentives to form coalitions to gain dominance over political structures in the same way that merchants have incentives to form cartels. Such strategies came to fruition in the United States following the Civil War. If politicians could dominate the slating process and offer slates of candidates for all legislative, executive, and judicial offices, the ones who controlled the winning slate could then exercise dominance over all instrumentalities of government and override the checks and balances inherent in the constitutional separation of powers. A surprising degree of success in putting together such coalitions was achieved during the era of machine politics and boss rule.

So long as competitive rivalry exists among political parties, they can contribute to maintaining polycentricity as part of the system. In those circumstances, politicians will attempt to advance proposals for collective action that will offer sufficient appeal to voters to win them the next election. Contestation yields information and critical assessments of alternative proposals. Tendencies exist to converge toward an appeal to median voters.

But success in gaining dominance over all decision structures can also yield extreme corruption, as revealed in the era of machine politics and boss rule. The method pursued by the Progressive reform movement was to reestablish conditions of polycentricity by constitutional modification of electoral arrangements in each of the states. With the introduction of systems of primary elections, which allowed any dissident to challenge the candidates offered by party leaders, and other electoral reforms, contestation was reestablished in electoral processes and strategies of dominance were sharply constrained. Every system of polycentric ordering is potentially vulnerable to circumstances where some achieve dominance at the cost of others. Spontaneity is not a sufficient condition for the maintenance of polycentric systems of order. A self-governing people need to understand when failures occur and how to reform their systems of order.

If polycentric arrangements were spontaneous systems of order, we might expect peace to occur spontaneously among the nations of the world. I do not expect that to occur. Rather, we can expect struggles for dominance to occur. We do, however, confront a challenge: If conditions of polycentricity were to apply through "the whole system of human affairs," how might such a system of relationships apply to all the nations of the world? As we turn to this question, we will also be exploring some of the implications that follow from the American experiment in constructing a federal system of governance.

Patterns of international order. Over the course of the past one thousand years the nations of Western Christendom have achieved some important degrees of polycentricity in their patterns of relationships with one another. I ascribe these developments, in their origin, to the quest by the Western clergy to establish the conditions for God's peace by renouncing retribution and to their efforts to establish the conditions of peace in the Western reaches of the Roman Empire after the fall of Rome. The papal revolution elicited by the dictate of Pope Gregory VII can be construed as one such effort to establish God's peace in Western Christendom. The constitution of the Holy Roman Empire evolved over a period of nearly a thousand years through processes of oath-taking mediated through the Church amid struggles for papal and imperial supremacy. The rituals of investiture in both ecclesiastical and secular offices involved the acknowledgment of obligations to others. Struggles over authority relationships were sustained both within the ecclesiastical realm, and within the secular realm as well as between these two realms. Popes, bishops, monks, and parishioners engaged these issues with reference to the governance of the Church just as emperors, kings, princes, dukes, counts, merchants, and villagers did with reference to secular affairs.

Wars persisted; but the presumptions of God's peace interposed limits against violating churches as places of refuge, of assembly, and of worship, and in establishing the presumption that rules of war applied among knights as the warriors of Western Christendom. Church officials, in their exercise of secular prerogatives, were not immune to participating in warfare, but they had an important place in maintaining a balance of power among contestants who aspired to imperial dominance.

Even such a limited system of order was marked by significant achievements. The basic contestability of the European balance-of-power system was marked by important advances in economics, science, and technology. In turn, authority relationships were continuously being altered in the struggles for empire mediated by balance-of-power strategies. While some of these struggles were marked by efforts to achieve dominance that might appropriately be labeled "absolutism," others were marked by successful forms of resistance. The American federal system, much like Bismark's Second Reich, can be regarded as a by-product of struggles for imperial dominance. The Americans were successful in resisting imperial dominance; and the Germans, in identifying the future of Germany with a system of imperial dominance, fashioned the Second and Third Reichs. The Swiss maintained their *Eidgenossenschaft* by resisting Austrian, French, and German imperialism. Whether Europe will be able to achieve constitutional arrangements under which its whole system of human affairs is ordered by principles of polycentricity remains to be seen.

The mediating place of polycentric systems of order in Western Christendom requires some comparative sense of proportion. The casualties—unarmed peasants—in Stalin's campaign to collectivize Soviet agriculture were as numerous as the total Russian casualties in World War II. Hitler's effort to create a Third Reich was met by an organized resistance that prevailed in a relatively few years against his imperial aspirations.

The world still faces the problem of achieving a peaceful order among its nations. The instruments of autocratic rule have been sufficiently well perfected that a so-called dictatorship of the proletariat exercised in the name of the workers of the world proved feasible for an extended period of time. But such a system of autocracy can be achieved only under conditions of servitude. Societies that place substantial reliance upon polycentric patterns of order present contestable options that must necessarily challenge systems organized on autocratic principles. The world cannot remain half free and half in servitude. Each is a threat to the other.

The irony is that the liberation of the world cannot be achieved by strategies of dominance: the world cannot be made safe for democracy by warfare. Liberation can be achieved only by building polycentric systems of order that can emerge in ways that, in Madison's words, apply through the "whole system of human affairs." There is no one strategy and no one way for building systems of polycentric ordering. We cannot expect such systems either to be constructed or to work in only one way. They have too much spontaneity and creativity to conform to a single mold. The American federal system suggests that polycentric systems can generally apply in human societies: human societies can exist without a monopoly of authority relationships. It is possible for societies to become self-governing rather than state-governed. The state, in such circumstances, withers away even when agents who may exercise limited authority are nominally designated as "heads of state."

If relationships among societies are to be achieved by extending principles of polycentricity through the whole system of human affairs, these conditions cannot be achieved when governments presume to govern other governments. Principles of polycentricity require critical attention to the equal standing of individuals with one another in a system of lawful relationships that meet the conditions of equal liberty and justice. The American way, however, is not the only way to achieve polycentric systems of order. Polycentric orders are open systems that manifest enough spontaneity to be self-organizing and self-governing. But the maintenance of such orders depends upon a sufficient level of intelligent deliberation to correct errors and reform themselves.

CONCLUSION

We can rule out the possibility that a polycentric system of order among the nations of the world will emerge spontaneously. Instead, it is necessary, as Tocqueville suggested, to draw upon a science and art of association in learning how to put polycentric systems of order together. Such systems can be expected to work well only under limited conditions. All are vulnerable to strategies of dominance. Difficulties arise because all polycentric systems of order are subject to counterintentional and counterintuitive patterns of relationships. The appearance of disorder, which is presumed to prevail at the surface, can be expected to generate emergent patterns of order that require deeper investigation.

Economists have long engaged in praise of competitive markets as systems of spontaneous order. But markets, like any other such systems, are vulnerable to the strategies of those who seek to acquire dominance over economic relationships. When the structure of human societies is conceptualized in terms of markets and states, there is strong reason to believe that the formal structure of economic relationships will succumb to dominance strategies pursued in collusion with state officials. Principles of polycentricity need to be extended through the whole system of human affairs. This applies to public economies as well as to market economies, to the constitution of particular units of government and to federal systems of government, to the conduct of elections and to the organization of political parties, to the operation of open public realms, to the deliberations of legislative bodies, to the function of executive instrumentalities, to communities of scholarship, to spiritual affairs, to institutions of education, and to the practice of professions—in short, to all of the conditions of life.

The radical implication of American federalism can be appreciated only if principles of polycentricity are to apply through the whole system of human affairs. It is then that we can begin to appreciate how that experiment was an effort "to construct society upon a new basis," why theories "hitherto unknown or deemed impracticable" were to have a special significance, and why that experiment was "to exhibit a spectacle for which the world had not been prepared by the history of the past." Tocqueville was one of the few observers who in the conduct of his analysis showed an appreciation for the way that principles of federalism, viewed as principles of polycentricity, might apply through the whole system of human affairs.

It is in that context, then, that I interpret his observation about the need for "a new science of politics" for "a new world" (Tocqueville [1835] 1945, 1: 7). We cannot rely upon spontaneity alone. Instead, human beings need to draw upon an art and science of association that will enable them to recognize the essential limits to every system of polycentric ordering, and see how strategies of dominance always pose threats. Contestation, innovation, and convergence toward mutually productive arrangements are the most likely ways to achieve progress in human societies. Once we accept this, we can begin to appreciate why the use of power to check power need not yield deadlock, stalemate, and immobility. Sufficient degrees of spontaneity exist to yield counterintuitive results. But such systems of order are always vulnerable to circumstances where bonds of mutual respect and methods of normative inquiry give way to efforts to gain dominance over others and to enjoy the fruits of victory by exploiting others.

IV

CONCLUSION

Federalism is not just a form of government; it is a method for solving problems, a way of life. Its attributes are manifold. Its creation and maintenance depend upon intelligent artisanship shared by citizens in federal societies, and those shared understandings and skills can be lost across successive generations. The viability of such a society is placed at risk when people presume that "the government" governs. How do mortals confront the challenge of keeping the craft of covenantal (collegial) problem-solving alive?

A political science, jurisprudence, journalism, or public administration for a democratic age cannot be confined to word pictures about what some choose to call "the government." People in a democratic society create their own social and political realities. People acting individually and in association with one another are required to know how to address themselves to problematical situations. They need to draw upon an art and science of association in addressing problems shared in diverse communities of relationships and to hold agents who act on their behalf accountable for the proper discharge of their public trusts. Critical reflections about citizenship in a democratic society should lead one to inquire more deeply about the meaning of federalism and its place in the unfolding of human civilization. When such inquiries, stimulated by intelligible communications, are used to resolve problems in constructive ways, the future remains open to new potentials.

TEN

1989 AND BEYOND

I have pursued an inquiry concerning the meaning of American federalism. In the course of that inquiry, I have also been concerned with a deeper puzzle about whether, in democratic societies, it is "governments" that "govern," or whether people "govern" in some fundamental sense that is more than an expression of demagoguery. Is there some sense in which people exercise self-organizing and self-governing capabilities in tending to common problems requiring collective decisions and collective actions?

This more general problem is not confined to the time-and-place exigencies of eighteenth- and nineteenth-century North America; it applies to much of the modern world. The events of 1989 and their implications for the future gave special cogency to the type of institutional arrangements that open opportunities for people to function as their own governors.

The year 1989, even more than 1848, is likely to have marked an important turning point in the emergence of modern civilization. This civilization has embarked upon an epoch that may significantly alter the course of human affairs. The responses to the aspirations of 1848 were accompanied by renewed imperial thrusts in the Austro-Hungarian empire; the France of Louis Napoleon; the

Germany of Bismarck and Hitler; and the Russia of Nicholas I, Lenin, and Stalin. Democratic aspirations have, however, persisted and, for the moment, appear to prevail. They have demonstrated a vitality in coping with the problems of life in the interval since World War II that allows for some modest measure of optimism.

There is also, however, reason for caution. Aspirations for democracy and reassertions of autocratic rule may only be manifestations of historical cyclicity like the rise and fall of dynasties or successions of revolutionary movements, coups d'état, and dictatorships of one form or another. This possibility is expressed in the closing paragraph of Robert Michels's *Political Parties* ([1911] 1966, 371), where he asserts:

> The democratic currents of history resemble successive waves. They break on the same shoal. They are ever renewed. This enduring spectacle is simultaneously encouraging and depressing. When democracies have gained a certain stage of development, they undergo a gradual transformation, adopting the aristocratic spirit, and in many cases also the aristocratic forms, against which at the outset they struggled so fiercely. Now new accusers arise to denounce the traitors; after an era of glorious combats and of inglorious power, they end by fusing with the old dominant class; whereupon once more they are attacked by fresh opponents who appeal in the name of democracy. It is probable that this cruel game will continue without end.

If I were to modify Michels's argument slightly, I would substitute the word "autocracy" for aristocracy and accept Milovan Djilas's (1957) thesis that a new ruling class can emerge without necessarily "fusing with the old dominant class." New ruling classes have the potential for becoming even more despotic than ancient aristocracies. Did 1989 represent the flowing of a democratic tide to be replaced, in due course, by new autocracies? In that case the cruel game continues: history repeats itself.

A possibility for avoiding or at least ameliorating the cruel game of history is to have recourse to new ideas that open the possibility of new patterns of development. This is why human cultural evolution offers the prospect of new opportunities and the emergence of new patterns of development in human civilizations. For democracies to break out of the perversities of revolutionary struggles and despotic orders it is necessary to achieve systems of governance where something other than "governments" actually "govern."

The issue to be considered, then, is whether ideas associated with the concept of federalism are innovations of a sufficient order of magnitude to transform Michels's cruel game of history. The issue is difficult to resolve because the analysis I have offered in Chapter 5 suggests the emergence of autocracy in the American system of government. The central-government trap places constitutional democracy at risk.

In what follows I shall state some conclusions about ideas associated with the concept of federalism, ideas that appear to be necessary for the constitution of order in self-governing societies. I presume that necessary and sufficient conditions can never be fully specified in the realm of public affairs without some reference to the appropriate use of human intelligence and artisanship to cope with practical problems. I shall then turn to the problem of "embodied intelligence" as a critical difficulty confronting all societies. Finally, I shall draw some conclusions about the future of federalism for a world that is open to new vistas of understanding.

SOME ESSENTIAL CHARACTERISTICS OF AMERICAN FEDERALISM

Simple definitions that refer to concepts associated with complex configurations of relationships do not contribute to human understanding. Systems of governance do not have interchangeable parts. The American federal system and the autocracy of the Soviet Union were based upon two different logics. Such systems cannot be simply defined. They have many attributes that must be taken into account with reference to systemic patterns of orderings. The association of American federalism with the coexistence of limited state and national governments is an incidental attribute of less than critical significance. Instead, it is important to clarify the basic elements of federalism as those elements were fashioned into a coherent system of governance. Among these elements I include (1) a covenantal approach, (2) plurality among the institutions of governance, (3) constitutional rule, (4) contestation as a way of processing conflicts and achieving conflict resolution, (5) active citizen participation in public entrepreneurship, (6) reaching out to new communities of relationships in open societies, and (7) achieving the reformability of patterns of association in complexly ordered societies. How a complementary fit among these elements is achieved is then considered.

A covenantal approach. The basic presuppositions of a covenantal approach are fundamental to the constitution of democratic societies; indeed, they are the root of what is meant by the term "federalism." How people stand both in their relationship to the universe of which we are a part and in their relationships to one another is basic to life in any society capable of self-organization. We draw upon our own resources to better understand ourselves, to reach out and develop an understanding of one another and of the world in which we live—but with a critical awareness that we are fallible creatures and vulnerable to error. Puzzles always remain about the nature of order, puzzles that transcend human understanding. Human beings always bear the burden of fallibility.

Tocqueville was correct, in my judgment, when he suggested that the critical idea at the core of American democracy was associated with the covenantal theology of the Puritans and the way that a covenantal approach could be applied in constituting civil bodies politic. The presuppositions of a covenantal approach are the foundation for the development of a method of normative inquiry grounded in the fundamental rule, "Do unto others as you would have others do unto you." This same rule can be used to civilize conflict so that human beings can engage in contestation with one another, as Jacob wrestled with God, to extend the frontiers of human understanding and build a unity of law that is compatible with diversity rather than uniformity. A covenantal approach might, thus, be viewed, using Montesquieu's expression, as "the spirit of the laws" in federal societies.

Human artisanship, in the practice of a covenantal approach, requires the use of diverse elements to create artifacts that serve human purposes. Ludwig Lachmann, in *Capital and Its Structure* (1978), has referred to this relationship as a principle of heterogeneity. Heterogeneous elements must be brought together to create any artifact. When this principle is applied to the time-and-place exigencies confronting any artisan, or teams of artisans, a challenge always exists about how best to achieve complementarity among those elements so as to realize the desired results to best advantage. This is a challenge facing not only artisans but also entrepreneurs and administrators: how to bring ideas into operation. The society that is open to more diverse ways of assembling heterogeneous elements and achieving effective complementarities is the one that allows for greater productive potentials. These principles apply not only to marketable commodities but to public facilities, common-pool resources and public services, and the patterns of rule-ordered relationships in self-governing associations of diverse sorts.

Plurality among the institutions of governance. If people are prepared to draw upon a covenantal approach in relating to one another, alternatives become available to the Hobbesian presuppositions that a unity of power by a sovereign authority is necessary to the peace and concord of a commonwealth. Instead, people can fashion multiple autonomous relationships capable of taking collective decisions appropriate to different ways of giving expression to human community. Diverse units of government tending to different communities of interest can coexist with one another in circumstances where each has recourse to multiple agency relationships in formulating and revising rules of conduct, monitoring the use and application of rules in relation to one another, and determining the proper application of rules and their enforcement. The plurality of such arrangements facilitates the development of a rule of law among people capable of fashioning their own rules and binding one another to mutually agreeable terms and conditions. Power that is widely shared in a democratic society must correlatively be broadly distributed. The fundamental authority of persons establishes one's authority to govern one's own affairs. Such authority is accompanied by correlative limits upon the authority of specialized instrumentalities of government. The latter are constituted by multiple agency relationships that manifest a division of labor in the exercise of authority relationships applicable to rule making (legislative authority), rule enforcement (executive authority), determining the proper application of rules (judicial authority), and monitoring performance (accounting, auditing, and investigative authority). No supreme authority exists; all authority is subject to challenge. Binding authority depends upon concurrence among multiple decision structures. Law, in an open society, acquires a publicness when no instrumentality of government is allowed to function as the supreme authority.

If the unity of law is to be achieved through a unity of power exercised by a sole agent as sovereign representative, then that agent is in a position to determine the authoritative allocation of values and exercise command over the lawful instruments of force in that society. Such agents cannot be held accountable to others within the society. They are the judges of their own cause in relation to the interests of others. Law is command, and the exercise of prerogative depends upon instrumentalities of control. This is the antithesis of federalism. People cannot govern in a system of command and control operating from a single center of ultimate authority in societies that reach out to continental proportions.

Constitutional rule. For a democratic society to exist, there must be both specifiable and commonly understood terms and conditions of governance under which people exercise basic prerogatives in the governance of their own affairs and can hold those who act as agents on their behalf accountable to limits implied in a proper discharge of their public trusts. Constitutions are meant to specify the terms and conditions of governance pertaining to the prerogatives of persons and citizens in the governance of their own affairs, to the discharge of public trusts in the exercise of governmental prerogatives, and to limits upon those prerogatives so that no one is allowed to exercise unlimited authority. Constitutional law can be treated as fundamental law. People can retain prerogatives to enforce limits and alter the terms and conditions of government through positive constitutional law. Federalism, then, as I have suggested elsewhere (1987, 25), can be conceptualized as "constitutional choice reiterated."

Contestation. The existence of a polycentric order among a great multitude of institutions of governance implies that principles other than domination through a command-and-control system are at work in a democratic society. In his treatment of the constitution of liberty, Montesquieu recognized that power should be used to check power if limits are to be maintained upon the proper discharge of political authority in a republic ([1748] 1966, 150). A similar doctrine applies where opposite and rival interests are to be arrayed so that different offices may be a check upon each other. "These inventions of prudence," Madison asserts, "cannot be less requisite in the distribution of the supreme powers of the State" (Hamilton, Jay, and Madison [1788] n.d., 337–38).

Such a system of governance is driven by contestation among opposite and rival interests in conflicts that extend to problematical situations beyond their mutual understanding. The institutions of governance, associated with collective deliberation, the taking of collective action, and the adjudication of conflicting interests, can be mobilized to use conflict in constructive ways; they can elucidate information, clarify alternatives, and stimulate innovations in order to find constructive resolutions and achieve a complementarity of interests.

The constitution of particular decision structures associated with legislative, executive, and judicial arrangements is thus intended to facilitate a due process of inquiry for transforming conflicts into constructive resolutions. The methods of normative inquiry derived from a covenantal approach are what enable people to civilize conflict, using it to open human understanding to new potentials for conflict resolution. Such potentials imply that it is more productive to endure temporary stalemates than to rely upon the preemptive dominance of a single center of ultimate authority.

Active citizen participation in public entrepreneurship. The basic test of a capacity for self-organization and self-government turns not upon voting and special pleading but upon participating in the organization of enterprises concerned with accomplishing some task—getting something done, in other words. This requires relating to others in the context of specific time-and-place exigencies in bringing together diverse elements that enter into productive activities, and in achieving the necessary complementarity among those diverse elements to get a job done.

The character of a democratic society is revealed by the willingness of people to cope with problematical situations instead of presuming that someone else has the responsibility for them. Anyone knowledgeable about affairs in the local community becomes aware of the resources that can be drawn upon in coping with a wide variety of problems. For many problems, concerted action through voluntary associations may be sufficient to accomplish what needs to be done. Other problems may require enduring forms of organization capable of overcoming holdout or free-rider strategies and using some potential for coercion to be exercised through limited forms of collective choice and action. Even in such situations, a covenantal approach implies achieving consensus as the basis for the organization of efforts that contribute to the functioning of local public economies. Such efforts bring people together on behalf of interests they share in common rather than to dominate others by forming coalitions to achieve dominance over others.

It is in the context of institutions of local government that people can come to terms with the difficulties and hazards of taking collective action, and so develop a deeper appreciation for how their interdependent interests affect their quality of life. Most people have the opportunity to be active citizens in their local communities in addition to being spectators watching the games of politics being played out in distant places. As Tocqueville recognized, municipal institutions are the basic source of vitality in a free society. Citizens cannot achieve self-organizing and self-governing capabilities without the experience of actively associating with their fellow citizens to accomplish tasks that require their joint efforts. Citizens are essential coproducers of the patterns of life constitutive of human communities.

Reaching out to new communities of relationships. Patterns of interdependencies in human societies imply diverse communities of relationships. Federal arrangements imply that people can avoid retreating behind political boundaries and viewing strangers beyond those boundaries as adversaries in a hostile world. Interdependencies require attention to how diverse interests get related to one another. Federal societies presume an openness that makes people able to relate to one another and explore latent communities of interest that might be constituted in diverse ways.

During the emergence of American federalism, towns associated themselves together in what eventually became states, and states associated themselves together in what became a federal union called the United States of America. Nation-states need not be viewed as the ultimate achievement in the organization of human societies. If patterns of associated relationships are to transcend national boundaries, rich networks of voluntary associations need to be complemented by rules that take account of communities of relationships that are multinational in character. It is federalism that provides the alternative to empire and opens opportunities in the light of 1989, for building upon and amplifying people's capacity for self-government.

Reformability. Self-governing societies depend upon achieving a capacity to reform themselves. Large-scale democratic societies in particular need to have a well-elaborated science of association that can be used both to engage in diagnostic assessments of problematical situations, and to explore how modifications in the structure of problematical situations can achieve improvements in human well-being that are complementary to other patterns of order in the world in which we live. In view of this need, democratic societies have to take account of diverse communities of interest in circumstances where new potentials are emerging as a function of advances in both knowledge and productive potential.

The ultimate challenge of a federal system of government is to mobilize the intellectual capacity to restructure patterns of human association in the context of diverse collectivities and communities of relationships. Human beings always stand exposed to the possibility that "they are unable to discern the causes of their own wretchedness and [so] fall sacrifice to ills of which they are ignorant" (Tocqueville [1835] 1945, 1: 231). Whether fallible creatures can mobilize the diagnostic and analytical capabilities to discern the causes of their own wretchedness and devise more constructive ways of life is problematical. Self-organizing and self-governing capabilities in human affairs depend upon capabilities for achieving the reordering of relationships through time.

The existence of many autonomous public enterprises and units of government allows greater opportunities for innovation and experimentation. A federal society is an experimenting society, where new ideas, including those that alter the structure of institutional arrangements, can be tried out as ways of alleviating problems of institutional weakness and institutional failure. Reformability is an essential attribute of a federal system of governance.

Complementary fit. The challenge of 1989 and beyond is to recognize that order and rivalry go together in fashioning human civilization. National boundaries need to become increasingly open to relationships in which individuals and associations of individuals build interpersonal networks that are constitutive of multinational societies. State-to-state relationships cannot suffice. The problems of interdependencies have potentials for conflict that require a level of communication and deliberation that is appropriate to the communities of interests that engender conflict. Institutional facilities for mediating and resolving conflict are necessary to complement the unfolding of relationships that emerge as communities of rule-ordered relationships.

Cooperation occurs when people act with reference to one another with a view to mutual advantage. Competition occurs when alternatives are available in choosing among potential partners with whom to cooperate. Conflict occurs when actors pose a potential threat or interfere with one another's activities. Conflict resolution occurs when those in conflict search out ways of securing complementarity among their diverse interests. That complementarity is achieved in constituting communities of relationships. Collective action occurs in light of what is presumed to have reference to whatever is shared in common by communities of people. How people act in governing their own affairs as individuals and in association with others is as essential to the constitution of a democratic society as is the action of those who make it their business to process conflict, facilitate conflict resolution, and act on behalf of the complementarities necessary for human communities. Complementarities are threatened when some uses of public space, for example, drive out other uses.

The larger the community, the greater the risks of oligarchical dominance inherent in democratic deliberations. The simple extended republic will always be dominated by oligarchical tendencies. The larger the community, however, the more important are constitutional constraints that confine the exercise of governing prerogatives to identifiable communities of relationships rather than presuming it to be omnicompetent. With reference to American democracy, my conclusion, then, is that democracy is at risk when "the government" is presumed to "govern." Tocqueville was correct when he recognized an absence in the United States of what the citizens of France would have termed "the government or the administration." In Tocqueville's words, "the hand that directs the social machinery is invisible," because each individual was first his or her own governor and each related himself or herself to others through voluntary associations and township institutions in tending to the exigencies of everyday life. The institutions of government were there to mediate and resolve conflicts and reach out to larger communities of relationships, but not to exercise command and control over all aspects of life.

To presume, in casual discussions, that "governments govern" is as theoretically naive in a democratic society as to presume that the sun rises and sets, rotating around the earth. Instead, it is people who govern in assuming responsibility for managing their own affairs, for learning how to relate to others, for setting the terms and conditions for taking collective decisions and collective actions, and for holding those who exercise authority on behalf of others accountable to fiduciary relationships. If states rule over societies, the burdens of life are quite different from when people assume responsibility for governing their own affairs and tending to what they share in common with others.

Karl Popper, in discussing the rationality principle, suggests that human rationality consists of acting in ways that are appropriate to situations (Popper 1967). Further, he suggests that the primary task of any analysis is to clarify the nature of the situation rather than to focus upon the cognitive characteristics of human beings. An actor acting in a way that is appropriate to a situation is characteristic of all forms of learning and adaptive behavior.

An important issue arises, however, because individuals acting in artifactual situations are required to have sophistication about how to act in those situations. Citizens in a democratic society need to know how to assume responsibility for their own lives, how to relate constructively to others, and how to govern human associations requiring collective decisions and collective actions. They must, among other things, be aware of the Faustian bargain that is inherent in the structure of rule-ordered relationships, of the dangers of autocracies, and of what it means to participate in the governance of a society organized in accordance with general theories of limited constitutions that are subject to revision through time.

It follows that the cognitive capabilities of human beings cannot be neglected in considering the constitution of order in self-governing societies. Peter Winch (1958) is correct in his emphasis upon the cognitive capabilities of human beings in his exploration of the relation of social science to philosophy. These refer to the domains of World II and World III that Popper (1972) elaborates in his later works on the three worlds of human cognition and human actions. The place of knowledge and its functioning in society, then, is critical for societies that presume to be self-governing. The nature of epistemic orders and how individuals learn to function in such orders is as important as how citizens learn to function in political orders—rule-orderings—that are self-governing.

Cognitive capabilities in self-governing societies place high levels of demand upon people to cope with the specificities of problematical situations. The generalization of a theoretical sort must be applied in the context of specific time-and-place contingencies (Hayek 1945) in which heterogeneous elements must be drawn upon in complementary ways to achieve practical results. We as human beings need to know what we are doing if we are to discern the causes of our difficulties and not fall prey to the ills of which we are ignorant. We are, however, always pressing limits, and errors are inevitable. Self-governing capabilities can be achieved only in a problem-solving mode, in which we order the exigencies of life so that we can learn from one another. This requires appropriate habits of the heart and mind and structural exigencies for transforming conflict into a problem-solving mode that facilitates conflict resolution.

When we naively presume that governments govern, we are likely to reveal a thorough misunderstanding of the basic foundations of democratic societies and of the steps appropriate for making transitions in the world beyond 1989. Paul A. Gigot, writing in the *Wall Street Journal* of June 29, 1990, indicates the magnitude of the problem when he finds that many Russians interviewed in Moscow make the plea: "Please don't help our government." He quotes comments by Ilya Zaslavsky, a member of the Interregional Group of Deputies in the Soviet parliament, who asserts: "Sometimes I think that the worst enemies of democracy in my country are democrats in the West. You are always trying to help our dictatorship."

National parliaments, national elections, and national political parties where governments govern are simply—with the possible exception of the Denmarks of this world—an inadequate basis for democratic systems of governance. The *Waterschappen* (water associations) of the Netherlands, the *Gemeinde* (village communities) in Switzerland, townships in New England, and the basic infrastructures for tending to community affairs in all societies are the institutions necessary to the nurturing of democratic ways of life. People can express themselves in town halls or village commons. It is impossible for each person in a hundred million to have a right to express oneself and be given a respectful hearing by everyone else.

When the "free world" depends upon government-to-government relationships, the best of intentions by Western democrats get transformed into the strengthening of dictatorships (autocracies). The presumption that governments govern is a serious error. The opening of societies to diverse interpersonal and inter-organizational relationships is much more fundamental to the emergence of democracies.

As human beings we each, to some significant degree, have the potential for becoming what we aspire to be and for shaping our own reality. What conceptions and calculations can we draw upon both in understanding ourselves, in making sense of our reality, and in establishing our aspirations for what might be achieved? This is the stuff from which human civilizations emerge and is what shapes the future.

THE PROBLEM OF EMBODIED INTELLIGENCE

Living with the systemic patterns of orderings in modern self-governing societies presses the limits of human intelligence. It is possible for human beings both to learn from the cruel game of history and from one another's experience to achieve self-governing capabilities; but human beings are always pressing the limits of human knowledge. Here we confront a fundamental dilemma: the use of knowledge can be exercised only by mortal creatures.

Jerry Fodor, the cognitive psychologist, has emphasized that human intelligence is *embodied* in the material conditions of life that come apart in a "ridiculously short time" when contrasted to "Eternity" (1987, 129). The exercise of learning and the use of intelligence occur only among living creatures. It is individuals who learn, think, act, and relate to others. The accumulation of learning and skill for each individual expires when life expires. The fact of mortality is a radical constraint upon human intelligibility. Human beings can draw upon language and communication through the use of language to transcend, to a limited degree, the absolute constraint that mortality would otherwise impose upon intelligible communications. With the use of language, it is possible to transmit knowledge from one individual to others so that learning can be accumulated across generations and specialization (division of labor) can accrue within generations. Both involve complex problems of coordination.

The acquisition of new knowledge in each generation requires its articulation and transmission to individuals in that generation. Specialization requires the acquisition not only of linguistically transmitted knowledge but also of the skills in artisanship that are entailed in putting knowledge to use in creative endeavors and, in turn, advancing the frontiers of learning in any given generation. Curiosity, the desire to learn and to know, and artisanship, the desire to use ideas to express oneself and to accomplish something, imply an active disposition to take a creative role in life.

The embodiment of intelligence in mortal beings requires that these processes occur within the constraints of mortality and apply to and among discrete individuals as mortals. Communication allows for the pooling of acquired learning as articulated knowledge, but the agencies through which the acquisition and transmission of knowledge occur are always discrete mortal beings. Knowledge and skills are neither aggregated nor transmitted as a single whole. The productive potential of a society depends upon the way that such processes are diffused and coordinated both through time and space. Human potentials for innovation—potentials for learning and the generation of new knowledge—mean that everyone's future must necessarily be uncertain. Long-term planning is an impossibility. The exigencies of nature are also subject to substantial variability. Achieving complementarity among the variabilities of time and place requires complex computations in every form of artisanship. The mortal embodiment of human intelligence requires extraordinary skills in communication, coordination, experimentation, and adaptation.

Grounds for constituting order in societies. A covenantal way of constituting order in human societies through self-organizing and self-governing capabilities turns upon whether human beings can most effectively resolve the problem of embodied intelligence among themselves as mortal creatures. Is there a way of diffusing knowledge, skills, learning, and problem-solving capabilities among the members of a society so that people can use methods of collegiality in addressing themselves to problems of conflict and conflict resolution? Or must they rely upon some ultimate center of authority to exercise dominance over society?

A response to these questions turns upon the analysis in Chapter 2. We can consider a theory of democratic governance fashioned by covenantal methods juxtaposed to a theory of sovereignty. The key issue turns upon the use of language to constitute rule-ordered relationships and how to make rules binding in human relations. To use principles of strong hierarchical orderings through command and control is one method. Another is to use a system of weak hierarchical orderings through concurrent and limited instrumentalities of governance under conditions of quasi-voluntary compliance (Levi 1988). The latter implies the diffusion of self-governing capabilities throughout a society with a presumption that each individual is responsible for governing his or her own affairs, achieving mutually productive relations with others, and learning how to achieve collective action in self-governing communities of relationships.

Amid changing conditions. The world itself is subject to radical transformation by the way in which embodied intelligence functions in human societies. The world of 1989 in American society was vastly different from the world of 1789. At the end of this century, science and technology have transformed the basic conditions of life. The "press" is no longer confined to the printed word. Railroads, highways, and airways have transformed space. Manufacturing and agriculture yield abundant varieties of goods. The realms of human organization and relationships have been subject to comparable transformations and elaborations.

The constitution of order in human relationships, for all this change, still depends upon making words binding in human relationships. A critical issue in contemporary legal scholarship turns upon debates over how to construe the language of constitutional rule in American jurisprudence. There are those who argue on behalf of an original intent and those who argue on behalf of some underlying value such as human dignity as a basis for construing a "living" constitution. The problem is one of translation; it cannot be simply discharged by recourse to a machine-like transformation. It requires recourse, in part, to original intention and plain meaning, but in the context of what is required to devise and maintain a system of democratic governance grounded in a general theory of limited constitutions. In turn, any general theory of limited constitutions needs to be grounded, first, in explicitly recognized methods of normative inquiry that enable human beings to make mutually understood interpersonal comparisons about the meaning of value terms; and second, in methods of positive inquiry that enable communities of people to acknowledge the existence of counterintuitive and counterintentional relationships in human affairs. James Madison's recognition of strong oligarchical tendencies in all democratic assemblies, for example, casts substantial doubt on the sufficiency of one-person, one-vote, majority-rule formulations for the constitution of extended democratic republics. "Living constitutions" dominated by ruling oligarchs can be expected to abandon the constraints of limited constitutions capable of maintaining systems of constitutional rule.

A narrow adherence to words like "press" in an era of electronic communication is not an intelligent exercise in translation. Neither is an exercise of free association grounded in discourse about human dignity an adequate basis for maintaining a system of constitutional rule in a democratic society. Lawyers motivated to win cases with reference to judges motivated to advance a variety of different policy agendas about human dignity can be expected to leave American jurisprudence in serious disarray.

Henry G. Manne, a leading scholar in law and economics, has likened such a system to a "constitutional lottery" (1990, 26). He correctly concludes that "we face the grave danger of losing the idea of a regime of law altogether" (ibid., 32). Majority rule unconstrained by constitutional limits is another form of constitutional lottery. Winning coalitions can be constituted in diverse ways. In large legislative assemblies, those exercising leadership prerogatives can be expected to dominate the agenda. Where winning coalitions are able to enjoy the fruits of victory, deprivations can be imposed upon minorities. The long-term interests of the community can be sacrificed to the temporary advantage of majority factions. To decide the fate of society by reference to winning and losing elections, and to fashion winning coalitions in legislative bodies, together amount to a constitutional lottery dominated by the exigencies of historical accident.

The challenge that students of contemporary jurisprudence face is comparable to the challenge confronting legal scholars in the twelfth and thirteenth centuries. Their achievement then was neither one of strict interpretations nor free associations about human dignity. Rather, they drew upon the achievements of Roman law interpreted by methods of normative inquiry derived from the Judaic and Christian traditions (Berman 1983; Tierney 1982). Roman concepts of empire are no longer appropriate. Instead, it is necessary to turn to general theories of limited constitutions that allow for a unity of law to be achieved with diversity rather than uniformity. Coherent systems of law can be fashioned through conflict and conflict resolution applied to problems arising from the conflict of laws.

Shared communities of understanding. Problems of interpretation and translation cannot be resolved by looking only at discrete words on paper. The meaning of symbols among mortal creatures of embodied intelligence always depends upon shared communities of understanding about the meaning of language. All languages depend upon the nesting of diverse levels of discourse grounded upon assumptions and presuppositions for achieving complementarity amid diversity. Constitutions can never be just words on paper. To be sure, words on paper are critical links for achieving embodied intelligence among mortal creatures, links that give meaning to their lives and to the way they relate to one another. But there always remain problems of tacit understanding about the meaning to be conveyed by words and of the fallibility characteristic of mortal human beings (Polanyi 1962).

A thorough knowledge of alternative possibilities is essential to a discriminating use of language. Otherwise, it is possible for people to talk to one another without communicating; they talk, but do not listen for a knowing response. Mass media are destructive of the essential reciprocity for intelligible communications.

Citizens, addressed en masse, no longer function as intelligent artisans in self-organizing and self-governing communities of relationships. The conditions of embodied intelligence can be breached; and civilization can be trampled under foot when intelligible communication as one of the necessary conditions of civilization is neglected.

A new and different way? The meaning of American federalism, as a design for the constitution of order in a self-governing society, is worthy of serious reflection by both the American people and by other peoples in the world of 1989 and beyond. What can be learned from Tocqueville's ([1835] 1945, 25) reference to a great experiment to "construct society upon a new basis"? What were the "theories hitherto unknown, or deemed impracticable [that] were to exhibit a spectacle for which the world had not been prepared by the history of the past"? What can be learned from that experiment? What in turn can be learned from the Soviet experiment and the multitudes of other experiments to construct societies upon new bases? How can such efforts to extend the frontiers of what can be learned be transformed into communicable bodies of knowledge to inform a human artisanship capable of exercising self-organizing and self-governing capabilities appropriate to the world of the future?

Are we in a position to respond to the question posed by Alexander Hamilton in the opening paragraph of essay 1 of *The Federalist*, namely, "whether societies of men are really capable or not of establishing good government from reflection and choice or whether they are forever destined to depend for their political constitutions on accident and force" (Hamilton, Jay, and Madison [1788] n.d., 3)? If political processes turn only upon winning and losing elections, building majority coalitions to dominate legislative decisions, and winning and losing lawsuits, then reflection and choice give way to constitutional lotteries and to accidental exigencies in the tragic dramas of history. If reflection and choice are to prevail, there are bodies of thought and manifestations of feelings that must stand behind and give meaning to the contestations that are also constitutive of democratic societies. Human communities cannot civilize conflict and achieve conflict resolutions without fundamental respect for one another. We contest with one another not to gain dominance over and destroy one another but to advance our own respective frontiers of understanding and compassion.

Perpetual quest. The dilemma of embodied intelligence confronting all human beings is challenged by the extraordinary faculty of imagination that drives innovation and inventiveness. Human imagination opens not only a wealth of creative possibilities but also vast realms of fantasy and delusion. The embodiment of intelligence among human beings can be used to generate images of universality and eternity. It is entirely possible for human beings to presume that they can transcend the constraints of mortality, function as omniscient observers, and know what represents the greatest good for the greatest number. These fantasies and delusions are commonplace and the source of many of the most profound errors and tragedies among human beings. They occur among the Benthams, the Engelses, and the Marxes of this world. They drive the Hitlers, the Lenins, and the Stalins. But they also drive the imaginations of the Spinozas, the Darwins, and the Einsteins.

How do we sort out the fantasies and delusions from the truly creative thrusts of the human imagination? The only way that I know of doing so is to fashion a culture of inquiry that is open to contestation mediated by an appreciation of the creative potential inherent in conflict and oriented to achieving conflict resolution. Even fantasies and delusions may contain the germs of creative impulses. If those germs are to be liberated from their encumbrances, the method by which a process of liberation can best be achieved is within the context of contestable argumentation and experimentation. Such a method is applicable to all forms of human artisanship and is not confined to academic halls and experimental laboratories. It is the method, appropriate to embodied intelligence, of allowing mortal creatures to strive for immortality by what they contribute to the emergence of enduring creativity. But caution must be exercised to sort out what is "excellently foolish" from what is "excellently wise," as Hobbes stated the problem ([1651] 1960, 22; cf. V. Ostrom 1990a). The advancement of human civilization depends upon making appropriate distinctions and discriminating choices.

DOES FEDERALISM HAVE A FUTURE?

When Tocqueville, some 150 years ago, wrote the second volume of his *Democracy in America,* he was concerned with a basic problem that afflicts embodied intelligence among mortal human beings. Would the institutional arrangements for constituting the American experiment in democratic governance enable American people to acquire, transmit, and diffuse the appropriate habits of heart and mind to sustain the principles of self-governance across future generations? If not, the American system of self-governance could not be expected to reproduce and sustain itself into the distant future.

In the two-century interval between 1789 and 1989, American society achieved a surprisingly creative thrust in human civilization. Can that thrust be sustained? My response is a cautious negative. There are two grounds for this judgment. The first is advanced by Tocqueville in his assessment of the dangers of democratic despotism. There is a transformation that occurs as citizens begin to think of themselves as like everyone else and to presume that they can address problems that apply to the society as a whole. They further presume that problems in the society as a whole can be addressed by central authorities identified as "the government." This "government," an illusion of the popular imagination, is presumed to be an omnicompetent problem-solver capable of addressing all problems arising in a society. No such creation can exist among mortal creatures of embodied intelligence. If it could, then, as Tocqueville recognized, it would become an "immense and tutelary power" that would be the "sole agent and the only arbiter" of a people's happiness. What, then, remains "but to spare them all of the care of thinking and all of the trouble of living" (Tocqueville [1840] 1945, 2: 318)? Such a system of democratic despotism would be destructive of the embodied intelligence necessary to the viability of a self-governing society. The affliction of democratic despotism, as I have indicated in Chapter 5, is beginning to take its destructive toll on American society.

If the path to democratic despotism is to be reversed, the people in American society will confront problems of reform reaching to basic constitutional considerations, that are comparable to the ones facing European peoples both east and west. In the American case, constitutional revisions will be required of the constitutional amendment process in Article V of the U.S. Constitution. Methods are necessary to allow the states to initiate constitutional amendments and to advance other amendments through a process of joint deliberation, formulation, and approval that does not allow Congress to exercise an absolute veto.[1] If there is no alternative to a congressional veto, then Congress becomes the ultimate judge of its own prerogatives in relation to the constitutional prerogatives of others and can obstruct the course of constitutional revision and reform. Such an amendment would be only a beginning in undertaking constitutional revisions and placing limits upon national authorities. Henry Manne is correct in presuming that a constitutional lottery places a regime of law at risk. Among societies of continental proportions, national governments are not competent to function as universal problem-solvers.

The other reason for a negative judgment about the place of American society in the future of human civilization is that the emergence of self-governing capabilities in other societies cannot occur under the dominance of American leadership. Thus the emergence of self-governing societies in other parts of the world may draw upon the ideas associated with American federalism, but those ideas must become a part of the cultural heritage that different peoples draw upon in shaping their own embodied intelligence. The future of democracy, then, turns upon the development of a collegiality where people draw upon one another's experience in constituting and reconstituting systems of self-governance that can be adaptive to time-and-space exigencies and that can achieve complementarities with others.

No one can anticipate the future of human civilization. We can, however, assume that its potential turns upon achieving a culture of inquiry that facilitates contestation amid processes of conflict and conflict resolution and allows for the emergence of complementary communities of relationships among fallible creatures capable of learning from experience. The future of Chinese, Russian, and other civilizations depends upon openness and potentials for restructuring that can be achieved only by such contestation, carried out in a respectful spirit that enables people to elucidate information, clarify alternatives, and facilitate innovation.

American federalism has important implications for achieving such cultures of inquiry. If the meaning of American federalism is construed in this way, then the United States can take its place in the emergence of a civilization grounded in principles of self-governance and in which reflection and choice function in human affairs subject to the burdens of fallibility that human beings can never transcend. The future will always pose a challenge. Meeting that challenge depends both on prior capabilities derived from the past and the use of human imagination to achieve new problem-solving capabilities that are constitutive of patterns of social order that, in turn, are complementary to other systems of order that are constitutive of the conditions of life in which we live. Those who conceive of themselves as omniscient observers and presume to know what represents the greatest good for the greatest number pose the most serious threat to the future of mankind. Those who neglect what can be learned from the past are not prepared to face the future.

These are the burdens that life imposes upon the exercise of intelligence. Federalism, as a way of structuring due processes of inquiry compatible with a due process of law, is commensurable with the limits of embodied intelligence. All systems of governance depend upon the exercise of human intelligence. We cannot escape the limits of mortality that each must bear. We can only advance by our willingness to build upon and extend each other's capabilities within the conditions that life makes available. All else is likely to be fantasy and delusion.

Federalism is a sham if covenants become mere words on paper. When the cares of thinking and the troubles of living are left to others, self-government is abandoned, democracy withers away, autocracy emerges, and people begin preying upon one another in the name of liberty and equality. The future belongs to those whose covenants are bonds of mutual trust grounded in principles of self-governance and who learn to use processes of conflict and conflict resolution to elucidate information, clarify alternatives, stimulate innovation, and extend the frontiers of inquiry to open new potentials for human development. Federalism has a future. Whether that future is associated with the United States of America is more problematical.

NOTES

Chapters 1–3 are not annotated.

Chapter 4

1. These theses are advanced in Martin Diamond's articles "*The Federalist*'s View of Federalism" (1961), "What the Framers Meant by Federalism" (1974), and "*The Federalist* on Federalism" (1977). Patrick Riley, in "Martin Diamond's View of *The Federalist*" (1978), further elaborates these theses by including reference to Diamond's unpublished lectures as well as published references. The Diamond theses are accepted by a large community of scholars. This essay was written with the objective of stimulating further consideration of these issues and in the hope that scholars might develop a greater critical consciousness of the problems involved in the language of political discourse.

2. Susanne Langer makes the following relevant observation:

> The process of philosophical thought moves typically from a first, inadequate, but ardent apprehension of some novel idea, figuratively expressed to more and more precise comprehension, until language catches up to logical insight. Really new concepts, having no names in current language, always make their initial appearance as metaphorical statements; therefore, the beginning of any theoretical structure is inevitably marked by fantastic inventions (1976, vi).

3. Riley ascribes the contention to Leo Strauss (1955, 202ff.). The Diamond theses are sometimes associated more generally with a Straussian interpretation of *The Federalist*.

4. Note the language used by Hamilton in essay 23 of *The Federalist*.

> If the circumstances of our country are such, as to demand a compound instead of a simple, a confederate instead of a sole government, the essential point which will remain to be adjusted, will be to discriminate the OBJECTS, as far as it can be done, which shall appertain to the different provinces or departments of power; allowing to each the most ample authority for fulfilling the objects committed to its charge (Cooke 1961, 149, emphasis in original).

Chapter 5

1. I have capitalized "Federal" wherever I construe the term to refer to the national government.

2. This tradition is exemplified by Walter Bagehot's *The English Constitution*, first published in installments from 1865 to 1867, and by Woodrow Wilson's *Congressional Government*, first published in 1885. Bagehot distinguishes between the "dignified" and "efficient" parts of a constitution. The dignified parts represent the facade that conceals reality as reflected in the efficient parts of a constitution. Wilson draws explicitly upon Bagehot in advancing his thesis that Congress exercises supremacy in the American system of government.

3. All parliamentary systems have distinguishable legislative bodies and processes. This is what the term "parliament" implies. Those bodies and processes are deliberative in nature and are not compatible with the performance of executive functions. The linkage achieved by constituting a leadership committee in a parliament to assume ministerial responsibility does not refute the existence of differentiable structures and processes of governance. Those who are ministers further differentiate themselves from their colleagues in parliament by becoming privy councilors for whom executive matters are subject to secrecy and, by that fact, create a realm of executive privilege that is not subject to parliamentary inquiry. Problems having to do with national security and external relationships make secrecy an essential feature of the government agencies responsible for them. Ministerial responsibility mediated by the requirements of secrecy implies that executive matters are not *res publicae*—public matters—but privy to the executive and confined to executive structures. The independence of the judiciary has become well established in all countries that are generally recognized as having a rule of law.

Chapter 6

1. The term is taken from Robert C. Wood (1958), who defines Gargantua as "the invention of a single metropolitan government or at least the establishment of a regional superstructure which points in that direction." We do not argue the case for big units versus small units as Wood does in his discussion of Gargantua versus grass roots. Rather, we argue that various scales of organization may be appropriate for different public services in a metropolitan area.

2. We use this term for want of a better one. An alternative term might be "multinucleated political system." We do not use "pluralism" because it has been preempted as a broader term referring to society generally and not to a political system in particular. Polycentric political systems are not limited to the field of metropolitan government. The concept is equally applicable to regional administration of water resources, regional administration of international affairs, and to a variety of other situations.

3. By analogy, the formal units of government in a metropolitan area might be viewed as organizations similar to individual firms in an industry. Individual firms may constitute the basic legal entities in an industry, but their conduct in relation to one another may be conceived as having a particular structure and behavior *as an industry*. Collaboration among the separate units of local government may be such that their activities supplement or complement each other, as in the automobile industry's patent pool. Competition among them may produce desirable self-regulating tendencies similar in effect to the "invisible hand" of the market. Collaboration and competition among governmental units may also, of course, have detrimental effects, and require some form of central decision making that considers the interests of the area as a whole. For a comprehensive review of the theory of industrial organization see Joe S. Bain (1959).

4. Krutilla and Eckstein develop the concept of "internalizing" external economies as a criterion for determining the scale of a management unit in the administration of water resources. But it is just as applicable to shopping centers, which in practice may also give favorable rents to large supermarkets as "traffic generators." This recognizes the externalities they create.

5. Dewey's use of the terms "acts" and "transactions" implies that only social behavior is contemplated in public action. But physical events, such as floods, may also become objects of public control.

6. See the discussion of "district boundaries and the incidence of benefits" in Stephen C. Smith (1956).

7. The boundary conditions of a local unit of government are not limited to its legally determined physical boundaries but should also include reference to extraterritorial powers, joint powers, and so forth.

8. This factor might be separately characterized as a criterion of equitable distribution of costs and benefits, but we have chosen to consider it here in the context of political representation.

9. The following analysis is confined to competition between units of government and makes no reference to competitive forces within a unit of government. Competition among pressure groups, factions, and political parties is a fundamental feature of the democratic political process, but is not within the primary focus of this paper and its concern with polycentric patterns of organization among units of government in metropolitan areas.

Chapter 7

1. The best single reference is U.S. Advisory Commission on Intergovernmental Relations (1987). See also notes by Vincent Ostrom, Robert L. Bish, and Elinor Ostrom (1988); Robert L. Bish and Vincent Ostrom (1973); Robert L. Bish (1971); Vincent Ostrom (1989); and E. S. Savas (1971). For those readers who would like to pursue a more extended bibliography, extensive bibliographic citations can be found in the above references and in Vincent Ostrom and Elinor Ostrom (1971).

2. The literature on public goods is quite large and in some cases quite technical. Readers who would like to pursue a preliminary set of readings related to the nature of goods could obtain a good overview by reading James M. Buchanan (1968) and Mancur Olson (1965). Some of the recent empirical studies in this tradition would include those by Roger Ahlbrandt (1973); Elinor Ostrom, William Baugh, Richard Guarasci, Roger Parks, and Gordon Whitaker (1973); James McDavid (1974); Bruce D. Rogers and C. McCurdy Lipsey (1974); Elinor Ostrom (1976); and E. S. Savas (1977b).

Chapter 10

1. The type of consideration that I have in mind is reflected in an informal proposal that I advanced in correspondence with a colleague on December 7, 1987:

> At the present time, Congress exercises control over the amendment process by either proposing specific amend-

ments or in calling a convention in response to the application of two-thirds of the state legislatures. What we need is an alternative process. We need to sort out an initiating process, from a deliberative process, and a ratifying process. An alternative to the present arrangements might be accomplished by having nine states take the initiative in proposing that constitutional amendments be formulated to address a problem of constitutional revision. When the first nine states have done so in relation to a common subject, then governors in each of these states might nominate, subject to ratification of the state legislature, a commissioner to constitute a commission on constitutional revision. The commission composed of nine commissioners might then organize itself with a chairman, temporary staff, etc., to undertake the task of holding hearings and conducting what inquiries may be necessary to advance a proposed amendment or set of amendments. Such a proposal might then be subject to ratification by resolution of the legislatures or conventions called for such a purpose in three-fourths of the states.

BIBLIOGRAPHY

Ahlbrandt, Roger. 1973. *Municipal Fire Protection Services: Comparison of Alternative Organizational Forms.* Beverly Hills: Sage.

Altshuler, Alan A. 1970. *Community Control: The Black Demand for Participation in Large American Cities.* Indianapolis: Pegasus.

Aristotle. 1942. *Politics.* Trans. Benjamin Jowett. New York: Modern Library.

Austin, John. 1955. *The Province of Jurisprudence Determined.* Ed. H. L. A. Hart. London: Weidenfeld and Nicolson. First published in 1832.

Bagehot, Walter. 1964. *The English Constitution.* Ed. R. H. S. Crossman. London: Watts. First published 1865–1867 as magazine articles.

Bain, Joe S. 1959. *Industrial Organization.* Berkeley: University of California Press.

Bárzel, Yoram. 1969. "Two Propositions on the Optimal Level of Producing Public Goods." *Public Choice* 6 (spring): 31–37.

Bentham, Jeremy. 1948. *The Principles of Morals and Legislation.* New York: Hafner. New edition of 1823 corrected by the author from the original 1780 publication.

Berman, Harold. 1983. *Law and Revolution: The Formation of the Western Legal Tradition.* Cambridge, Mass.: Harvard University Press.

Bish, Robert L. 1971. *The Public Economy of Metropolitan Areas.* Chicago: Markham.

Bish, Robert L., and Hugh O. Nourse. 1975. *Urban Economics and Policy Analysis.* New York: McGraw-Hill.

Bish, Robert L., and Vincent Ostrom. 1973. *Understanding Urban Government: Metropolitan Reform Reconsidered.* Washington, D.C.: American Enterprise Institute.

Bish, Robert L., and Robert Warren. 1972. "Scale and Monopoly in Urban Government Services." *Urban Affairs Quarterly* 8 (Sept.): 97–120.

Boskin, M. J. 1973. "Local Government Tax and Product Competition: The Optimal Provision of Public Goods." *Journal of Political Economy* 78 (Jan./Feb.): 203–10.

Boulding, Kenneth E. 1963. "Toward a Pure Theory of Threat Systems." *American Economic Review* 53 (May): 424–34.

Breton, Albert. 1974. *The Economic Theory of Representative Government*. Chicago: Aldine.

Buchanan, James M. 1968. *The Demand and Supply of Public Goods*. Skokie, Ill.: Rand McNally.

———. 1970. "Public Goods and Public Bads." In *Financing the Metropolis*, ed. John P. Crecine. Beverly Hills: Sage.

———. 1975. *The Limits of Liberty: Between Anarchy and Leviathan*. Chicago: University of Chicago Press.

Buchanan, James M., and Gordon Tullock. 1962. *The Calculus of Consent: Logical Foundations of Constitutional Democracy*. Ann Arbor: University of Michigan Press.

Burns, James MacGregor. 1963. *The Deadlock of Democracy*. Englewood Cliffs, N. J.: Prentice-Hall.

California Governor's Task Force on Local Government Reform. 1974. *Public Benefits from Public Choice*. Sacramento: Governor's Office.

Commons, John R. 1968. *Legal Foundations of Capitalism*. Madison: University of Wisconsin Press. First published in 1924.

Cooke, Jacob E., ed. 1961. *The Federalist*. Middletown, Conn.: Wesleyan University Press.

Crozier, Michel. 1964. *The Bureaucratic Phenomenon*. Chicago: University of Chicago Press.

Custine, Marquis de. 1989. *Empire of the Czar: A Journey through Eternal Russia*. New York: Doubleday. First published in 1839.

Dales, J. H. 1968. *Pollution, Property and Prices*. Toronto: University of Toronto Press.

Dardess, John W. 1983. *Confucianism and Autocracy: Professional Elites in the Founding of the Ming Dynasty*. Berkeley and Los Angeles: University of California Press.

Dewey, John. 1927. *The Public and Its Problems*. New York: Holt.

Diamond, Martin. 1961. "*The Federalist's* View of Federalism." In *Essays on Federalism*, ed. George S. Benson, 21–64. Claremont, Calif.: Institute for Studies in Federalism, Claremont Men's College.

———. 1974. "What the Framers Meant by Federalism." In *A Nation of States*, ed. Robert A. Godwin, 25–42. Chicago: Rand McNally.

———. 1977. "*The Federalist* on Federalism." *Yale Law Journal* 86 (May): 1273–85.

Djilas, Milovan. 1957. *The New Class*. New York: Praeger.

———. 1969. *The Unperfect Society*. New York: Harcourt, Brace.

Dye, Thomas R. 1990. *American Federalism: Competition among Governments.* Lexington, Mass.: Lexington Books.

Elazar, Daniel J. 1971. "Community Self-Government and the Crisis of American Politics." *Ethics* 81 (Jan.): 91–106.

Elazar, Daniel J., and John Kincaid. 1980. "Covenant, Polity and Constitutionalism." *Publius* 10 (fall), especially 3–30.

Elkin, Stephen L. 1987. *City and Regime in the American Republic.* Chicago: University of Chicago Press.

Eucken, Walter. 1951. *The Foundations of Economics.* Chicago: University of Chicago Press.

Fodor, Jerry F. 1987. *Psychosemantics: The Problem of Meaning in the Philosophy of Mind.* Cambridge, Mass.: MIT Press.

Fromm, Erich. 1941. *Escape from Freedom.* New York: Farrar & Rinehart.

Goodnow, Frank J. 1900. *Politics and Administration.* New York: Macmillan.

Greene, Vernon L. 1978. "The Metaphysical Foundations of Constitutional Order." Ph.D. diss., Dept. of Political Science, Indiana University, Bloomington.

Gregg, Phillip M. 1975. *Problems of Theory in Policy Analysis.* Lexington, Mass.: Heath.

Hamilton, Alexander, John Jay, and James Madison. n.d. *The Federalist.* Ed. Edward M. Earle. New York: Modern Library. First published in 1788.

Hayek, F. A. 1945. "The Use of Knowledge in Society." *American Economic Review* 35 (Sept.): 519–30.

———. 1973. *Rules and Order.* Vol. 1 of *Law, Legislation and Liberty.* Chicago: University of Chicago Press.

Hirsch, Werner. 1964. "Local versus Areawide Urban Government Services." *National Tax Journal* 17 (Dec.): 331–39.

———. 1968. "The Supply of Urban Public Services." In *Issues in Urban Economics,* ed. Harvey S. Perloff and Lowden Wingo, Jr., 435–75. Baltimore: Johns Hopkins University Press.

Hobbes, Thomas. 1949. *De Cive or the Citizen.* Ed. Sterling P. Lamprecht. New York: Appleton-Century-Crofts. First published in 1642.

———. 1960. *Leviathan or the Matter, Forme and Power of a Commonwealth Ecclesiasticall and Civill.* Ed. Michael Oakeshott. Oxford: Blackwell. First published in 1651.

Hochman, Harold M., ed. 1976. *The Urban Economy.* New York: Norton.

Huang, Ray. 1981. *1587: A Year of No Significance.* New Haven, Conn.: Yale University Press.

Huckfeldt, Robert. 1990. "Structure, Indeterminacy and Chaos: A Case for Sociological Law." *Journal of Theoretical Politics* 2 (Oct.): 413–33.

Hume, David. 1948. *Hume's Moral and Political Philosophy.* Ed. Henry D. Aiken. New York: Hafner.

Kaminski, Antoni. 1992. *The Institutional Order of Communist Regimes.* San Francisco: ICS Press. Forthcoming.

Kaufmann, Franz-Xavier, Giandomenico Majone, and Vincent Ostrom, eds. 1986. *Guidance, Control, and Evaluation in the Public Sector.* Berlin and New York: de Gruyter.

Koestler, Arthur. 1959. *The Sleepwalkers: A History of Man's Changing Vision of the Universe.* New York: Macmillan.

Kotler, Milton. 1969. *Neighborhood Government: The Local Foundations of Community Life.* Indianapolis: Bobbs-Merrill.

Krutilla, John V., and Otto Eckstein. 1958. *Multiple Purpose River Development: Studies in Applied Economic Analysis.* Baltimore: Johns Hopkins University Press.

Lachmann, Ludwig M. 1978. *Capital and Its Structure.* Kansas City: Sheed Andrews and McMeel.

Landau, Martin. 1969. "Redundance, Rationality and the Problem of Duplication and Overlap." *Public Administration Review* 29 (July/Aug.): 346–58.

Langer, Susanne K. 1976. *Philosophy in a New Key.* 3rd ed. Cambridge, Mass.: Harvard University Press.

Lasswell, Harold, and Abraham Kaplan. 1950. *Power and Society: A Framework for Political Inquiry.* New Haven, Conn.: Yale University Press.

Lenin, V. I. 1932a. *State and Revolution.* New York: International Publishers.

———. 1932b. *What Is To Be Done?* New York: International Publishers.

Levi, Margaret. 1988. *Of Rule and Revenue.* Berkeley: University of California Press.

Lindblom, Charles E. 1955. *Bargaining: The Hidden Hand in Government.* Research Memorandum RM-1434-RC. Santa Monica, Calif.: RAND Corporation.

———. 1965. *The Intelligence of Democracy: Decision Making through Mutual Adjustment.* New York: Free Press.

Locke, John. 1947. *Two Treatises of Government.* New York: Hafner. First published in 1690.

Long, Norton E. 1970. "Rigging the Market for Public Goods." In *Organizations and Clients: Essays in the Sociology of Service*, ed. William R. Rosengren and Mark Lefton. Columbus, Ohio: Merrill.

Lutz, Donald. 1988. *The Origins of American Constitutionalism*. Baton Rouge: Louisiana State University Press.

Mandeville, Bernard. 1970. *The Fable of the Bees*. New York: Penguin. First published in 1714.

Manne, Henry G. 1990. "A Proposal for Reconciling Different Views About Constitutional Interpretation." Working paper, School of Law, George Mason University, Alexandria, Va.

Martin, Dolores T. n.d. "The Institutional Framework of Community Formation: The Law and Economics of Municipal Incorporation in California." Ph.D. diss., Dept. of Economics, Virginia Polytechnic Institute and State University, Blacksburg.

McDavid, James. 1974. "Interjurisdictional Cooperation among Police Departments in the St. Louis Metropolitan Area." *Publius* 4 (fall): 35–58.

McKean, Roland N. 1965. "The Unseen Hand in Government." *American Economic Review* 55 (June): 496–506.

Michels, Robert. 1966. *Political Parties*. Ed. S. M. Lipset. New York: Free Press. First published in 1911.

Mishan, E. J. 1969. "The Relationship between Joint Products, Collective Goods, and External Effects." *Journal of Political Economy* 77 (May/June): 329–48.

Montesquieu, Charles Louis de Secondat. 1966. *The Spirit of the Laws*. New York: Hafner. First published in 1748.

Musgrave, Richard. 1959. *The Theory of Public Finance*. New York: McGraw-Hill.

Mushkin, Selma, ed. 1972. *Public Prices for Public Products*. Washington, D.C.: Urban Institute.

Niskanen, William A., Jr. 1971. *Bureaucracy and Representative Government*. Chicago: Aldine.

Oakerson, Ronald J. 1978. "The Erosion of Public Highways: A Policy Analysis of the Eastern Kentucky Coal-Haul Road Problem." Ph.D. diss., Dept. of Political Science Indiana University, Bloomington.

Olson, Mancur. 1965. *The Logic of Collective Action*. Cambridge, Mass.: Harvard University Press.

———. 1969. "The Principle of 'Fiscal Equivalence': The Division of Responsibility among Different Levels of Government." *American Economic Review* 59 (May): 479–87.

Ostrogorski, Moisei. 1964. *Democracy and the Organization of Political Parties*. Vol. 2, *The U.S.* Garden City, N. Y.: Anchor Books. First published in 1902.

Ostrom, Elinor. 1971. "Institutional Arrangements and the Measurement of Policy Consequences: Applications to Evaluating Police Performance." *Urban Affairs Quarterly* 6 (June): 447–75.

————. 1972. "Metropolitan Reform: Propositions Derived from Two Traditions." *Social Science Quarterly* 53 (Dec.): 474–93.

————. 1975. "On Righteousness, Evidence, and Reform: The Police Story." *Urban Affairs Quarterly* 10 (June): 464–86.

————. 1976. "Size and Performance in a Federal System." *Publius* 6 (spring): 33–74.

————. 1986. "An Agenda for the Study of Institutions." *Public Choice*, 48: 3–25.

————. 1990. *Governing the Commons: The Evolution of Institutions for Collective Action.* New York: Cambridge University Press.

Ostrom, Elinor, William Baugh, Richard Guarasci, Roger Parks, and Gordon P. Whitaker. 1973. *Community Organization and the Provision of Police Services.* Beverly Hills: Sage.

Ostrom, Elinor, and Roger B. Parks. 1973. "Suburban Police Departments: Too Many and Too Small?" In *The Urbanization of the Suburbs*, ed. Louis H. Masotti and Jeffrey K. Hadden, 367–402. Urban Affairs Annual Reviews, vol. 7. Beverly Hills: Sage.

Ostrom, Elinor, Roger B. Parks, and Gordon P. Whitaker. 1973. "Do We Really Want to Consolidate Urban Police Forces? A Reappraisal of Some Old Assertions." *Public Administration Review* 33 (Sept./Oct.): 423–33.

————. 1974. "Defining and Measuring Structural Variations in Interorganizational Arrangements." *Publius* 4 (fall): 87–108.

Ostrom, Elinor, and Dennis C. Smith. 1976. "On the Fate of 'Lilliputs' in Metropolitan Policing." *Public Administration Review* 36 (Mar./Apr.): 192–200.

Ostrom, Elinor, and Gordon P. Whitaker. 1974. "Community Control and Governmental Responsiveness: The Case of Police in Black Communities." In *Improving the Quality of Urban Management*, ed. David Rogers and Willis Hawley, 303–34. Urban Affairs Annual Reviews, vol. 8. Beverly Hills: Sage.

Ostrom, Vincent. 1953. *Water and Politics.* Los Angeles: Haynes Foundation.

————. 1968. "Water Resource Development: Some Problems in Economic and Political Analysis of Public Policy." In *Political Science and Public Policy*, ed. Austin Ranney. Chicago: Markham.

————. 1969. "Operational Federalism: Organization for the Provision of Public Services in the American Federal System." *Public Choice* 6 (spring): 1–17.

————. 1971. *Institutional Arrangements for Water Resource Development.* Springfield, Va.: National Technical Information Service.

————. 1973. "Can Federalism Make a Difference?" *Publius* 3 (fall): 197–238.

———. 1980. "Artisanship and Artifact." *Public Administration Review* 40 (July/Aug.): 309–17.

———. 1985. "The Meaning of Federalism in *The Federalist:* A Critical Examination of the Diamond Theses"; and "Historical Circumstances and Theoretical Structures as Sources of Meaning: A Response." *Publius* 15 (winter): 1–21, 55–64.

———. 1986. "A Fallibilist's Approach to Norms and Criteria of Choice." In *Guidance, Control, and Evaluation in the Public Sector,* ed. F. X. Kaufmann, G. Majone, and V. Ostrom, 229–49. Berlin and New York: de Gruyter.

———. 1987. *The Political Theory of a Compound Republic: Designing the American Experiment.* Rev. ed. Lincoln: University of Nebraska Press.

———. 1989. *The Intellectual Crisis in American Public Administration.* 2d ed. Tuscaloosa: University of Alabama Press.

———. 1990a. "Problems of Cognition as a Challenge to Policy Analysts and Democratic Societies." *Journal of Theoretical Politics* 2 (July): 243–62.

———. 1990b. "Religion and the Constitution of the American Political System." *Emory Law Journal* 39 (winter): 165–90.

Ostrom, Vincent, Robert Bish, and Elinor Ostrom. 1988. *Local Government in the United States.* San Francisco: ICS Press.

Ostrom, Vincent, David Feeny, and Hartmut Picht, eds. 1988. *Rethinking Institutional Analysis and Development: Issues, Alternatives, and Choices.* San Francisco: ICS Press.

Ostrom, Vincent, and Elinor Ostrom. 1965. "A Behavioral Approach to the Study of Intergovernmental Relations." *Annals of the American Academy of Political and Social Science* 359 (May): 137–46.

———. 1971. "Public Choice: A Different Approach to the Study of Public Administration." *Public Administration Review* 31 (Mar./Apr.): 302–16.

———. 1977. "Public Goods and Public Choices." In *Alternatives for Delivering Public Services: Toward Improved Performance,* ed. E. S. Savas, 7–49. Boulder, Colo.: Westview Press.

Ostrom, Vincent, Charles M. Tiebout, and Robert Warren. 1961. "The Organization of Government in Metropolitan Areas: A Theoretical Inquiry." *American Political Science Review* 55 (Dec.): 831–42.

Pennock, J. Roland. 1959. "Federal and Unitary Government: Disharmony and Frustration." *Behavioral Sciences* 4 (Apr.): 147–57.

Piaget, Jean. 1969. *The Moral Judgment of the Child.* New York: Free Press. First published in 1932.

Pipes, Richard. 1974. *Russia under the Old Regime.* New York: Scribner.

Polanyi, Michael. 1951. *The Logic of Liberty: Reflections and Rejoinders.* Chicago: University of Chicago Press.

———. 1962. *Personal Knowledge: Toward a Post-Critical Philosophy.* Chicago: University of Chicago Press.

Popper, Karl R. 1967. "Rationality and the Status of the Rationality Principle." An English translation of "La rationalité et le statut du principe de rationalité." In *Les fondements philosophiques des systèms économiques: Textes de Jacques Rueff et essais rédigés en son honneur,* ed. E.M. Classen, 145–50. Paris: Payot.

———. 1968. *Conjectures and Refutations: The Growth of Scientific Knowledge.* Harper Torchbooks ed. New York: Harper & Row.

———. 1972. *Objective Knowledge: An Evolutionary Approach.* Oxford: Clarendon Press.

Rheinstein, Max, ed. 1954. *Max Weber on Law in Economy and Society.* Clarion Book ed. New York: Simon and Schuster.

Riker, William H. 1964. *Federalism: Origin, Operation, Significance.* Boston: Little, Brown.

Riley, Patrick. 1978. "Martin Diamond's View of *The Federalist.*" *Publius* 8 (summer): 71–101.

Riordon, William L. 1963. *Plunkitt of Tammany Hall.* New York: Dutton.

Rogers, Bruce D., and C. McCurdy Lipsey. 1974. "Metropolitan Reform: Citizen Evaluation of Performances in Nashville-Davidson County, Tennessee." *Publius* 4 (fall): 19–34.

Rousseau, Jean-Jacques. 1978. *On the Social Contract.* Ed. Roger D. Masters. New York: St. Martin's Press. First published in 1762.

Savas, E. S. 1971. "Municipal Monopoly." *Harper's Magazine,* Dec., 55–60.

———. 1974. "Municipal Monopolies versus Competition in Delivering Urban Services." In *Improving the Quality of Urban Management,* ed. David Rogers and Willis Hawley. Beverly Hills: Sage.

———ed. 1977a. *Alternatives for Delivering Public Services: Toward Improved Performance.* Boulder, Colo.: Westview Press.

———. 1977b. "Policy Analysis for Local Government: Public vs. Private Refuse Collection." *Policy Analysis* 3: 49–84.

Savas, E. S., and S. Ginsburg. 1973. "The Civil Service: A Meritless System?" *The Public Interest* 32 (summer): 70–85.

Sawyer, Amos. 1992. *The Emergence of Autocracy in Liberia* [working title]. San Francisco: ICS Press. Forthcoming.

Schelling, Thomas C. 1978. *Micromotives and Macrobehavior.* New York: Norton.

Shields, Currin V. 1952. "The American Tradition of Empirical Collectivism." *American Political Science Review* 46 (Mar.): 104–20.

Smith, Adam. n.d. *The Theory of Moral Sentiments.* Indianapolis: Liberty Press. First published in 1759.

———. n.d. *The Wealth of Nations.* London: Ward, Lock & Tyler. First published in 1776.

Smith, Stephen C. 1956. "Problems in the Use of the Public District for Ground Water Management." *Land Economics* 32 (Aug.): 259–69.

Sproule-Jones, Mark. 1990. *Governments at Work: Canadian Parliamentary Federalism and Public Policies.* Working paper. Bloomington: Workshop in Political Theory and Policy Analysis, Indiana University.

Stigler, George S. 1952. "The Tenable Range of Functions of Local Government." In *Private Wants and Public Needs Surrounding the Size and Scope of Government Expenditure,* ed. Edmund S. Phelps. New York: Norton.

Strauss, Leo. 1955. *Natural Right and History.* Chicago: University of Chicago Press.

Sundquist, James L. 1969. *Making Federalism Work.* Washington, D.C.: Brookings Institution.

Teilhard de Chardin, Pierre. 1961. *The Phenomenon of Man.* New York: Harper & Row.

Tiebout, Charles M. 1956. "A Pure Theory of Local Expenditures." *Journal of Political Economy* 64 (Oct.): 416–24.

Tierney, Brian. 1982. *Religion, Law and the Growth of Constitutional Thought 1150–1650.* Cambridge: Cambridge University Press.

Tocqueville, Alexis de. 1945. *Democracy in America.* Ed. Phillips Bradley. New York: Knopf. First published in 1835 and 1840.

———. 1955. *The Old Regime and the French Revolution.* Garden City, N. Y.: Doubleday. First published in 1856.

———. 1959a. *The Recollections of Alexis de Tocqueville.* Ed. J. P. Mayer. New York: Meridian Books. First published in 1893.

———. 1959b. *Journey to America.* New Haven, Conn.: Yale University Press.

Tolley, G. S. 1969. *The Welfare Economics of City Bigness.* Urban Economics Report no. 31. Chicago: University of Chicago Press.

Tullock, Gordon. 1965. *The Politics of Bureaucracy.* Washington, D.C.: Public Affairs Press.

———. 1970. *Private Wants, Public Means: An Economic Analysis of the Desirable Scope of Government.* New York: Basic Books.

U.S. Advisory Commission on Intergovernmental Relations. 1987. *The Organization of Local Public Economies.* Washington, D.C.

U.S. Congress. House. Committee on Interior and Insular Affairs. 1956. *Central Valley Documents.* 84th Cong., 2d sess. H. Doc. 436.

———. 1957. *Central Valley Documents.* 85th Cong., 1st sess. H. Doc. 246.

Warren, Robert O. 1964. "A Municipal Services Market Model of Metropolitan Organization." *Journal of the American Institute of Planners* 30 (Aug.): 193–204.

———. 1966. *Government in Metropolitan Regions: A Reappraisal of Fractionated Political Organization.* Davis: Institute of Governmental Affairs, University of California.

———. 1980. "Federal-Local Development Planning: Scale Effects in Representation and Policy Making." *Public Administration Review* 30 (Nov./Dec.): 584–95.

Webb, Sidney, and Beatrice Webb. 1922. *English Local Government: Statutory Authorities for Special Purposes.* London: Longmans, Green.

Weissberg, Alex. 1952. *Conspiracy of Silence.* London: Hamish Hamilton.

Weschler, Louis F., and Robert Warren. 1970. "Consumption Costs and Production Costs in the Provision of Antipoverty Goods." Paper read at 66th annual meeting of the American Political Science Association, Los Angeles, Sept. 8–12.

Wildavsky, Aaron. 1966. "The Political Economy of Efficiency." *Public Administration Review* 26 (Dec.): 292–310.

———. 1976. "A Bias toward Federalism: Confronting the Conventional Wisdom on the Delivery of Governmental Services." *Publius* 6 (spring): 95–120.

Williamson, Oliver. 1985. *The Economic Institutions of Capitalism: Firms, Markets, Relational Contracting.* New York: Free Press.

Wilson, Woodrow. 1887. "The Study of Administration." *Political Science Quarterly* 2 (June): 197–200.

———. 1956. *Congressional Government.* New York: Meridian Books. First published in 1885.

Winch, Peter. 1958. *The Idea of a Social Science and Its Relation to Philosophy.* London: Routledge & Kegan Paul; New York: Humanities Press.

Wood, Robert C. 1958. "The New Metropolis: Green Belts, Grass Roots or Gargantua." *American Political Science Review* 52 (Mar.): 108–22.

Yang, Tai-Shuenn. 1987. "Property Rights and Constitutional Order in Imperial China." Ph.D. diss., Dept. of Political Science, Indiana University, Bloomington.

Zimmerman, Joseph F. 1972. *The Federated City: Community Control in Large Cities.* New York: St. Martin's Press.

INDEX

Adjudication. *See* Courts; Judiciary; Law
Administrative officer, local, 154
Administrative Reorganization Act, 117
African
governance systems, 18
societies, relationships in, 60
Ahlbrandt, Roger, 276n2
Air pollution abatement, 143, 146
America, federalism in. *See* Federalism
American national government
instrumentalities of, 115–22
insufficiencies of, 122–26
See also Democracy; Federalism
American Revolution, 58–59
American society, changing conditions in, 264
Aquinas, Thomas, 55
Aristotle, 164–65, 172
Articles of Confederation, 6, 44, 104
Articles of peace (Hobbes), 35, 36–37
Artisanship, 253, 263
Assembly, democratic characteristics of, 205–6

government by 41–42, 74–75
Associations
assessments by, 174–75
voluntary, 192, 257
Austin, John, 131
Austro-Hungarian empire, 249
Authority
of Congress, 100, 107, 118, 237, 276–277n1
among government instrumentalities, 238–40
of individuals, 253–54
limited, 242
Autocracies, 262

Bagehot, Walter, 19, 30, 274n2
Bain, Joe S., 275n3
Balkanization, 193
Bargaining, among consumption and production units, 192
Baugh, William, 276n2
Bentham, Jeremy, 19, 131, 204
Berman, Harold, 24, 58, 235
Bills of rights. *See* Rights, constitutional
Bish, Robert L., 276n1(ch7)
Bismarck, Otto von, 241, 250
Blackmun, Harry A. (Justice), 21, 99–100

About the Author

Vincent Ostrom is Arthur F. Bentley Professor Emeritus of Political Science and codirector of the Workshop in Political Theory and Policy Analysis at Indiana University. He received his Ph.D. in political science from UCLA in 1950 and has long studied and written about the nature and constitution of order in human societies. Besides scores of papers, articles, and chapters in edited volumes, he has published fourteen books and monographs. One of his most important works, *The Political Theory of a Compound Republic*, first printed in 1971, has been translated into Serbo-Croatian and published in Yugoslavia. Ostrom is the senior author of *Local Government in the United States* and coeditor of *Rethinking Institutional Analysis and Development*, both published by ICS Press.